ETHNICITY, COMMODITY, IN/CORPORATION

ETHNICITY, COMMODITY, IN/CORPORATION

EDITED BY
GEORGE PAUL MEIU, JEAN COMAROFF,
AND JOHN L. COMAROFF

INDIANA UNIVERSITY PRESS

This book is a publication of

Indiana University Press
Office of Scholarly Publishing
Herman B Wells Library 350
1320 East 10th Street
Bloomington, Indiana 47405 USA

iupress.indiana.edu

Manufactured in the United States of America

Cataloging information is available from the Library of Congress.

ISBN 978-0-253-04792-2 (hdbk.)
ISBN 978-0-253-04794-6 (pbk.)
ISBN 978-0-253-04796-0 (web PDF)

1 2 3 4 5   25 24 23 22 21 20

CONTENTS

EDITORIAL NOTE

THIS VOLUME BEGAN LIFE ON October 15, 2015, as a conference held at Harvard University by the African Studies Workshop (ASW) under the sponsorship of the Center for African Studies. Entitled "Ethnicity, Inc. Revisited"—which we retain for the title of the introductory essay—it was the second ASW conference. The first, two years earlier, resulted in the publication of *The Politics of Custom: Chiefship, Capital, and the State in Contemporary Africa* (University of Chicago Press, 2018). We would like to thank the staff of the center—especially its then executive director, Susan Cook, who is also a contributor to this volume, and associate director, Maggie Lopes—for their invaluable assistance in creating and coordinating the event. Our appreciation also goes to Alma Medina, our administrative assistant in the Department of African and African American Studies, for her unstinting efforts in bringing both the conference and the book to fruition, and to our research assistant, Sebastian Jackson.

ETHNICITY, COMMODITY, IN/CORPORATION

INTRODUCTION

Ethnicity, Inc., Revisited

GEORGE PAUL MEIU, JEAN COMAROFF,
AND JOHN L. COMAROFF

IN ITSELF, THE PHENOMENON OF ethnicity is hardly new. As a slippery, polyvalent concept of collective being-and-interest, ethnicity had already troubled Max Weber (1968, 387) a century ago—although, as a common noun, it only appeared in *Webster's Third New International Dictionary* in 1961 and entered the anthropological lexicon quite recently (Surak 2010, 152; Comaroff and Comaroff 2011, 68–72). Neither is the marketing of ethnic difference unprecedented: trade in the emblems, effects, and embodiments of "Otherness" dates back deep into to the mists of time. But what provoked the writing of *Ethnicity, Inc.*—to which this collection is both a sequel and a good deal more—was the sudden intensification, across the late twentieth-century world, of the commodification of culture and the corporatization of identity.

The significance of ethnicity, however—of ethnicity understood as the biocultural basis for forging selfhood, for feelings of primal attachment and shared affect, for claiming rights and defending interests—has grown greatly over the past few decades. At stake in the original study was not just the heightened incidence of such things as cultural tourism and casino capitalism. Or the sale of heritage and the predisposition of diverse populations to buy into it—to buy in, that is, in both senses of the phrase. It was that ethnic identity itself was being repurposed, taking on more objectified, commodified form—and, in so doing, animating novel species of value, novel claims to sovereignty, territory, and property, novel kinds of sociality and sensibility.

Ethnicity, Inc. sought to explore the impact of these transformations on the people and populations caught up in them, on the sense of selfhood, sociality, ownership, and belonging they conjured into existence, on the emotive energies they engendered, on the conscience collective they shaped. It strove, in other

1

words, to plumb the generative effects of the commodification of difference in terms that, pace Bruce Kapferer's (2018, 10) reading of the study, went well beyond reducing ethnicity, inc. to the spreading tentacles of global neoliberalism: terms that addressed the reifying, rationalizing effects of commerce—and also the slippages, spillages, and mutations it spawns—in an epoch in which the very nature of being and belonging, of economy and society, of nation and state, has been under reconstruction. In this spirit, the study insisted that, in the selling of ethnicity, "just as culture is being commodified, so the commodity is being rendered explicitly cultural," a process that appeared to be potentiating new social and productive relations, revitalized affiliations, and refigured aspirations.

At the time of writing, however, over a decade ago, some of the larger political, social, and economic implications of this process remained to be determined—were, indeed, still very much in the making. These new developments have taken the phenomenon in directions that move beyond the original framing in many respects. Nonetheless, *Ethnicity, Inc.* sought to challenge conventional thinking about identity, sui generis, and the worlds configured in its name, concluding with a set of yet-to-be-answered questions about what might be at stake in this historic and historical turn; about the imbrication of ethnic enterprise in the changing shape of the global order; about whether the identity business could, or would, deliver on the empowerment it promised, and, if it did, for whom; about the sustainability of the relations of production, distribution, investment, and ownership it conjured into existence; about when and where it failed to take root or to flourish. At stake, too, were the sorts of ambitions authorized by identity-as-business and how they might relate to other kinds of ethnopolitics, including those inflamed by violence.

What light has been cast on these issues by the passage of time? Did *Ethnicity, Inc.* alert us to a truly significant shift in the economic, judicial, expressive, and existential nature of cultural identity? Or were the phenomena it described merely a "sideshow"—interesting, perhaps, but peripheral to "real action" in the social world in recent times, especially the action of ethnonationalist movements? In other words, did the volume slight the continuing political significance of ethnicity by stressing its material, moral, and economic dimensions or the claims to sovereign autonomy made in its name through processes of incorporation[1]—that is, of it taking on the shape and values of a business, a limited liability company? Was it not the overarching sovereignty of the nation-state that actually gave "legal lebensraum," and life, to ethnic assertions of self-determination (Surak 2010, 156–57)? In point of fact, these critiques, which continue to treat the political and the economic, in the spirit of orthodox liberal theory, as discrete domains, misread the very essence of ethnicity, inc.: that, in the new order of things, the political, the economic, the social, and the cultural dissolve into each other, mediated by the juridical, the frame of reference that validates economic rights and political claims.

In the age of deregulation, in sum, when capital subdues labor and state-craft is increasingly shaped by the logic and imperatives of the market, it is impossible any longer to treat "the political" as anything like an autonomous sphere.[2] Nor is it viable, in these times, to regard the nation-state—itself ever more corporate in form and function, increasingly living in "collaboration" with for-profit firms—as a fully independent actor, willing or able to wield tight control over the *trans*national regimes of law and business that contest its sovereignty. States may seek to condone or constrain, license or limit, tolerate or tax corporate ethnicity. But the expansion of global enterprise, international property law, the digital commons, and social media has breathed life into the marketing of difference, its capital assets and forms of "indigenous knowledge," in ways that, as often as not, bypass the dictates of national administrations.

THE ENDURING, THE EMERGENT,
AND THE UNFORESEEN

In light of the literature to which it has given rise, *Ethnicity, Inc.* appears to have proven good to think with as the twenty-first century moved through its teens. Its core argument has been taken up by a wide range of scholars, variously exploring the interplay of culture and commodification, identity and political economy, across the world. These interventions attest cogently to the versatile, often surprising ways in which ethnicity has provided both a basis for belonging and a source of value of diverse sorts—a process that is often reciprocally reinforcing, even where it flares into conflict, contestation, excess, or disappointment. Not only have forms of corporate identity continued to manifest themselves among peoples marked by their difference, but in the age of mass production and global circulation, the advantage conferred on com-modities produced locally, and authenticated under the sign of indigeneity, has also interpolated many of the features of ethnicity, inc. into the economic mainstream, sometimes revitalizing industrial margins and struggling com-munities (Colloredo-Mansfield 2011).

A growing number of fine-grained ethnographies of such processes have also begun to address questions left open by *Ethnicity, Inc.*: about when cor-porate ethnicity fails to emerge where or how one might expect it—in this volume, for instance, in Australia, where government crushed the attempts of Aboriginal people to trade culture (Darian-Smith, chap. 8), or among Madhesi (lit., "plains-dwellers") in Nepal (Shneiderman, chap. 7)—or about contexts in which it provokes frank ambivalence, as among Roma in Edirne, Turkey, who doubt whether they actually *have* customs in common, despite strong encouragement by UNESCO to "reclaim" their intangible heritage and fear a political backlash against minorities (Blignaut n.d.). For identity to be minimally viable as the stuff of enterprise, some recognition of the rights to ethnic difference must exist in the wider political context. New studies have underscored, too, that the branding of culture-as-commodity, its "enclosure," is seldom free of argument, often sparking bitter dispute and invariably requiring careful choreography to disambiguate the messages it conveys; this is a point persuasively made by Tatiana Chudakova (chap. 2, see also discussion that follows) in respect to the contested effort to market Buddhist merit in Buryatia, eastern Siberia, and by Finola Kerrigan, Jyotsna Shivanandan, and Anne-Marie Hede (2012) on the ongoing struggle of officials in charge of the *Incredible India Campaign* to brand the kaleidoscopic, volatile, hybridizing cultural facts of the world's largest democracy. It is also made evident in Andrew Graan's (2013) analysis of the fractious local response to efforts by Macedonia's rulers to refigure Skopje as a historic European capital, a case to which we shall return. These rich accounts permit us to develop a more nuanced understanding of what is at stake in the pragmatic production of ethnocommodities, in the symbolic and material labor invested in making and marketing the tangible stuff of difference, thus to transform identity into a capital resource (see Cook, chap. 5). They also underline the fact that the more power it packs, the more millenary its promise, the more the process of incorporation itself is subject to critique and to argument over its ownership, efficacy, and implications.

In a revealing examination of what is actually entailed in establishing a trade in goods construed as cultural assets, Rudi Colloredo-Mansfield (2011) drew on four detailed cases—Russian salmon (Gerkey 2011), Peruvian ceramics (Chan 2011), Indonesian textiles (Aragon 2011), and Bolivian quinoa (Ofstehage 2011)—to cast light on the ways in which their commodification depends on particular kinds of activity.[3] The success of bringing ethnic objects to the market and securing a sustainable niche for them, he shows, rides on a number of things: among them, intensified levels of local production, the mastery of new technologies and expertise, and the engagement with external sources of investment and merchandising. The viability of ethnocommerce is quite frequently threatened from *within* by efforts to privatize shared knowledge, skill, or hereditary status—and from *outside* by those who seek to profit from that commerce by investing in it on highly exploitative terms. Drawing further on those four case studies, Colloredo-Mansfield (2011) adds something else: the intellectual property law used to appropriate (i.e., "enclose") shared cultural practices and possessions can *also* be mobilized in the name of the commons—what some have termed the "substantive grounds for collective life" (Reid and Taylor 2010, cited in Colloredo-Mansfield 2011, 52)—to protect joint heritage from individual entrepreneurs.

But it is primarily against something larger, against what is seen to be the rapacious tendencies of global capital that indigenous movements have grown up all over the planet to champion indigenous stewardship of the commons: to wit, local communities have increasingly taken strong, often eloquent, stands against the commercial erosion of their territories. Witness, in this connection, the quest of the "native" population of Haida Gwaii to preserve the custody of their terrain in British Columbia, Canada (Weiss 2018). Or the eight-year-long battle of Saami (also rendered Sami or Sámi) reindeer-herding cooperatives in northern Finland to retain control of their historic grazing lands (Sanders 2015), this in the face of a complex relationship of Saami to the commodification of their culture and the indigenous tourist industry (Kelly-Holmes and Pietikäinen 2014). Such cases lead Colloredo-Mansfield (2011, 53) to make another important claim: that, rather than being regarded as opposed spheres, markets and commons ought to be seen as "growing up together." The very idea of the commons, in its contemporary sense, he suggested, is often a *consequence* of market development, not a vestige of precapitalist relations. Hence the conviction of many resource activists that, if the commercial success of ethnopreneurs can be sustained, it would enhance their power in negotiations seeking—on behalf of the collective good—to limit the potential damage wrought by commodification, especially at the hands of outsiders.

This strange symbiosis of market and (ethno)commons is evident, too, in contemporary development discourse. For some time, and increasingly, global marketing strategists have stressed the competitive advantage of rooting production, even of mainstream commodities—as Apple, Inc. has done in Cupertino, California, for instance—in locally grounded sites. This is said to confer on them a distinctive "geographical indication," or GI, a tag recognized by the World Intellectual Property Organization (WIPO) to denote "the possess[ion] of qualities or a reputation . . . due to [their] origin."[4] In enhancing product identity, "geographical indication" is thought, in prospect at least, to invigorate the local cultural *terroir* (Colloredo-Mansfield 2011, 51)—and, with it presumably, ethnicity, inc. But not always. In practice, resort to GI may be, and often is, quite strained. Michele Fontefrancesco (2012), for example, testifies to the fact that the "crafting of locality" in Valenza, Italy—where distinctive jewelry is manufactured in ostensibly traditional fashion—is belied by the rigid enforcement of new techno-scientific norms from above. In the age of finance capital and deregulation, the narrative of the commons and commonality is often just that: a *narrative* that, with ever greater intensity, romances vernacular authenticity, productivity, creativity, and togetherness—while still being commandeered by those who take control of the means of manufacture and marketing. Meanwhile, the policies of more traditional development agencies, those aimed at populations on the margins of established economies, display a newfound emphasis on the capacity of *inalienable* heritage to generate alienable value. In the upshot, they have taken to urging people/s marked by their difference to regard alterity *itself* as a species of monopoly capital, an "abundant," profitable source of wealth waiting to be harvested (see Hirsch, chap. 3).

The very intangibility of ethnocultural heritage enables and enriches the rhetoric of value without limit, of the conjuring of money from nothing (cf. James 2015). Precisely because it does, investors and developers also have continued to push financialization, encouraging competitive ethnoprise and the recognition of indigeneity as a site of abstract investment capital (Nakassis 2013, 118), however uncertain it may be to yield returns of any magnitude. All too often, the discourse of natural abundance reverberates cynically, often alchemically, in marginal environments, those already stripped of other assets or employment opportunities. In such places, as noted in *Ethnicity, Inc.* (2009, 41–42), the concept of "human capital" can take on ever more unnerving concreteness. Not only their culture or their natural habitat, but the very bodies of ethnic subjects increasingly become the source of exploitable—and for venture capital from outside, sometimes highly profitable—value in the form of branded raw material: for genomic and pharmaceutical research (Abu El-Haj 2012; Benjamin 2015; Petryna 2009), for "natural" prowess in sports,[5] for innate musicality (Copeland n.d.), military force (May, chap. 4), and exotic sexuality (Meiu 2017; also this volume, chap. 1).

It seems clear, then, that, over the past decade or so, ethnicity, inc. has been on the rise in many places, some of them unexpected, as in the case of the Griqua, a marginal population in the South African interior (see Schweitzer 2015), who at one point in their history were said scarcely to exist at all and who have based their "reinvention of indigeneity . . . [and] the commodification of [their] ethnic history and culture" in a struggle for land rights (Zips 2015). Or, halfway across the world, in Indonesia, where "the production and consumption of Chineseness as an ethno-commodity" had long been obscured by "a singular preoccupation with identity politics" (Siew-Min Said and Chan-Yau Hoon 2013, 17). Or in Tibet, where, Martin Saxer (2013, 201) has told us, being Tibetan "serves as a commodity or asset . . . [as] actors engage, willingly or not, in the economy of Tibetanness." Some mass media have picked up on the global story: the *Vancouver Sun*, for one, published a report in early 2018 under the title "The Rapid Growth of Ethnic Economies." These economies, it said, had increased dramatically in both their geographical scatter and their visible incidence over the previous few years.[6] We could go on ad infinitum: the phenomenon, patently, has entered the realm of the new normal. Tellingly, the phrase *ethnicity, inc.* generated 134 million results on Google at the time of writing and *ethnic economies*, 15.4 million—hardly, to close the circle, "a sideshow" in the history of the present.

This is not to deny, as we have already made plain, that the spread of ethnicity, inc., founded conjointly on the commodification of culture and the incorporation of difference, has been *very* uneven; that, where it has manifested itself, it has been demonstrably variable in its form and substance; or that, in a number of contexts, it has been flatly repudiated or iconoclastically redeployed or paid no heed. Self-evidently, moreover, it has had positive effects for some and steep downsides for others—indeed, for *many* others, typically along pre-existing lines of inequality and, worse, of brute exclusion. All of these things continue to be true. But at base, there is no question that ethnicity, inc., sui generis—as a constructed sociological, political-economic, affective, and ethical reality—has sunk deep roots and, however haphazardly, is spreading. Nor only spreading. Its framing logic, that of *identity*, inc., is also extending itself further and further into the heartland of collective consciousness and material life. Just as it is radiating out horizontally across the geoscapes of the planet, so is it upscaling vertically, to more embracing forms of being in the world. And in both its horizontal and its vertical extensions, it is interpolating itself ever more deeply into the contours of the labile, constantly mutating global economy. In fact, the increasingly elaborate efforts by marketers everywhere to invest commodities and brands with distinctive identities, to root them, as we have noted, in a particular atmospheric terroir, underlines a core insight from *Ethnicity, Inc.*: that contra clichés about economic reductionism, commodification is a queer process: the more that culture is made marketable, the more the commodity itself is being rendered cultural and made into a recognizable, customized complement to the distinctively desiring subject (Mazzarella 2017).

ETHNOECONOMICS: SCALING OUT, SCALING UP

Perhaps the most immediate expansion of the reach of ethnicity, inc. is to be found in its original locus classicus: ethnocommunities in postcolonial states and settler colonies, emergent "nationalities" in postsocialist societies, and culturally marked minorities in (more or less) liberal democratic polities. Here ethnic corporations tend to do more than just persist where they can. In addition to making bold claims for political and legal recognition, many of them have widened their horizons in pursuit of business opportunity, some of it new, some of it an intensification of older kinds of commerce: in heritage, eco-, and thanatourism;[7] in enclaved enterprises such as gambling and licensed big-game hunting; in mining, forestry, transport, and communication; in leasing vast swathes of arable land to foreign firms and states; in "living museums" that offer "menus" to visitors to consume culture at "fixed prices" (Zips 2018, 22).

In Africa, for instance, there is now wide acknowledgment of the "rebirth" of the "kingdom of custom," the sovereign terrain of indigenous kings and chiefs, a number of whom—anticipated, in *Ethnicity, Inc.* by the case of the ruler of the Royal Bafokeng Nation—have emerged as powerful corporate figures, even CEOs (Comaroff and Comaroff 2018). The liberalizing thrust of structural adjustment policies, under the Washington Consensus, played a significant role in this turn of events. It actively encouraged the devolution of aid and investment away from national capitals toward so-called local communities, thereby (re)legitimizing their rulers as their sovereign representatives—with fiduciary jurisdiction over their often considerable material and cultural interests (Comaroff and Comaroff 2018; Geschiere 2018). It is no wonder that many of these resurrected rulers have become skilled dealers in ethnic patrimony, willing real estate brokers with mining companies, and adept venture capitalists on their own account (Coyle 2018; J. Smith 2018) or that, emboldened by a mix of authority at once corporate and customary, some have come to challenge the sovereignty of the state, to the point, at times, of national emergency (Buthelezi and Skosana 2018). These cases illuminate, yet again, the entanglement of politics and economy at work in ethnicity, inc., how it can potentiate unprecedented inflows of value and, in so doing, reconfigure "traditional" modes of empowerment. This while opening the door to new, or repurposed, vectors of inequity, exclusion, even despotism (Darian-Smith, chap. 8).

Outscaling: From the Country to the City

As we have already seen, identity-based enterprise has also continued to move beyond its "traditional" terrain, having become ever more visible in towns, in the metropole, and in the force-fields of mainstream national and transnational economies. Here commodified ethnicity frequently takes shape at the interface with regional and state-level institutions, giving rise to remastered categories of subjectivity and belonging. Thus Falina Enrique's (2012) narrative of the rivalry between two popular music groups in Recife, northeastern Brazil, each trying in its own way to make its urbane, youth-oriented style resonate with the emergent category of *cultura*, an official, artistically expressed form of "regional identity." The state-sponsored cultura scene endorses a specific understanding of culture and national inclusion, one that shapes a sense of citizenship, even democracy, among its participants. A similar process of ethnopreneurial citizenship is evident in the "staging of authenticity" and "internal orientalism" in mainland China's ethnotourist industry (Wang 2012). Buyi people in a village in the southwest have responded to local government development initiatives by establishing an ecological museum that has turned everyday household goods into protected cultural artifacts. There is nothing new in this, of course, but, as Mengqi Wang shows, the attempt to make the surrounding village *itself* into a timeless open-air diorama has been undermined by the very process of museumization. For the largely script-based rendering of Buyi life as ossified essence, to be consumed by outsiders, has thrust their microworld into the currents of national history. The villagers have begun to appropriate and enact these scripts both in their daily interactions and in their dealings with the state, enabling them to become energetic agents of their own commercial enterprise—thereby proving, too, that "they needed to be traditional first if they want to be modern and 'developed'" (452).

As it expands and embeds itself, ethnoincorporation often challenges national sovereignty and belonging, not least by (re)fashioning identity-modulated forms of citizenship; of this, more in a moment. The interpolation of ethnic subjectivity into the *conscience collective* of the larger body politic has also become a rapidly growing concern of the mass-marketing industry; palpably more so than it was in the early years after the millennium.[8] The emerging practices of this industry are revealed in a burgeoning literature on ethnicity and advertising: Shalini Shankar's (2012, 2015) studies of Asian American merchandising, for instance, suggest that mainstream copywriters aim to index brand identities in ways that seek to reconcile common stereotypes of a homogenous Asian identity with more subtle characterizations that acknowledge internal diversity. But the overriding aim of their messaging is to transform this population from "model minority producers" into "model minority consumers"; this by way of a process of "racial naturalization" that makes them visible as legitimate citizens on the US popular cultural landscape (2015, 15). Here, as minority populations come to constitute lucrative target markets, ethnic publicists become engaged as much in the business of selling their culture to coethnics as to others. Arlene Dávila (2012) has alerted us to the ambiguous implications of this endeavor in her path-breaking *Latinos, Inc.*, which explored the multibillion-dollar Hispanic advertising industry in the United States. Insider efforts to harness the potential of the Latin American "nation within a nation" (4) and to brand its diversity, she observed, have turned out to be only a little less reductive, homogenizing, and exoticizing than the exertions of mainstream marketers—threatening to render the Latino population marginal to the larger (i.e., white) consumer public.

Not surprisingly perhaps, the reception by Hispanic Americans of these vernacular marketing strategies has been deeply ambivalent. They have provoked estrangement, anger, bemusement, and, simultaneously, vigorous debate not merely about the politics of Latino identity but also about the perverse, self-referential pleasures of consumer recognition. Like other instruments of merchandising, advertising seeks to mobilize the creativity of market forces as an abstract form of capital, one that has the capacity, in and of itself, to generate value. As such, it has emerged as both a means *and* an object of collective action. Not surprisingly, then, the argument of images within Latino marketing has become complicated, ironic, and sophisticated as widening cultural and class diversity among Hispanics resists stereotypy or encompassment. And as "Hispanic business" becomes more and more entangled with the US and the transnational economy.

Upscaling: From Ethnicity, Inc. toward Nationality, Inc.

Talk of the Hispanic "nation within a nation" points to a further dimension of the upscaling of the identity economy—namely, nationality, inc., a phenomenon that has gained a good deal more visibility and scholarly attention of late. In some contexts, ethnicity, inc. and nationality, inc. merge seamlessly into one another, notably in those polities actually constituted as ethnonations—by contrast to civic nations—whose citizens, united in blood and soil, are held to share unique biocultural substance, most famously, perhaps, being Germany (Brubaker 1992), although there are many others. But even modern civic nations, as Benedict Anderson (1983, 7) reminded us, hold to the fantasy of cultural homogeneity and deep "horizontal comradeship." What is more, nation-states of both sorts long foreshadowed ethnicity, inc. in as much as they have always acted as corporations, possessing sovereign territory, investing themselves in signs of distinction, and marshaling their interests by recourse to law and war. Orthodox political theory, of course, has matters the other way around, at least in part. It takes ethnicity-as-polity to be a primordial form of association, derived from "hot" attachments of ancestry and consanguinity—and destined, with the advent of modern government, to give way to cooler ties of solidarity, vested in a social contract and rational-legal authority (cf., e.g., R. Smith 1986; Kamenka 1975). Critics have long been skeptical of this telos and the categorical opposition on which it rests. Even in western Europe, heartland of the liberal polity, ethnic and civic nationalism typically infuse each other, their difference, despite often shrill claims to the contrary, more a matter of degree than kind (Weber 1968, 925; Povinelli 2006, 197; Tilly 1990).

Ethnicity and nationalism, to be sure, are political artifacts of a similar sort (Weber 1968, 392), both being mythopoetic fictions sustained by idioms of genealogy and family. The former, moreover, is seldom erased by the latter (Corrigan and Sayer 1985), *itself* a perpetual work-in-progress. As Renan (1992) famously quipped, the existence of a nation, is a "daily plebiscite,"[9] not least because, to a greater or lesser extent, ethnic heterogeneity is always present to trouble it. This is most overtly so in postcolonies, precisely because they were bequeathed an imperial legacy of divide-and-rule. But at the turn of the twenty-first century, as capital has freed itself from state regulation—and as labor has been outsourced, government privatized, and the social contract undermined—the sovereignty of civic nations has been challenged by claims made against it in the name of difference, diversity, and minority rights.

This, in turn, has evoked energetic pushback in those civic nations, resistance being framed in ever more ethnonationalist-sounding terms: hence Brexit Britain, Trump's USA "base," Kaczynski's Poland, Erdogan's Turkey, and any number of strident neonationalist movements elsewhere—all of them fueled by the worldwide increase, under economic and political duress, of migration and other kinds of traffic across state boundaries. These movements invoke the nation-as-identity, claiming to defend the culture, heritage, and patrimony of the homeland against difference-as-dissolution; indeed, as one astute observer put it, by asserting "a sense of rightful ownership."[10] Asked another: "What drove Brexit if not the anger that some genuine British identity—remembered or misremembered—was being drowned within the shallow waters of the European Union?"[11] The same spirit is evident in the rallying cries of popular neonationalism across the globe: in *russkii* (Russian culture, language, and traditional values [Blakkisrud 2016]), in *Hindutva* (Hindu nationalism [Basu 1996]), in the call to limit "Germany for the Germans"[12] and "Make American Great Again."

It is in this context that the contemporary salience of nationality, inc., as a distinctive, late modern phenomenon, is to be understood. While the state might always have been a corporation in the broadest sense of the term, in recent times it has become corporate sensu stricto: a metabusiness, so to speak, acting *an und für sich*, franchising out its operations to the private sector, husbanding its assets, commodifying its collective *Geist* to attract commerce, and creating a conducive fiscal environment for those who fund the election of its officeholders—and, to a more limited extent, constitute its tax base. No longer simply a custodian of the commonweal or a guarantor of the welfare of its citizens, government, under "neo-liberal political rationality" (Brown 2003), has largely relinquished its role as a mediator among "class and sectarian interests" in the name of a greater public good (Harvey 1990, 108); it is *itself* ruled by the logic of the market, now taken to be the archetypical instrument for the production of social and material value (Foucault 2008; see above). As the state takes on the form of a holding company, as the line between politics and economics gives way, as the population becomes a body of consumer citizens and the social contract is rewritten, so nation branding and mass politics converge. And so, increasingly, ruling regimes are charged by their subjects: market us (Graan 2013, 281).[13] Thus do heads of state become businessmen, and some businessmen heads of state, be they Silvio Berlusconi or Donald Trump, Emmanuel Macron or Cyril Ramaphosa, Mark Rutte or Tihomir Orešković.[14]

Branding . . . and Its Discontents

Nation branding, noted *Ethnicity, Inc.* (2009, 122–36), is an integral aspect of the incorporation of identity. It reimagines twenty-first-century nationhood through the lens of the commodity form in a manner at once highly self-conscious, widely theorized, and thoroughly fetishized—and has opened up a privileged site for contemporary state-making.[15] As an upscaled version of the commodification of ethnicity, it is its analogical extension in a digital era: an era in which civic (neo-)nationalism, as we intimated a few moments ago, begins ever more to mimic ethnonationatism. Yet conjuring the civic nation in these terms always poses a challenge as, on the face of it, this species of polity lacks the essential, and essentializing, coherence that ethnicity presumes. It has to forge homogeneity and fraternity in the face of social difference and cultural heterogeneity; in the face, also, of the fact that the metaphors of kinship and genealogy on which it draws tend to stretch rather thinly across its typically diverse scapes. Which is why politicians, confronted by centrifugal forces that pull against national integrity—global capital, world religions, transnational movements, social media, and the electronic commons—invoke the emotive power of autochthony: of inalienable belonging rooted in birth, heritage, locality, destiny (Geschiere 2009). Hence the impetus, too, when seeking to assert collective identity, to enlist the force of the market, the persuasiveness of commodity images, and the cunning seductions of branding.

Recent work on nation branding makes clear how pervasive it has become, not least as a form of governance, in what Noam Chomsky[16] has dubbed the age of "corporate mercantilism": one in which trade and its trappings are taken to be the prime engine of wealth, in which international diplomacy gives way to professional marketing and the enchantments of advertising (Coombe 2012; Marsh and Fawcett 2011). The global order, structured hitherto as an articulated system of national economies, melts into a planetary market for transacting the emblems of national je ne sais quoi, reputation, and the capacity for creating value— "fame" in the vocabulary of classic Melanesian kula exchange (Munn 1986).

Pioneering copywriter Simon Anholt claims to have coined the phrase *nation branding* in 1996 (Kaneva 2011), although he recently expressed remorse that poor countries are encouraged to "blow wicked amounts of money on futile propaganda programmes" to the sole benefit of "beastly PR agencies."[17] But publicists are adept at hyping their own commodifed essence, their "indispensable" ability to engender communicable esteem, trust, and investment potential, especially in uncertain times.[18] The *Anholt-GfK Nations Brand Index*, published annually by major corporate players in the industry—Anholt himself remains one—rates and ranks the brand images of fifty countries, offering complex computations of fluctuations in "national reputation."[19] It is widely cited and debated by business publications across the planet. Self-publicizing advocates of rebranding point to a catalog of achievements: how EU neophyte Croatia shed its shady Balkan associations for a pleasing patina of Mediterranean chic; how stagnant, strife-torn Tatarstan elevated itself from the dreary Russian periphery by rediscovering a masterful medieval history and sense of national purpose; how Cape Verde, an arid archipelago off the African coast, became an attractive "melting pot of cultural flavour"; how the minuscule West Indies polity of Saint Kitts and Nevis became the world's most patronized—but, as the World Economic Forum notes, far from the only[20]—purveyor of belonging (i.e., "economic citizenship," full heritable nationality) acquired in exchange for local investment.[21]

As this suggests, branding promises to defy ordinary means and ends; in so doing, it is like the transformative magic of ritual. Take, for one especially dramatic example, *Guerrilla Marketing* in Colombia (Fattal 2018, xi). Here local publicity professionals, with a nudge from US counterparts, mounted antiguerrilla warfare by way of "weaponized advertising." Their multimedia campaign was vested in the faith that branding can "reconcile the irreconcilable"—in this case, that it could make counterinsurgency into a humanitarian project and conjure the Colombian armed forces into agents of peace. By laboring, often very creatively, to depict the strife-torn present into a time of "post-conflict," they sought to will the future into existence. This, after all, was "Colombia, land of magical realism."

Not only has the high-tech end of the identity business grown by leaps and bounds, but it has also provided a site of sociopolitical experimentation with complicated consequences. Graan's (2013) account of nation branding in Macedonia casts sharp light, in this regard, on the skill and deception involved in staging nationality, inc.—and the dialectics of reception and rejection to which it can give rise. In 2010, the Macedonian government embarked on Skopje 2014, an extensive, expensive project to make the city over as a properly European capital. Eager to shed its jaded Yugoslav past and defuse challenges to its status as an independent nation-state, the architects of the scheme refashioned the urban center around a giant equestrian statue of Alexander the Great, in a style held to embody haute Euromodernity. For Graan, this assertion of historic, ethnonationalist identity, unceremoniously erasing archives of the Ottoman and socialist past, was more than just an iteration of nineteenth- and twentieth-century state-making (161–62, 165). Those who commissioned the scheme saw it as pivotal to the production of an ethnonational brand: an identity-as-commodity-image capable of evoking worldwide recognition, recalibrating the relation between national polity and global economy. As an engine of financial value and "soft power," the project was taken as the sine qua non of neoliberal statecraft. But many locals were skeptical. Vocal opposition decried its cost, its embarrassing turn to Euro-kitsch, and its provocative erasure of Muslim, Albanian, and Greek legacies, sparking a counterpolitics among those who saw the exercise as a misguided effort to flog the country. It also drew forth parodic comment: one sardonic postcard depicts the city as an empty wilderness beneath that rearing steed of Alexander the Great (174). Yet the protesters, Graan noted, seemed less concerned that their rulers had branded the nation than with the fact that they had failed to brand it well. If anything, popular outrage reinforced a common faith in the fetishistic promise of identity-as-commodity image.

But are the enchantments of brand-making ever unambiguously efficacious? Branding—be it ethnic, national, regional, or any other—is never without surfeit, writes Nakassis (2013), never without an excess of meaning that defies attempts to discipline its intelligibility. As semiotic confections, brands invariably run up against other signs circulating in the world. As a result, they frequently spawn unforeseen associations. We have already noted that efforts to interpolate ethnic consumers by marketing techniques seldom take place without friction, often producing ambivalence, doubt, dispute, or censorship.

Like all advertising, such efforts ride on hype, on a partially acknowledged con, on the hope that some will be taken in, and on the reality that there is always a yawning gap between what a brand promises and what it can deliver. Nation branding, like ethnic branding, traffics in a double abstraction. On one hand, it calls into being a collective identity, a concrete imagining. On the other, it turns the putative substance of that identity into a currency, a species of rentier capital (Nakassis 2013, 117). But as a medium of investment and speculation, its fetishized capacity to vitalize commodities and power wealth production is open to demystification the moment it fails to deliver.

And it *has* failed to deliver, quite visibly, with recurring economic crises driven nowadays largely by the excesses of speculative finance capital—of capital detached from "real" production—and exacerbated by rising rates of mass debt and government-by-austerity. This failure, in turn, has drawn outspoken cynicism about the traffic in national and ethnic identity, some of it from insiders in the business. Jose Torres, a Spanish counterpart of Simon Anholt, recently declared that most nation-branding strategies "fail miserably . . . because, mainly, governments don't have the capabilities to manage [them]"[22]; bluntly, they cannot back up hype with substance and thus cannot make good on the vaunted power of commodity images to stimulate production and consumption—especially where marketing seeks to breathe life into postindustrial urban wastelands and postcolonial peripheries.

But failure does not only occur in poor countries or the poor reaches of rich ones. When, in 2002, amid the War on Terror, the US administration looked to Madison Avenue to upgrade its tarnished image abroad, Naomi Klein retorted: "America's problem is not with its brand—which could scarcely be stronger—but with its product."[23] Her critique went beyond the conceit that geopolitics is merely a matter of effective communication. It argued against the pretense that branding could make a corporate monologue into a social dialogue. While resorting to a reliable, homogeneous brand image might make sense for purposes of marketing washing powder, "selling" a nation in the same manner—especially one claiming to embrace diversity within a democracy—was "not only futile but dangerous." Yet despite Klein's mass-mediated outrage, corporate monologues *can* and do become social dialogue. Indeed, corporate nation branding, in the age of market fetishism, seeks to replay the elemental relationship, identified by Durkheim and those who followed him (e.g., Turner 1970), among enchantment, collective conscience, and sociality: the conjuring by charismatics—priests or politicians, shamans or statesmen, advertising "creatives" or "cult" figures—of messages that take on transcendent vitality, condensing diverse signs into an effervescent experience of shared being, predicament, and purpose; conjurings that, like fetishes, have the capacity to enchant and command but also to come apart under their own excess. Or simply to fail (Mazzarella 2017).

Ethnicity and nationality, inc., then—primed by the logic of the market and by prevailing political, material, and social rationalities—are here to stay, be it as accomplished social facts, active aspirations, unrealized fantasies, or failed fetishes. So, too, are other modes of incorporation that replicate them in substance and/or spirit. Indeed, the temporalities and trajectories of the identity economy lead in all directions, from nation to ethnicity, ethnicity to nation, and both to many other species of imagined community: locality, region, religion, and so on, all alike vested in the commodification of culture and putatively shared being in the world. It is these trajectories and temporalities, many of them mutated or magnified or multiplied, that anchor the chapters to follow.

INTERSECTIONS, (DIS)ARTICULATIONS, AMBIVALENCES

The chapters in this volume uncover ways in which the commodification and incorporation of ethnicity, through their myriad entanglements with various life worlds—worlds at once social, political, and economic—have generated new kinds of identity and alterity, new forms of value and belonging, new temporalities, new modes of historicity, new space-time configurations. Exploring the presence of ethnicity, inc.—at times spectacular, at times spectral—in Australia, Fiji, Kenya, Mali, Nepal, Siberia, and South Africa shows, among other things, how the intersection of different domains of life at once expand and undermine the possibilities of producing ethnobrands; how emerging forms of value, struggles over autochthonous attachments, and asynchronous temporalities trouble the distinction between the market and the ethnocommons; how new media, advertising, and violent conflict may further a sense of collective ownership of ethnicity; and how ambivalence, excess, and exclusion simultaneously destabilize and enable the production of fetishized difference. We also attempt to pursue ethnicity, inc. to its margins, to places where it remains a path not taken or where its objectifications are rerouted through other kinds of ethnopolitics.

Intersectional Commodities, Uncertain Brands

The ethnocommodity is often a scene of odd historical convergences and cultural intersections, and therefore also a site of deep ambivalence. As a commodity fetish, ethnicity promises something essential, primordial, immutable.

Yet, contrary to its promises, it often manifests historically shifting *confluences* and *convergences* of distinct realms in social life, intersecting transregional styles, or the outcomes of competing geopolitical and cultural orientations. As suggested earlier, what comes to be "enclosed" as an ethnocommodity—the concrete objects and practices contained under its brand image—can be assemblages of multiple, competing dimensions of social and cultural life, each with its own, complex origins. The ethnocommodity, to be sure, thrives through identities rendered intersectional both in the terms of the poststructuralist concept of *intersectionality* (Crenshaw 1989) and also more broadly. Inseparable from race, gender, sexuality, and class (Nagel 2003), in its commodified form, ethnicity often derives its value from the naturalized logics of global white supremacy (Pierre 2013) and patriarchy. These historical intersections often work to reaffirm the ethnocommodity's quality of difference and to enhance its desirability. But, as we shall see, they can also undermine the very possibility of its reproduction.

George Paul Meiu (chap. 1) describes how the image of the young male Maasai or Samburu *moran*, or warrior, became a best-selling brand of Kenya as a tourist destination, thus foregrounding a particular gender, generational, and sexual subject position as emblematic of ethnicity. Since the 1980s, men from the Samburu ethnic group in northern Kenya have migrated seasonally to the country's beach resorts to sell souvenirs, dance for tourists, and engage in sexual intimacies with women from European countries. They have drawn on an older colonial paradigm of the Maa-speaking warrior as a young, tall man with both a culturally distinct appeal and an erotic allure. In this context, embodying the brand image of the touristic moran has become a complex, yet uncertain pursuit. Meiu argues that stabilizing and embodying cultural difference—in this case, the fetishized *image* of erotic masculinity and ethnosexuality—represents a nebulous process that requires constant reiterative claims. Those claims, in turn, also open up the possibility of conflict and violence.

As Samburu men come to understand the image of the moran as a *brand* that they *own*, various tensions emerge. On the one hand, this image excludes Samburu women and aging men from the possibilities of ethno-erotic commodification, generating new internal conflicts. On the other hand, Samburu migrants often violently attack young men from coastal ethnic groups—so-called fake morans—who embrace the appearance of the Maa-speaking moran to make money in tourism. In response, in recent decades, young coastal men have also attacked Samburu migrants, urging them to "return home." Meiu argues that to understand interethnic violence in this context it is necessary to pay close attention to how difference is actually produced as part of ethnicity, inc.

(see also above). If the difference of the Maa-speaking warrior holds the promise of spectacular wealth, it is the imagined essence of this identity that coastal people then seek to "divinate"—to use Arjun Appadurai's (1989, 99) phrase—through the macabre spectacle of violence. Here, commodity fetishism enables the fetishistic logic of ethnicity (and indeed ethnosexuality) *as a hidden essence*. For, in violence, bodies are dismembered to reveal (the impossibility of) difference as an ontological given, a process that is itself ambivalent, generative of repetition and reiteration.

Tatiana Chudakova (chap. 2) describes how, over the last decade, in Buryatia, an ethnic-minority republic in southeastern Siberia, numerous local social actors have struggled to articulate a distinct local identity to attract tourists. They hope that tourism will help the region overcome its relative marginality within the Russian federal state. Since 2007, regional and state leaders have seen Buryatia's remoteness as an appealing exotic destination for cultural, ecological, and medical tourists. Branding experts and nonexperts alike have struggled to place its Buddhism, traditional herbal medicine, and environment at the forefront of its tourist economy.

The Buryat ethnocommodity, Chudakova shows, draws value from being *betwixt* and *between* spatial and social realms, with various, unexpected outcomes. Intersections, here, are of two kinds. First, in Buryatia, the ethnocommodity emerges at the convergence of the distinct genres of religion, healing, ecological imaginaries, and tourism. For example, local hospitals may take their visiting practitioners on cultural tours; schools of Tibetan medicine involve ecotourists in collecting herbal remedies; and religious objects sometimes double as touristic souvenirs. Second, the Buryat commodity is also a product of the historical and geopolitical confluence of a pan-Buddhist world, a pan-Mongol ethnicity, and a post-Soviet lifeworld in a region that is simultaneously positioned as a margin of the Russian federation and "the Heart of Asia in Russia." These diverse and complex historical intersections make it patently difficult to brand local products simply as "Buryat." Except, of course, if what is branded is precisely their "derivative hybridity"—that is, the distinction of their intersectional quality.

The success of the Buryat brand, Chudakova shows, rests in part on its ability to "stake out the region's political connections"—to point, that is, to the historical mobility of things, ideas, and people. The brand's interpretative possibilities are here open-ended, its semiotic volatility sustaining some of its key promises. But this volatility also animates the haunting possibility of the brand's demise. As Chudakova notes "liminal mixtures" generate ambiguities that render the brand fragile, unstable. Here then is a central paradox of the ethnocommodity's intersectional qualities: On the one hand, the ambivalence of odd intersections makes the commodification of difference slippery and fragile. On the other hand, the commodity reinvents itself precisely through this ambivalence, deriving value from the *distinction* of its odd mixings.

Similar intersectional paradoxes emerge with the Fijian male warrior-cum-global soldier (May, chap. 4) or the Malian male hunter-musician turned into a repository of the nation's "local culture" (Schulz, chap. 6). Meanwhile, in Nepal, efforts to objectify ethnic difference converge with complex struggles over caste and class in the arena of national politics (Shneiderman, chap. 7). But the intersections explored in the following chapters also push us to think beyond the narrower identity categories of intersectionality. For, as the logics of ethnicity, inc. permeate spheres of social, economic, and political life, value is derived from the complex *convergences* of religion, medicine, finance, kinship, sex, security, art, and activism, among other things. Such intersections animate diverse idioms, grammars, and domains that allow difference to be assembled and reassembled, always in new, albeit never fully stable ways. Here, as ethnicity, commodification, and incorporation are implicated ever more deeply in the minutiae of particular life worlds, difference can emerge precisely from the unexpected intersections generated by the market's inextricable social embeddedness.

Ethnocommons: Social Articulations

Immediate manifestations of ethnicity, inc. often come to reverberate across social fields in ever wider concentric circles of influence. In some places, the new possibilities engendered by ethnicity, inc. transform social relations—sometimes quite radically—producing new lines of inequality, new subject positions, or, at times, revitalizing and repurposing older forms of custom, kinship, and belonging. Meanwhile, rules and rhythms of social life also inform the specific terms and trajectories of ethnobusiness. What it means to belong to a place or a people, what forms of moral worth and material wealth are desirable, or what collective futures are imaginable are all questions people address, implicitly or openly, as they participate in ethnobusiness. The commodification and incorporation of ethnicity and the production of an ethnocommons are caught up in a dialectical relationship. If, as pointed out above, it would be erroneous to extricate the economic from the political dimensions of ethnicity, inc., so too—it is worth remembering—are market dynamics inextricable from sociality. *Together* they constitute ethnoeconomies (see also Meiu 2017).

Eric Hirsch (chap. 3) shows how, in southern Peru, ethnoeconomies bring developmental logics of finance and the cultural dynamics of social value into the same space of the market, generating new social positions and orientations. Since 2010, in Peru, nongovernmental organizations (NGOs) have shifted away from pursuing development projects focused on poverty alleviation, emphasizing instead how people can manage and maximize a kind of wealth that inheres in individuals, groups, and—in this case, also—their ethnic identities. In the Colca Valley, NGOs have deployed the idea that, for many poor rural residents, ethnicity is the only option for significant economic empowerment. NGO workers imagine Collaguas and Cabanas individuals as already wealthy—wealthy, that is, *if* they learn how to actualize the abundant value of their ethnicity through the market skills of entrepreneurialism. And so, Peruvian and international tourists encounter members of the Collaguas and Cabanas ethnic groups engaging in staged competitions that convert local products—alpaca weavings, traditional dishes, guinea pigs, or ecotouristic experiences, among other things—into sustainable ethnopreneurial ventures. Through such competition, development workers and their beneficiaries reimagine ethnicity as a kind of extant, collective wealth, a prized asset or abundant resource, to which any ethnic subject always already has access simply by virtue of *being* ethnic.

And so the idea of *ethnicity-as-abundance*—a living fetish of fecundity—has come to permeate social life, generating new forms of subjectivity, cooperation, and attachment. Hirsch argues that, as a consequence of these practices of entrepreneurial self-fashioning, subjects and communities are transformed in important ways. For example, ventures into ethnobusiness also prompt "a [collective] passion for continuing ancestral traditions," a nostalgia for autochthonous attachments, as well as the possibility of imagining new kinds of futures in rural areas. The advent of ethnicity-related projects has led people to revive and redeploy older (sometimes dormant) forms of village sociality, including the custom of *ayni*, a practice of reciprocal lending used by people throughout the Andes, or the custom of *faenas*, the organization of local communal work parties for the completion of large projects. Not surprisingly, such customs are now repurposed to help individuals start their own ethnobusinesses. The ensuing relations, notably, are at once mundane forms of sociality *and* business networks, blurring distinctions between economic production and social reproduction, between ethnicity, inc. and an ethnocommons.

Simon May (chap. 4) shows how, in Fiji, autochthonous attachments are anchored in the image of the male warrior-cum-soldier. This image has become emblematic both of Fijian identity on the transnational military market and of ideal forms of masculinity and social reproduction in the Fijian archipelago. Over the past two decades, the rise in the global demand for outsourced military service has coincided with rampant unemployment in Fiji, prompting many Fijians, mostly men, to turn to an older stereotype of their identity as a "warlike people" to work as soldiers abroad. Many have been recruited to fight for the British army, the United Nations, and the United States in Afghanistan, Iraq, and elsewhere. Others have worked, among other things, as security guards for Nigerian oil pipelines or Australian immigration detention centers. The money obtained in military service abroad, even by those in low-ranking, entry-level positions, has often amounted to more than most Fijians could earn at home.

May shows that Fijians use their success on the military market to invest in social and cultural attachments in Fiji, attachments that, in turn, sustain the global image of Fijian men as "born soldiers." Military migrants remit money to their families to invest in practices constitutive of kinship relations and forms of local belonging, in what locals refer to as *vaka i taukei*, "the Fijian way of life." Yet military money also animates new inequalities, allowing migrants' families to engage in forms of redistribution that exceed social expectations at a time when other locals can barely afford to meet their own material needs. Thus, Fijian migrants produce (sometimes in excess) forms of sociality and belonging that make their identity legible as *Fijian* in a wider global arena. At the same time, this legibility of military service as ethnic enables the transnational outsourcing of violence, risk, and death in an economy premised on the bodies of Others. May argues that nativist attachments and global networks of military labor are dialectically entangled, making Fijianness ever more about the value and virtues of warriorhood and thus readily available for global extraction. By bringing the ethnocommodity of the "Fijian warrior" to the global marketplace, the Fijian state encourages local practices of strategic self-essentialization that render local male bodies into militarized ethnocommodities and that drive the neoliberal privatization of military power worldwide.

The dialectics of ethnobusiness and ethnofutures reveal new kinds of *articulations* that are important for understanding the social implications of ethnicity, inc. First, the production of value involves an ongoing dialectic linking the logics of microfinance, entrepreneurialism, abundance, and the moral imperatives to reciprocity and mutuality associated with local belonging in the ethnocommons. How money is produced, stored, and circulated are questions addressed at once through entrepreneurial considerations *and* concerns over reproduction, sociality, and futurity. Second, struggles over belonging in ethnicity, inc. recalibrate relations between scales (local, national, and global) and spaces (centers and peripheries, towns and villages). Schulz (chap. 6) describes this well for Mali, where the relations between rural areas and towns, between locality and the nation, are coopted, through media, in the production and commodification of culture. Similarly, Meiu (chap. 1) shows how, in Kenya, since the 1980s, tourist resorts and remote ethnoregions, though far apart, have been growingly implicated in one another—socially, culturally, and economically. Third, much of what is at stake in these articulations and recalibrations plays out in everyday struggles to coordinate the *temporalities* and *rhythms* of social action. Chudakova (chap. 2), for example, demonstrates how, in Buryatia, the commodification of culture generates a "new calculus of time" as people struggle to reconcile the perceived shortage of the religious ethnocommodity with the karmic time of reincarnation. Similarly, in Kenya, Samburu men engaged in "ethno-erotic economies" produce temporal asynchronies as they try to reconcile contradictory expectations associated with bodily aging, age-set relations, and the rhythms of wealth accumulation (Meiu 2015, see also chap. 1). How people synchronize, attune, or orchestrate different, competing temporalities while navigating the multiple scales and spaces of ethnicity, inc., and, generating value from doing so, are central questions for understanding the emergence of ethnocommons in these contexts. Because it is so deeply implicated in the making of social life, ethnicity, inc. may also have drastic effects on the ethnocommons in contexts in which its economies fail.

Divining Difference, Collective Consciousness

An important intervention of this volume is to open up the microdynamics of the production of ethnic identity and cultural difference to careful ethnographic scrutiny. A key aspect of these dynamics is the relationship between the production of difference and emerging forms of collective consciousness—a set of issues that requires close observation of lived experience. As pointed out above, the production of difference is an uncertain process. Difference is often established against the backdrop of complex, even contradictory (and intersectional) discourses, political orientations, economic contingencies, risks and realities, all of which can render representations of difference in excess of that which they claim to represent. The production of difference—its identification, performance, standardization—is therefore a continuous process. Within the practical logic of ethnicity, inc. producing, fixing, and pinning down the quality of difference involves a wide variety of new media and modes of communication while engendering new excesses, exclusions, and erasures. Struggles over how the collective past is reimagined, over who comes to represent the ethnic group or over who is left out in the process, are often made manifest and addressed in such contexts. In the ensuing contestations, people often revisit their past, find new ways to narrate their identity, and attempt to figure out—not just for themselves but also for their global audiences—who they *really* are.

Susan Cook (chap. 5) shows how the 2010 World Cup represented a unique opportunity for the Royal Bafokeng Nation of South Africa, an ethnic kingdom turned into a mining corporation, to build a global reputation and thus diversify its economic activities. Since the early 2000s, the Royal Bafokeng Nation has solidified its status as landowner and major player in the platinum-mining industry, rendering quite blurry the distinctions between the community and the ethnocorporation. Cook's account offers invaluable insights into the corporation's struggles with ethnic branding. Having carried out anthropological fieldwork in the region since 1995, she became a personal advisor and research and planning executive for the Royal Bafokeng, a position she held for six years. In this chapter, an exercise in reflexive ethnography, she describes the challenges she encountered when faced with the corporation's rush to market itself in anticipation of the World Cup. The relatively short time span during which the tournament would turn international audiences toward South Africa represented a window of immense potentiality for the Bafokeng administration. But to capture the interest of global sports media required "tailoring a simplified narrative" describing who the Tswana of Bafokeng were and what made them attractive to consumers around the world.

The production of ethnic brands and cultural difference means resorting to new means of historicity—that is, new ways of reckoning the past and of producing knowledge about it for the present. Cook and her team commissioned, among other things, two books and a documentary that told the story of the Bafokeng. While primarily concerned with avoiding (and refuting) primitivist representations of Bafokeng, the team also had to leave out competing historical narratives of the region. This prompted other Tswana to resort to social media as alternative sites to question the historical representations put forth by Bafokeng, Inc. What is ultimately questioned is not the singularity of the narrative or the foreclosure of heterodox discourse or the global media through which this history is disseminated. Rather, it is who authors and benefits from collective identity. Although the relative success of this marketing campaign has continued to spark controversy on the ground, it also created new means of collective consciousness; as people now come together to debate how the corporation depicts their history, they all nonetheless claim belonging to what is now a globally renowned and, for them, collectively owned identity.

Dorothea Schulz (chap. 6) introduces an interesting case that complicates in important ways our understanding of the concrete terms in which difference works in ethnicity, inc. She shows how, in Mali, ethnicity, inc. does not play out through ethnic identity per se. Rather, central here is a more diffuse notion of local culture (or tradition), an idiom understood to entail a rural cultural stratum on which national belonging is predicated. Since the 1990s, government has supported a television program that broadcasts traditional dance and songs from across the country. Called *Terroir*, or "from the earth," the show has tried to conflate national belonging with a generic notion of local culture—rather than, say, ethnicity—thus depicting various groups as horizontally integrated in the nation-state and depoliticizing their social and cultural differences. In this context, efforts that bring local culture into the national mass media often foreground particular performances—such as the hunters' musicians—while also producing new means for standardizing and evaluating authenticity. Schulz argues that, in Mali, the logics of ethnocommodification (and incorporation) permeate even though not under the sign of ethnicity.

What local culture is here remains highly contested. For one thing, as people come to be involved in its performance, tensions emerge between, on the one hand, the state's attempts to foreground ideologically a nonethnic local culture and, on the other hand, an uneven geopolitical distribution of the concrete contents of that which is included in the category of culture. There is more focus, we learn, on traditions from southern Mali, for example, and much less on northern peoples, like the Tuareg. In the production of local culture, Schulz argues, difference also requires practices to undergo processes of *standardization, selection,* and *adaptation* to mass media and market dynamics. Yet these processes make cultural difference ambivalent, an ambivalence also attenuated by the fact that the homogenous population it is seen to depict does not exist as such. Meanwhile, performers and audiences themselves contest the authenticity of hunters' musicians along lines of generation, aesthetic corruption by commercialization, and fear over the possibility of cultural depletion. Schulz argues that, while the state seeks to reassert its power of horizontal integration through the ideology of local culture, the tensions associated with its geopolitics and ethnolocalities also undermine this possibility.

A few important observations emerge from the juxtapositions of these case studies. They all demonstrate how, first, the production of cultural difference involves complex, mostly asymmetrical sociologies, in which government officials, local elites, and ethnopreneurs play distinct, sometimes conflicting roles. If in Mali and among the Bafokeng, the ruling regime plays a central role in sanctioning authenticity, in other contexts described throughout this book, ethnicity, inc. projects emerge through local elites or from below, at times supported, at times foreclosed by the state. Second, the means through which difference is produced and circulated are growingly globalized. They involve mass media, advertising campaigns, television shows, documentary films, books, and social media, among other things. These prevailing means of constructing and narrating difference invite everyone, in an imagined global public, to share the same ground, as it were, for viewing and consuming difference, assessing its authenticity, and determining its value. Third, this inevitably leads to loci of difference that are more and more about similar things, including bodies, clothes, dances, music, narratives about the past, and whatever else might be easily recognizable as "culture." Fourth, and most importantly, despite the growing globalization of the means of producing difference, difference remains an uncertain quality, ridden with ambivalence and ambiguities. In this context, contestations of hegemonic formations of identity and alterity dialectically produce competing attempts to claim, own, and defend culture from commercialization and vulgarization. Those not directly engaged in it are nonetheless in conversation with it—not so much questioning its means and purposes as the particularities of its contents.

Absences, Specters, Margins

The last two chapters of our volume theorize from these margins of ethnicity, inc.—that is, from contexts in which it is violently contained or, simply, manifests itself as a path not taken, abandoned, stalled, or deferred. If ethnicity, inc. has the potential to both animate and annihilate, both to empower and to marginalize, the circumstances that allow for one set of potentialities to materialize over another are not equally manifest in all places at all times. In some places, only few people have access to the means of ethnoincorporation or cultural commodification. With the rise of the security state, military interventions, and moral securitization as central modalities of governmentality (Amar 2013), ruling regimes may prevent the emergence of ethnobusiness and ethnocommons. How then can we expand our understanding of ethnic commodification and incorporation from contexts in which these processes do not happen as we might expect them to? What can we learn from situations in which the state works to suppress the assertion of cultural difference? And how can we think of the *limits* and *failures* of ethnicity, inc. more generally?

Sara Shneiderman (chap. 7) shows how, in Nepal, it was initially a desire for national integration and more direct participation in state politics that determined the objectification of ethnic identity and not so much a desire to assert sovereignty against the state. Yet the failures of such quests for full citizenship have had surprising outcomes. Marginal pan-ethnic groups, such as the

Madhesi and the Janajati, have sought state recognition as ethnoterritorial entities. In recent years, Madhesi and Janajati activists hoped that upcoming constitutional reforms would allow them to overcome their long-standing exploitation at the hand of elites. Janajati hoped to move toward an "identity-based federalism," while Madhesi hoped to break free from the control of high-caste Hindu nationalists. At the same time, however, the latter sought to suppress expressions of ethnicity. Following the promulgation of a new constitution in 2015, political elites and state leaders succeeded in reconsolidating a conservative state structure, further marginalizing the Madhasi and the Janajati. But while the new constitution kept high-caste Hindu majorities in the leadership of each province—thus solidifying elite strategies to appropriate land—marginal indigenous groups actually became aware that their identity was vested in territory.

At first, Madhesi and Janajati groups tried to have their difference recognized by government. But unlike the Janajati who had stronger ties to elites, the state saw the Madhesi as culturally more alike to Indians than Nepalis—or, in other words, not sufficiently different from Nepal's neighbors to represent its ethnonational identity. When Shneiderman asked one of her Madhesi interlocutors why they did not commodify their culture for tourists, he said: "How can we try that when anything we do is seen to be Indian?" The state here played a central role in legitimizing manifestations of ethnic identity and cultural difference. Yet, as the elite hijacking of the new constitution crushed the hopes of indigenous ethnic activists, suddenly, among Madhesi, a desire emerged to assert cultural difference in new ways, often against the state. "It's only now that we have been rejected as Nepali by this constitution," one informant told Shneiderman, "that we are freely claiming our own culture." In this case, the potential for ethnicity, inc.—which is yet to be realized among Madhesi—emerges precisely out of the failures of citizenship and disappointment with the state.

Eve Darian-Smith (chap. 8) argues that new social and political dynamics in the global order make the annihilating potentialities of ethnicity, inc. more likely to realize themselves in most parts of the world. Focusing on the case of Australian Aborigines under violent forms of state intervention, militarization, and land alienation, she shows how these people, like asylum seekers, serve as targets of domination meant to uphold a form of nationalism premised on white supremacy. Driven by rising international inequalities, an intensified displacement of people (refugees, migrants), and militarization of state, there emerges a context in which, Darian-Smith argues, "increasingly marginalized people of the world have less, not more, access and opportunity to take advantage of the manifestations and implications of ethnicity, inc." Ethnicity, inc. is not absent in such contexts, but very present in its spectral form, as a fantasy, an abandoned trajectory, a path not pursued.

Starting in the 1970s, for example, indigenous dot painting became an important medium through which Aboriginal people commodified their culture. Throughout the following two decades, dot painting quickly became emblematic of Australian indigenous people, generating a large market that involved, among other things, a government-sponsored company, indigenous artists cooperatives, and NGOs supporting art centers. However, not only did indigenous people quickly realize that they could not control the interpretation of their work in the national and international arenas, but colonial stereotypes of indigeneity have also worked to legitimize ideologically violent state interventions that have come to reduce the possibility of empowerment through ethnicity. Since 2007, for example, the Australian federal government has initiated the so-called Northern Territory National Emergency Response, an emergency program deploying exceptional forms of governance in Aboriginal communities. Claiming to respond to allegations of sexual abuse and neglect of Aboriginal children, the state called up the military to control Aboriginal people, altered welfare services and land tenure regulations to their detriment, and thus limited the economic resources and political rights of these communities. Darian-Smith argues that "both permanent Afghani detainees and impoverished Aboriginal communities share a common future in Australia in that both must be kept out of sight and out of mind under policies of neocolonial management." Efforts to keep indigenous people "out of sight and mind" prevent them from achieving empowerment through the commodification of their culture, or indeed, ethnicity, inc. more generally.

What these examples suggest is that there are numerous, different paths into—or, indeed, *around*—ethnicity, inc. Most importantly, they show that this phenomenon need not manifest itself in its most identifiable forms—immediate commodification or incorporation—to be *present*, as a *real* potentiality, in any particular context. Therefore, ethnicity, inc. also resides as a *specter*: that is, as a path-not-yet-taken, a path-abandoned or deferred, a fantasy of worlds built otherwise. And, in all these instances, it nevertheless exists as a possibility objectified in language and practice, in relation to which people imagine other livelihoods, other futures.

NOTES

1. Our attention has been drawn to the fact that the term *incorporation* does not imply "constituting a company, city, or other organization as a

legal corporation" in many languages other than English (i.e., in addition to meaning "inclusion of something as part of a whole"; Peter Geschiere, personal communication).

2. Witness the insistence of the likes of Wilbur Ross, secretary of commerce to Donald Trump, that "economic security is military security" and hence valorizes all sorts of (political) action under its sign. See Martin Kettle, "Trump's Trade War Threatens Global Peace," *The Guardian*, June 2, 2018, 5.

3. Significantly for present purposes, these and other studies on the topic were published together, under Colloredo-Mansfield's (2011) editorship, as a special issue of *Anthropology of Work Review*, under the title "Work, Cultural Resources, and Community Commodities in the Global Economy."

4. See "Geographical Indications," World Intellectual Property Organization, accessed July 24, 2018, http://www.wipo.int/ geo_indications/en/.

5. Gregory Warner, "How One Kenyan Tribe Produces the World's Best Runners," *Parallels*, November 1, 2013, https://www.npr.org/sections /parallels/2013/11/01/241895965/how-one-kenyan-tribe- produces-the-worlds -best-runners.

6. Douglas Todd, "The Rapid Growth of Ethnic Economies," *Vancouver Sun*, February 19, 2018, https://vancouversun.com/news/staff-blogs/the-rapid-growth -of-ethnic-economies. The definition of "ethnic economies" offered in the report, as well as the term itself, was taken from Light and Gold (2000).

7. The complex, ambivalent relationship between the rise of thanatourism—aka disaster, dark, and grief tourism—and heritage tourism has garnered a growing literature in recent years; see, for example, Hartmann (2014) and Light (2017).

8. That is, at the time of writing *Ethnicity, Inc.* (see 16–18).

9. This quip was part of a conference talk, "What Is a Nation?," delivered at the Sorbonne on March 11, 1882. An online copy can be found at http://ucparis.fr /files/9313/6549/9943/What_is_a_Nation.pdf.

10. Tim Haughton, "It's the Slogan, Stupid: The Brexit Referendum," *Perspectives*, accessed May 24, 2018, https://www.birmingham.ac.uk/research /perspective/eu-ref-haughton.aspx. Those in favor of leaving the EU noted that they sought control over "our money and our economic policy."

11. Samanth Subramanian, "How to Sell a Country: The Booming Business of Nation Branding," *The Guardian*, November 24, 2017, https://www.theguardian .com/business/audio/2017/nov/24/how-to-sell-a-country-the-booming -business-of-nation-branding-podcast.

12. This is the contentious motto of the right-wing party, Alternative for Germany (AfD).

13. In *Ethnicity, Inc.* a number of early examples of this—among them, one remarkable one from Kenya (125–26)—were already put forward.

14. Of these, the last two are the least well-known internationally. Mark Rutte, three-time prime minister of the Netherlands, had been an executive in Unilever and a number of its subsidiaries before taking office; Tihomir Orešković became head of state in Croatia in 2016, having been CEO of his nation's largest pharmaceutical company and head of financial management for Teva, a multinational pharma. Of course, a number of US presidents before Donald Trump had been businessmen, but, unlike him, they had political careers before being elected.

15. It was in this sense, rather than the simple reduction of Nationality, Inc. to marketing (*pace* Surak 2010, 157), that the issue of nation branding was discussed in *Ethnicity, Inc.* (117).

16. Noam Chomsky, "Free Market Fantasies: Capitalism in the Real World," lecture delivered at Harvard University, April 13, 1996, https://chomsky.info /19960413/.

17. Subramanian, "How to Sell a Country."

18. "The image and reputation of countries can be a real deal maker—or breaker. How your country and nation is perceived by overseas audiences has implications for your success as destination, your economic development, public diplomacy and talent attraction," notes a report titled "Country Brands: 2017 Anholt-GfK Roper Nation Brands Study Reveals Winners, Losers and Trends." The report highlights features like the "welcoming . . . progress in world's image of Latin American nations, a region that experienced decades of turmoil and now making strides towards progress and stability" (*The Place Brand Observer*, November 22, 2017, https://placebrandobserver.com/anholt-gfk-nation-brands -index-2017-highlights).

19. See Anholt-GfK Nation Brands Index, accessed June 5, 2018, https:// nation-brands.gfk.com/.

20. The World Economic Forum offers a chart of "Countries Where You Can Buy Citizenship," replete with details of prevailing prices (starting at $100,000), residency requirements (often none), and qualifying period (also often none). It is striking how the number of these countries has risen since 2011 (Joe Myers, "Countries Where You Can Buy Citizenship," World Economic Forum, July 28, 2016, https://www.weforum.org/agenda/2016/07/countries-selling -citizenship).

21. Subramanian, "How to Sell a Country." See also "Cape Verde Holidays," SAGA, accessed June 20, 2018, https://travel.saga.co.uk/holidays/destinations /africa/cape-verde.aspx?; "Belong: St Kitts and Nevis," *High Life* (British Airways), June 2018, 35.

22. Subramanian, "How to Sell a Country."

23. Naomi Klein, "America Is Not a Hamburger," *The Guardian*, March 14, 2002, https://www.theguardian.com/media/2002/mar/14/marketingandpr .comment.

REFERENCES

Abu El-Haj, Nadia. 2012. *The Genealogical Science: The Search for Jewish Origins and the Politics of Epistemology*. Chicago: University of Chicago Press.

Anderson, Benedict. 1983. *Imagined Communities: Reflections on the Origin and Spread of Nationalism*. London: Verso.

Appadurai, Arjun. 1998. "Dead Certainty: Ethnic Violence in the Era of Globalization." *Development and Change* 29: 905–25.

Aragon, Lorraine V. 2011. "Where Commons Meet Commerce: Circulation and Sequestration in Indonesian Art Economies." *Anthropology of Work Review* 32 (2): 63–76.

Blakkisrud, Helge. 2016. "Blurring the Boundary between Civic and Ethnic: The Kremlin's New Approach to National Identity under Putin's Third Term." In *The New Russian Nationalism: Imperialism, Ethnicity and Authoritarianism 2000–2015*, edited by Pål Kolstø and Helge Blakkisrud, 249–74. Edinburgh: Edinburgh University Press.

Basu, Amrita. 1996. "Mass Movement or Elite Conspiracy?: The Puzzle of Hindu Nationalism." In *Contesting the Nation: Religion, Community, and the Politics of Democracy in India*, edited by David Ludden, 56–80. Philadelphia: University of Pennsylvania Press.

Benjamin, Ruha. 2015. "The Emperor's New Genes: Science, Public Policy, and the Allure of Objectivity." *Annals of the American Academy of Political and Social Science* 661 (1): 130–42.

Blignaut, Margarite. n.d. "Valuing Roma: Articulations of Development and Heritage in Turkey." Prospectus for Doctoral Dissertation Research, Department of Anthropology, Harvard University, 2018.

Brown, Wendy. 2003. "Neo-Liberalism and the End of Democracy." *Theory and Event* 7 (1). http://muse.jhu.edu/article/48659.

Brubaker, Rogers. 1992. *Citizenship and Nationhood in France and Germany*. Cambridge, MA: Harvard University Press.

Buthelezi, Mbongiseni, and Dineo Skosana. 2018. "The Salience of Chiefs in Postapartheid South Africa: Reflections on the Nhlapo Commission." In *The Politics of Custom: Chiefship, Capital, and the State in Contemporary Africa*, edited by John L. Comaroff and Jean Comaroff, 110–33. Chicago: University of Chicago Press.

Chan, Anita Say. 2011. "Competitive Tradition: Intellectual Property and New Millennial Craft." *Anthropology of Work Review* 32 (2): 90–102.

Colloredo-Mansfield, Rudi. 2011. "Work, Cultural Resources, and Community Commodities in the Global Economy." *Anthropology of Work Review* 32 (2): 51–62.

Comaroff, John L., and Jean Comaroff. 2009. *Ethnicity, Inc.* Chicago: University of Chicago Press.

———. 2011. "*Ethnizität.*" In *Lexikon der Globalisierung*, edited by Fernand Kreff, Eva-Maria Knoll, and Andre Gingrich, 68–72. Bieleveld: Transcript.

———. 2018. "Chiefs, Capital, and the State in Contemporary Africa: An Introduction." In *The Politics of Custom: Chiefship, Capital, and the State in Contemporary Africa*, edited by John L. Comaroff and Jean Comaroff, 1–48. Chicago: University of Chicago Press.

Coombe, Rosemary. 2012. "Managing Cultural Heritage as Neoliberal Governmentality." In *Heritage Regimes and the State*, edited by Regina F. Bendix, Aditya Eggert, Arnika Peselmann, and Sven Mißling, 375–89. Göttingen Studies in Cultural Property. Vol. 6. Göttingen: Göttingen University Press.

Copeland, Ian. n.d. "Sonic Humanitarianism: Affect, Altruism, and Musical Aid in Malawi." Prospectus for Doctoral Dissertation Research, Department of Music, Harvard University, 2018.

Corrigan, Philip R. D., and Derek Sayer. 1985. *The Great Arch: English State Formation as Cultural Revolution*. Oxford: Blackwell.

Coyle, Lauren. 2018. "Fallen Chiefs and Sacrificial Mining in Ghana." In *The Politics of Custom: Chiefship, Capital, and the State in Contemporary Africa*, edited by John L. Comaroff and Jean Comaroff, 247–78. Chicago: University of Chicago Press.

Crenshaw, Kimberle. 1989. "Demarginalizing the Intersection of Race and Sex: A Black Feminist Critique of Antidiscrimination, Doctrine, Feminist Theory and Antiracist Politics." *University of Chicago Legal Form* 1: 139–67.

Dávila, Arlene. 2012. *Latinos, Inc.: The Marketing and Making of a People*. Updated edition with a new preface. Berkeley: University of California Press. First edition, 2001.

Enrique, Falina. 2012. "The Ins and Outs of *Cultura*: How Bands Voice Their Relationships to the State-Sponsored Music Scene in Recife, Brazil." *Journal of Popular Music Studies* 24 (4): 532–53.

Fattal, Alexander L. 2018. *Guerrilla Marketing: Counterinsurgency and Capitalism in Colombia*. Chicago: University of Chicago Press.

Fontefrancesco, Michele F. 2012. "Crafting the Local: GIs, Jewelry, and Transformations in Valenza, Italy." *Social Analysis* 56 (3): 89–107.

Foucault, Michel. 2008. *The Birth of Biopolitics: Lectures at the Collège de France, 1978–1979*. Edited by Michel Senellart. Translated by Graham Burchell. New York: Picador.

Gerkey, Drew. 2011. "Abandoning Fish: The Vulnerability of Salmon as a Cultural Resource in a Post-Soviet Commons." *Anthropology of Work Review* 32 (2): 77–89.

Geschiere, Peter. 2009. *The Perils of Belonging: Autochthony, Citizenship, and Exclusion in Africa and Europe*. Chicago: University of Chicago Press.

———. 2018. "African Chiefs and the Post-Cold War Moment: Millennial Capitalism and the Struggle over Moral Authority." In *The Politics of*

Custom: Chiefship, Capital, and the State in Contemporary Africa, edited by John
  L. Comaroff and Jean Comaroff, 49–78. Chicago: University of Chicago Press.

Graan, Andrew. 2013. "Counterfeiting the Nation? Skopje 2014 and the Politics of
  Nation Branding in Macedonia." *Cultural Anthropology* 28 (1): 161–79.

Hartmann, Rudi. 2014. "Dark Tourism, Thanatourism, and Dissonance in
  Heritage Tourism Management: New Directions in Contemporary Tourism
  Research." *Journal of Heritage Tourism* 9 (2): 166–82.

Harvey, David. 1990. *The Condition of Postmodernity: An Enquiry into the Origins of
  Cultural Change*. Oxford: Blackwell.

James, Deborah. 2015. *Money from Nothing: Indebtedness and Aspiration in South
  Africa*. Stanford: Stanford University Press.

Kamenka, Eugene, ed. 1975. *Nationalism: The Nature and Evolution of an Idea*.
  Canberra: Australian National University Press.

Kaneva, Nadia. 2011. "Nation Branding: Toward an Agenda for Critical Research."
  International Journal of Communication 5: 117–41.

Kapferer, Bruce. 2018. "Introduction: Crises of Power and the State in Global
  Realities." In *State, Resistance, Transformation: Anthropological Perspectives on the
  Dynamics of Power in Contemporary Global Realities*, edited by Bruce Kapferer.
  Canon Pyon, Herts, UK: Sean Kingston.

Kelly-Holmes, Helen, and Sari Pietikäinen. 2014. "Commodifying Sámi Culture in
  an Indigenous Tourism Site." *Journal of Sociolinguistics* 18 (4): 518–38.

Kerrigan, Finola, Jyotsna Shivanandan, and Anne-Marie Hede. 2012. "Nation
  Branding: A Critical Appraisal of Incredible India." *Journal of Macromarketing* 32
  (3): 319–27.

Light, Duncan. 2017. "Progress in Dark Tourism and Thanatourism Research: An
  Uneasy Relationship with Heritage Tourism." *Tourism Management* 61: 275–301.

Light, Ivan Hubert, and Steven J. Gold. 2000. *Ethnic Economies*. Bingley, UK:
  Emerald Group.

Marsh, David, and Paul Fawcett. "Branding, Politics and Democracy." *Policy
  Studies* 32 (5): 515–30.

Mazzarella, William. 2017. *The Mana of Mass Society*. Chicago: University of
  Chicago Press.

Meiu, George Paul. 2015. "'Beach-Boy Elders' and 'Young Big-Men': Subverting
  the Temporalities of Aging in Kenya's Ethno-erotic Economies." *Ethnos* 80 (4):
  472–96.

———. 2017. *Ethno-erotic Economies: Sexuality, Money, and Belonging in Kenya*.
  Chicago: University of Chicago Press.

Munn, Nancy D. 1986. *The Fame of the Gawa: A Symbolic Study of Value
  Transformation in a Massim (Papua New Guinea) Society*. Cambridge: Cambridge
  University Press.

Nagel, Joane. 2003. *Race, Ethnicity, and Sexuality: Intimate Intersections, Forbidden
  Frontiers*. London: Oxford University Press.

Nakassis, Constantine V. 2013. "Brands and Their Surfeits." *Cultural Anthropology* 28 (1): 111–26.

Ofstehage, Andrew. 2011. "Nusta Juira's Gift of Quinoa: Peasants, Trademarks and Intermediaries in the Transformation of a Bolivian Commodity Economy." *Anthropology of Work Review* 32 (2): 103–14.

Petryna, Adriana. 2009. *When Experiments Travel: Clinical Trials and the Global Search for Human Subjects.* Princeton, NJ: Princeton University Press.

Pierre, Jemima. 2013. *The Predicament of Blackness: Postcolonial Ghana and the Politics of Race.* Chicago: University of Chicago Press.

Povinelli, Elizabeth A. 2006. *The Empire of Love: Toward a Theory of Intimacy, Genealogy, and Carnality.* Durham, NC: Duke University Press.

Reid, Herbert, and Betsy Taylor. 2010. *Recovering the Commons: Democracy, Place, and Global Justice.* Champaign: University of Illinois Press.

Renan, Ernest. 1992. *Qu'est-ce qu'une nation?* Translated by Ethan Rundell. Paris: Presses-Pocket.

Sanders, Emily. 2015. "Saami vs. Metsähallitus: The Case for Corporate Recognition of Indigenous Rights." *Cultural Survival Quarterly Magazine* 39 (1): 16–17.

Saxer, Martin. 2013. *Manufacturing Tibetan Medicine: The Creation of an Industry and the Moral Economy of Tibetanness.* New York: Berghahn.

Schweitzer, Erwin. 2015. *The Making of Griqua, Inc.: Indigenous Struggles for Land and Autonomy in South Africa.* Vienna: Lit Verlag.

Shankar, Shalini. 2012. "Creating Model Consumers: Producing Ethnicity, Race, and Class in Asian American Advertising." *American Ethnologist* 39 (3): 578–91.

———. 2015. *Advertising Diversity: Ad Agencies and the Creation of Asian American Consumers.* Durham, NC: Duke University Press.

Siew-Min Sai and Chang-Yau Hoon. 2013. "Introduction: A Critical Reassessment of Chinese Indonesian Studies." In *Chinese Indonesians Reassessed: History, Religion and Belonging,* edited by Siew-Min Sai and Chang-Yau Hoon, 1–26. New York: Routledge.

Smith, James. 2018. "Colonizing Banro: Kingship, Temporality, and Mining of Futures in the Goldfields of South Kivu, DRC." In *The Politics of Custom: Chiefship, Capital, and the State in Contemporary Africa,* edited by John L. Comaroff and Jean Comaroff, 279–304. Chicago: University of Chicago Press.

Smith, Rogers. 1986. *The Ethnic Origin of Nations.* Oxford: Blackwell.

Surak, Kristin. 2010. "The Business of Belonging: Review of *Ethnicity, Inc.,* John L. Comaroff and Jean Comaroff." *New Left Review* 63 (May–June): 151–59.

Tilly, Charles. 1990. *Coercion, Capital, and European States, AD 990–1990.* Oxford: Blackwell.

Turner, Victor W. 1970. *The Forest of Symbols: Aspects of Ndembu Ritual.* Ithaca, NY: Cornell University Press.

Wang, Mengqi. 2012. "The Social Life of Scripts: Staging Authenticity in China's Ethno-Tourism Industry." *Urban Anthropology and Studies of Cultural Systems and World Economic Development* 41 (2/3/4): 419–55.

Weber, Max. 1968. *Economy and Society: An Outline of Interpretive Sociology*. 3 vols. Edited by Guenther Roth and Claus Wittich. New York: Bedminster Press.

Weiss, Joseph. 2018. *Shaping the Future on Haida Gwaii: Life beyond Settler Colonialism*. Vancouver: University of British Columbia Press.

Zips, Werner. 2015. "Ethno-Marketing—Indigenous Cultures on Sale: A Foreword." In *The Making of Griqua, Inc.: Indigenous Struggles for Land and Autonomy in South Africa*, edited by Erwin Schweitzer, 5–11. Vienna: Lit Verlag.

———. 2018. "Preface: 'Stars of their Own Show': Close Readings of Ju/'Hoansi San Performances of Culture and Tradition." In *Tracking Indigenous Heritage: Ju/'Hoansi San Learning, Interpreting, and Staging Tradition for a Sustainable Future in Cultural Tourism in the Tsumkwe District of Namibia*, edited by Salomé Ritterband, 15–32. Vienna: Lit Verlag.

GEORGE PAUL MEIU is John and Ruth Hazel Associate Professor of the Social Sciences in the Department of Anthropology and the Department of African and African American Studies at Harvard University. He is author of *Ethno-erotic Economies: Sexuality, Money, and Belonging in Kenya.*

JEAN COMAROFF is Alfred North Whitehead Professor of African and African American Studies and of Anthropology and Oppenheimer Research Fellow in African Studies at Harvard University. She is Honorary Professor of Anthropology at the University of Cape Town. She is coauthor of *Theory from the South: or, How Euro-America Is Evolving toward Africa, The Truth about Crime: Sovereignty, Knowledge, Social Order,* and *The Politics of Custom: Chiefship, Capital, and the State in Contemporary Africa.*

JOHN L. COMAROFF is Hugh K. Foster Professor of African and African American Studies and of Anthropology and Oppenheimer Research Fellow in African Studies at Harvard University. He is Honorary Professor of Anthropology at the University of Cape Town and Affiliated Research Professor at the American Bar Foundation. He is coauthor of *Theory from the South: or, How Euro-America Is Evolving toward Africa, The Truth about Crime: Sovereignty, Knowledge, Social Order,* and *The Politics of Custom: Chiefship, Capital, and the State in Contemporary Africa.*

ONE

ON BRANDING, BELONGING, AND THE VIOLENCE OF A PHALLIC IMAGINARY

The Maasai Warrior in Kenyan Tourism

GEORGE PAUL MEIU

MY STORY BEGINS WITH A touristic postcard I bought in Nairobi, sometime in August 2008 (fig. 1.1). At first sight, it is a postcard like any other that one may encounter in airports or souvenir shops in Kenya. It depicts the portrait of a young, slim, black man, smiling, somewhat shyly, while looking away from the camera. The man is probably in his late teens or early twenties. His bodily decorations are of the kind foreign tourists and Kenyans alike recognize as traditional or ethnic. Linear geometric patterns painted horizontally with red ochre sharpen the features of his cheeks and eyebrows. Strings of colored plastic beads and metal chains tied across his forehead and around his neck accentuate his facial shape. His left earlobe is pierced and stretched on a white, ivory cylinder. A short, beaded accessory hangs from the top of his ear. The text on the postcard describes this man as an "African warrior." It does not specify his tribe or ethnicity. But this generic description is sufficient to sell the card. For, together with the image, it echoes long-standing primitivist ideas of Africa and its warrior traditions. Despite the postcard's generic nature, however, most tourists will readily recognize the young man as Maasai. They will have already encountered the prototypical image of the Maasai warrior, or *moran*, on travel websites, airport banners, and safari vans; in brochures and coffee-table books; or in souvenir stores (in the form of wooden sculptures, metal candlesticks, or plastic fridge magnets). The typical Maasai warrior appears throughout as tall and slim, decorated with beads and ochre, dressed only with a red loincloth, his youthful body exuding erotic appeal. From these contexts, most tourists learn that the red color of the warrior's dress is emblematic of his ethnic identity. It is no coincidence then that on the postcard I discuss here, the description

35

Fig. 1.1. Touristic postcard,
"African Warrior," Kenya.
(Fair use; © Sampra
M.M., Nairobi.)

AFRICAN
WARRIOR

"African warrior" appears in red letters. Thus, the postcard at once invites its viewers to discover the young man's identity on their own while hinting implicitly to his unmistakable Maasainess.

When I bought this postcard, I was researching how the commodification of the Maasai warrior in Kenyan tourism shaped ethnic group and state belonging. One phenomenon interested me in particular. Since the early 1980s, men of the Samburu ethnic group, from northern Kenya, migrated to coastal beach resorts, south and north of the town of Mombasa, to make a living in tourism. They drew on their cultural and linguistic relatedness to the more famous Maasai (who reside mostly in southern Kenya and northern Tanzania)—including their shared custom of the initiation of men as morans—to introduce themselves to tourists as Maasai or, as they would have it, as a more authentic subgroup thereof. At the coast, Samburu men dressed in traditional attire, sold souvenirs at the beach, and performed dances in tourist hotels. Their cultural

Otherness and erotic appeal attracted women from western Europe, who now desired intimate relationships with them. Some women sought Maasai warriors for one-night stands; others, for long-term relationships, including marriages. Through such relationships, some Samburu men gained wealth. With money they obtained from their partners, they returned to northern Kenya, where they acquired houses, land, businesses, and cars, and achieved authority as influential "big men" (Meiu 2015). Indeed, at the time of my research, some of the richest in Samburu were men in relationships with European women. Over the years, this prompted hundreds of young men to migrate to the coast. Between 2005 and 2015, I carried out twenty-five months of research in Kenya exploring how these men performed warrior masculinity in tourism, invested their money, and tried to negotiate emerging conflicts over their respectability and belonging. During my research, I collected postcards like the one described because they exemplified the image that potentially generated spectacular value in tourism. Tourist companies used the image of the Maasai warrior as a logo for their ads, young men I worked with performed this image in different ways to attract Europeans, and tourists themselves sought to meet "real-life" warriors in order to authenticate their sojourns. In these ways, the warrior image had become emblematic of Maa-language speakers like Maasai and Samburu and a successful brand of East Africa as a tourist destination.

But, as I was to discover, the story of the man depicted on the postcard also spoke of another, darker side of the exchanges I was studying. When I showed it to my research assistant, Lteipan, a Samburu man in his early thirties who had been seasonally migrating to coastal resorts for almost fifteen years, he immediately recognized the man in the image. His name was Losolia Lelenguia, though he used to introduce himself as Peter, a name that tourists were more likely to remember. Peter, Lteipan told me, had died in 1997, when "coastal people" (Swahili[1]: *watu wa pwani*)—that is, ethnic groups claiming to belong to the coast—rose to chase away so-called upcountry people (S: *watu wa bara*), or migrants and migrant settlers originating in Kenya's interior regions. I decided then to find out more about Peter and the events that led to his death. I looked up newspapers and reports of the time and interviewed Samburu who had known him.

In April 2011, I met Leramat, Peter's former friend. The two of them had been initiated as morans in the late 1970s and then, since the 1980s, had traveled together to the coast. He recalled in detail how, on the evening of September 5, 1997, he and Peter, along with twenty-five other Samburu men, had been preparing to perform dances in the Shelly Beach Hotel, a major tourist resort south of Mombasa. While they were waiting for the time of their scheduled performance in a small bar across the street from the hotel, a group of some hundred young men attacked them with machetes and guns. The attackers were members of the so-called Kaya Bombo uprising, a violent youth movement through which young men, mainly of the coastal Digo ethnic group sought to expel upcountry people. Kaya Bombo youth felt that coastal people had lost land and jobs to migrants from upcountry (see also Mahoney 2017, chap. 2). Most Samburu men, including Leramat, survived the incident, despite severe injuries. One had been killed on the spot. Peter sustained machete cuts on his head and leg and died in a hospital sometime later. After he finished telling me Peter's story, Leramat removed the red cloth that covered his upper body. "You see these scars?" he asked me. His chest, back, and waist were covered in long, pronounced, linear scars. "These are all from that day. They cut me with the machetes. I was lucky I survived."

Leramat's story and Peter's death prompted me to think of the potential for conflict and violence that lay behind the serene erotics of the Maasai warrior on touristic postcards. Violent events, such as those of 1997, are not instances of timeless tribal feuds as they often figure in the international media. Nor, for that matter, can they be reduced to the attempts of Kenyan political leaders to incite violence between different ethnic groups, by way of manipulating electoral demographics. This, of course, was part of the problem. That year, Daniel Arap Moi, who had been Kenya's president since 1978, was coming up for reelection, and KANU, his party, was trying to secure coastal votes. Some accused KANU and Moi of inciting coastal youth to violently evict migrants, because they knew the latter would most likely not vote for them. However, the meanings and sentiments that informed these violent incidents were not merely a function of political manipulation. Rather, such events were part of a wider spectrum of conflicts over belonging. Among these were conflicts emerging as some people, like Samburu and Maasai, discovered they could market their culture and ethnic sexuality and thus earn money in ways that others could not.

This chapter explores how interethnic violence of the kind that Peter, Leramat, and other Samburu encountered on the coast relates to their attempts to generate value by speculating on and enacting touristic imaginaries of the Maasai warrior. I wish to understand the historical concurrence of the warrior's marketability with the violent events that accompanied his touristic performance. I ask how Samburu migrants in tourism imagine themselves through a more general pan-Maa identity and through the youthful masculinity of the prototypical warrior? How does a certain image of identity shape belonging and ethnic regionalism? How does the commodification of warrior sexuality as part of the Maasai brand shape how migrants and coastal people experience belonging—whether violently or otherwise? And what work does violence do in contexts of ethnic commodification?

BRANDING, BELONGING, AND VIOLENCE

In the conclusion of *Ethnicity, Inc.*, John and Jean Comaroff (2009, 143) reflect on how violence may figure in the process of ethnic incorporation and commodification. "Does the incorporation of identity not bear within it a dark energy," they ask, "the potential to foment division, dissension, even homicidal hatreds?" "How, more generally does the commodification of cultural being relate to the kinds of violent confrontation so often associated with assertions of ethnic consciousness, belonging, and birthright?" The marketing of culture and identity, the Comaroffs argue, carries multiple, contrasting potentialities. It has "*both* insurgent possibility *and* a tendency to deepen prevailing lines of inequality, the capacity *both* to enable *and* to disable, the power *both* to animate and annihilate" (139). How different potentialities materialize in any given context is mostly a question of historical contingency. Yet, although ethnic commodification and incorporation unfold differently in different contexts, they also play out, as the Comaroffs show, by logics that are similar across the world. Branding, for example, now offers people everywhere a means for producing, assessing, and contesting social and economic value. Meanwhile, a preoccupation with belonging has risen globally, sometimes manifesting itself through political conflict and violence. But the concrete ways in which branding and belonging intersect in practice and relate to violence require further theorization.

Belonging has become a hot topic worldwide in recent decades. With late capitalism, people and goods have been circulating more intensively within and across borders, and displacement and mobility have become generalized conditions of social life. But this trend has also produced a counter movement. Following neoliberal economic reforms, in Africa and elsewhere, more and more people have turned to autochthony, ethnoregionalism, ethnicity, or indigeneity as dominant criteria of social attachment. These are not mere attempts to close off social worlds and defend them from foreigners. Nor are they naive ways of shutting out the outside world—quite the contrary. They represent ways to benefit more fully from global flows of capital. Being rooted in land or being attached to seemingly immutable identities are now more effective ways to position oneself, claim rights and recognition, and access resources in national and global arenas. Since the late 1970s, the retraction of the welfare state, the effects of structural adjustment programs, and the rise of an ethos of speculation and entrepreneurialism have fueled a return to the local. Peter Geschiere (2009) argues that throughout Africa, democratization and state decentralization have led to a rising preoccupation with autochthony or local belonging. Various polities, regions, and social groups now claim autochthonous attachments. Both politicians and commoners, the rich and the poor, find new meanings in the idea of a primordial attachment to land, ethnicity, and culture. Amid intensified flux, such attachments promise not just profit and power, but a sense of stability, durability, and rootedness.

The pursuit of belonging, however, often takes the routes of violence, exclusion, and displacement. A central irony, Geschiere notes (2009, 5), animates contemporary understandings of local belonging. On the one hand, it seems natural, self-evident, embedded in blood and emotion. On the other hand, it remains ambiguous, uncertain, constantly requiring validation and reiteration. Under these circumstances, as Vigdis Broch-Due (2005, 1) suggests, "violence is often employed as a futile quest to produce certainty, a means to reinforce essentialized ideas about identity and belonging." Violence, Broch-Due argues, is more than the sum of its destructive qualities. It is also a means of identification and differentiation that is meaningful, if read through the "thick" social relations in which it plays out. As the state retracts and global resources shift course in seemingly unpredictable ways, violence becomes a means to claim belonging and appropriate vital forces in the face of people's growing sense of disconnection, loss, and exclusion (Geschiere and Meyer 1998). In this context, violence also represents a way to disambiguate the social differences between autochthons and foreigners (Appadurai 1998).

Like violence, the branding of collective identities is also driven by a quest for certainty. With the commodification and incorporation of ethnicity, branding becomes a means—at once semiotic and sentimental—for owning identities and establishing new parameters for belonging. Martin Chanock (2000, 26) argues that "the international market . . . does not make cultures disappear, but it manipulates them in particular ways, using cultural essences to create loyalty to the universal brand. The cultural element is important because it is the manipulation of identity that creates the attachment." In other words, through branding, culture must become reducible to a set of essential(izing) features that secure both its distinctiveness and its universal recognizability. Cultural belonging is then established through such essences-*cum*-brands. Building on Chanock's point, the Comaroffs (2009, 24) suggest that "those who seek to brand their otherness, to profit from what makes them different, find themselves having to do so in the universally recognizable terms in which difference is represented, merchandised, rendered negotiable by means of the abstract instruments of the market: money, the commodity, commensuration, the calculus of supply and demand, price, branding. And advertising." This means that culture and the commodity are more and more inflected with each other's logics or less and less easy to tell apart (28). As Chanock (2000, 26) puts it, nowadays, "successful and sustainable cultures are those which brand best."

Branding culture, however, is not a straightforward undertaking. Anthropologists have described brands as inherently unstable, indeterminate semiotic processes, which are prone to encounter gaps and failures while circulating or being consumed (Manning 2010; Mazzarella 2003; Moore 2003; Nakassis 2012, 2013). Brands refer to performed relations of signification between the concrete objects or things that one consumes—that is, the *brand tokens*—and the categories, names, or images that the tokens are said to instantiate, that is, the *brand types*. Consuming brands, people also come to inhabit worlds in particular ways, thus generating *brand ontologies* (Nakassis 2012, 631). The semiotic relations between brand types, tokens, and ontologies are often slippery. In various contexts, brands are counterfeited, their names may dissolve into common nouns, or their material components may turn into other branded goods. Or they may fail to generate any desires altogether. In other words, brands are inherently "vulnerable to contingency" (Moore 2003, 334). And if their parts have long been managed by professional specialists, following market liberalization, brands are often strategically left open and inarticulate to allow consumers to become part of—or discover themselves in—the making of these brands (Mazzarella 2003, 194; Nakassis 2012, 629). Recall, for example, the postcard that I described at the beginning of this chapter: While its value is premised on the brand type of the Maasai warrior, it allows viewers to discover themselves that the man in the image is indeed Maasai. Viewers can thus become cultural explorers of their own, as it were.

But what happens when the vulnerability of the brand—the slippery semiotic articulation of its parts—intersects with the uncertainties that haunt contemporary quests for belonging, that is, with the social anxieties that inform people's desires to know who really belongs and who does not? And what happens when, in the process of marketing identity, a specific brand type—such as the young male warrior—suddenly comes to anchor claims to collective belonging, creating new opportunities for some but not for others?

A central contradiction animates my analysis—namely, that ethnic subjects seek to fix, stabilize, and make durable brands of collective identity that promise spectacular wealth, while the reality of their social life in the present is in excess of, or cannot be adequately represented through, their brand image. First, the primitivist fantasies signified by the Maasai moran of touristic postcards do not reflect contemporary social realities among Maasai or Samburu (although, indeed, the marketing of this brand image now shapes social life there in unexpected ways). Second, in the case of Samburu, what drives the influx of capital and, with it, new pursuits for belonging is a specific body image that is male, young, and sexual. But it is impossible—to state the obvious—that all Samburu suddenly become young, male warriors or that even young men can fully inhabit the narrow contours of their erotic brand image. This body image thus excludes women, children, or older men while also posing myriad challenges for young men who try to perform and assume it. Inspired by Jacques Lacan's concept of the imaginary and the mirror stage and his notion of the phallus, I examine struggles that emerge when men try to embody the image of the ethnic warrior and when a young male body comes to brand ethnicity as a whole. After I examine how these struggles transform the means and terms of ethnic attachment, I return to violence to explore how it makes manifest uncertainties of both branding and belonging. But before I proceed, some background is necessary.

TOURISM, MIGRATION, AND ETHNIC REGIONS IN KENYA

Beneath a widespread political discourse of national unity in Kenya, ethnicity plays an important role in regional belonging and national citizenship. Since the country's independence in 1963, ethnic categories transformed and solidified by the British colonial administration have shaped access to state resources, land ownership, and political authority. More populous ethnic groups, such as Kikuyu, Luo, Kalenjin, and Kamba, have dominated state governance and, at different times, controlled the distribution of national resources and development (Lynch 2011; Oucho 2002). Ethnicity has also served as a key criterion of patronage relations between political leaders and the populations of different regions of the country, thus informing the geopolitical distribution of wealth. Consequently, electoral practices—as well as, for example, the violence that took place around election time in 1997 or 2008—have been anchored in networks of patronage based on ethnicity (Mwakikagile 2001; Ouchu 2002). In this national context, different ethnic groups and their regions did not interact on equal terms. Drawing on colonial and development discourses of progress, some, such as Kikuyu, have appeared modern and progressive, while pastoralists like Maasai, Samburu, Pokot, or Turkana have persistently been seen as backward, underdeveloped, and primitive. Such dominant perceptions have played an important role in legitimizing ideologically the political and economic marginalization of various ethnoregions.

Both the Coast Province and the Samburu District have been largely marginal to the state. But their respective marginalities have been of different kinds and magnitudes. The coast is important economically yet has remained peripheral in national politics. The coastal city of Mombasa, for example, has been an important international port and a major employer in the region (Cooper 1987). What is more, its engagement in trade relations with the Middle East and India have been central sources of revenue for both local elites and the government. Beach tourism too—the most popular attraction in Kenya—has been a significant source of national revenue. Yet coastal politicians have remained marginal (Mahoney 2017). The predominance of Islam in the region and its rule by Arab or Swahili elites has prompted upcountry politicians, most of them Christian, to be wary of the participation of coastal leaders in government. Since independence, those coastal leaders—like Ronald Ngala—have critiqued upcountry politicians for alienating the coast. They have repeatedly called for a form of regional federalism, known as *majimboism*, hoping for greater political self-determination. If only the coast were independent, they reasoned, it would have abundant resources to become self-sufficient.

By contrast to the coast, Samburu and northern Kenya, more generally, have been marginal to the state both politically *and* economically. British colonials saw little potential for profit in the region's semiarid savannah environment. They also saw its mostly pastoralist populations as culturally conservative and reluctant to embrace modernization. Hence, they closed off what was then the Northern Frontier District and governed it—mostly through military repressive power—as a zone of exception (Simpson 1994). Following independence, the Kenyan government continued to neglect the region, postponing investments in infrastructure or economic development. Its administrators were appointed by the central government until very recently; these men came mostly from dominant ethnic groups that were already in power. In this context, stereotypes of Samburu cultural backwardness proliferated and informed how foreign leaders governed them. For Kenya's elites, Samburu were primitive, violent, and sexually promiscuous. And, for them, Samburu morans seemed to congeal these properties most saliently. But, for tourists, their cultural distinctiveness held greater value than that of other Kenyans, creating new possibilities for some Samburu to subvert national ethnic hierarchies by commodifying their culture.

Tourism has grown spectacularly in the past four decades. Throughout the seventies, the tourist arrivals in Kenya leveled at 350,000 per year (quoted in Schoss 1995, 36–38); over the following decades it grew steadily, reaching 1.7 million in 2011 (KIPPRA 2013, 26). In addition to safaris (undertaken mostly in the southern reserves of Maasai Mara, Tsavo, and Amboseli), the beaches along the Indian Ocean brought in the majority of visitors. The coast, therefore, became central to the tourism industry. Samburu District, however, was far removed from these sites of touristic encounters. Cattle rustling and carjacking also deterred foreigners from venturing into the region. Here, then, was a central conundrum for Samburu: while their ethnic identity was more marketable to tourists than that of other Kenyans, its convertibility into cash required access to regions of the country where tourism thrived, yet these were regions where most of them felt they did not belong.

Samburu, in short, like southern Maasai, had something that visitors wanted. In particular, the image of the Maasai warrior, hunting lions, dancing in vertical thrusts, holding a spear and a club, has long been part of Euro-American fantasies of East Africa. It appeared on postcards, in coffee-table books, and in Hollywood movies (Kasfir 1999, 2007), congealing the authenticity of an African culture untainted by modernity and colonialism. Since the mid-twentieth century, some Maasai and Samburu have benefited, in various ways, from the desires of foreigners to photograph and film them. Some have appeared as extras in movies and others—like Peter, whom I introduced at the beginning of this chapter—are pictured on postcards. But such opportunities have been relatively rare in the north. If they were to be involved more fully in marketing their appearance, Samburu had to participate directly in tourism. In the 1960s, several men worked on the farm of a white settler in Limuru, near Nairobi, where they occasionally danced for tourists (Bruner and Kirshenblatt-Gimblett 1994). With the rise of beach tourism, however, they soon saw more possibilities for selling culture at the coast.

At the time of their first migration to the coast, most Samburu men were members of the moran age grade. In Samburu District, men are initiated through circumcision into moranhood once every fourteen years or so. In this ritual process, initiates aged fifteen through twenty-five come to form an age set. Over the next fourteen years, until the initiation of a new age set, morans are not allowed to marry and are expected to fend for themselves (Spencer 1965, 102–72). Some herd cattle, others are employed as soldiers and policemen, and yet others work informally in tourism. So, since 1979, many morans have migrated seasonally to the coast. There, they live together in small ethnic enclaves in Diani, Mtwapa, Watamu, and Malindi, where they rent and share small rooms. During the day, they sell crafts along the beach or dance in cultural villages, and in the evenings, they perform in tourist hotels. Many of them have had relationships with European women. The image of these men at the coast was truly sensational when they first arrived. In 1980, for example,

Kenya's major national newspaper, *Daily Nation*, published a photograph of two morans resting on the white sands at Serena Beach amid foreign visitors, and looking toward the ocean. The caption read: "They're a long way from home ... but for these Masai [*sic*] morans, complete with traditional spears and rungus [clubs], the sight of surf pounding on a silver beach is just as fascinating as it is for the tourists."[2]

BECOMING MAASAI MORANS:
BRAND IDENTITY AS PHALLIC BODY IMAGE

Samburu men who arrived at the beach for the first time quickly found that, in order to access tourist spaces, meet foreign women, and build relationships with them, there was much to be learned. One told me that before he started migrating to the coast, he had heard from friends that "in Mombasa, a white woman can fall in love with you even if you don't talk to her." The very sight of the bodies of young men dressed in traditional attire, he implied, often led female tourists to initiate intimate relationships with them. Indeed, in Samburu District, there were many stories of how these young men had arrived on the coast—often without speaking a word of English—and immediately found rich foreign partners. While such stories motivated many of them to migrate, the reality of their first arrival on the coast was more complicated. As Samburu migrants put it, a man had to learn first how to become a "moran of business" (Maa: *lmurrani lolbiashara*). They had to learn English and Swahili, a bit of German and Italian, how to calculate and negotiate prices for artifacts, and how to entertain foreigners. "The first time I came to the beach I was very *primitive*," one told me in Maa (italicized word in English). "I didn't even know how to speak to a tourist. But one gains *experience* slowly, slowly." Many of my informants saw the time they spent at the coast as part of becoming "modern" or cosmopolitan. Ironically perhaps, to achieve this cosmopolitanism, they had first to learn how to look "primitive" by performing as Maasai warrior in specific ways.

Becoming a moran of business presupposed, among other things, assuming the body image and bodily theatricality—gestures, posture, smiles—that instantiated the kind of erotic warrior desired by tourists. When Zakayo began migrating to the coast in 2005, he was in his late teens and close to finishing high school in Maralal, Samburu District. But because his parents could no longer afford tuition, he decided to make money in tourism. "I was very uncomfortable dressing up in traditional clothes," he told me in an interview in 2008. "At home, in Maralal, I always wore pants and shirts. Only bush people dressed like that. I thought that people would laugh at me." But Zakayo soon learned to be proud of "his" traditional attire; it was what, in the eyes of visitors, made him distinct from other Kenyans. Every day, before going to the beach, he tied a red loincloth around his waist, placed two strings of colored beads diagonally across his bare chest, and covered his forearms with beaded bracelets and other decorations. He tied a handkerchief on his head and placed several strings of beads around his forehead. When tourists stopped by the beach stand where he sold souvenirs, he adopted a distinctive posture. He stood up straight, shoulders pushed back, smiled and looked his interlocutors in the eye. When female tourists asked him for permission to photograph themselves with him, he often hugged them gently. Smiles, soft touches, and intensive glances were all part of what produced the ethno-erotic persona of the moran.

This bodily performance, my informants told me, did not always come naturally to them. "You know," Zakayo explained, "when you go to the beach for the first time, you are shy. You fear to go up to the white person and talk. So, you have to learn how to present yourself." While some gestures, gaits, and bodily postures were part of the habitus of moran masculinity in the north, much was new at the coast (cf. Kasfir 2007). Here, men seek to perform moranhood in ways that appeal to foreigners. The likes of Zakayo, who had been in high school, told visitors stories of lion hunts in which they had participated; how they had never worn pants or modern clothes; and also reevaluated their own notions of intimacy and bodily proximity. "In Samburu, you cannot just hold a woman's hand or kiss her when she comes up to you," Zakayo said. "But at the beach, that's how it works." Furthermore, while at the coast, some of my informants had also joined gyms, working out to lose weight or stay in shape to fit the image of the slim, strong moran.

Thus, I argue, many Samburu men encountered the "European" image of the moran body, at first, as patently foreign to themselves. The postcard moran was something to which they have to aspire, its successful assumption materializing through the tourists' desires. I read this assumption of a body image, as I have already intimated, in light of what Jacques Lacan describes as the processes of the imaginary in the mirror stage. In the mirror stage, Lacan (1977, 76–80) argues, we encounter our body image as something alien from us—a representation that appears outside us, in the mirror. But soon we desire to *be* that image, to have its tidy contours to fully represent our lived being. This, however, is never possible, since the turbulent corporeal flows and affects—the Sturm und Drang of our existence—are always in excess of the self-contained image in the mirror. So, Lacan wrote, "the mirror stage is a drama whose internal pressure pushes precipitously from insufficiency to anticipation . . . and to the final donned armor of an alienating identity that will mark [the subject's] entire mental development with its rigid structure" (78). This assumption of an alienating identity produces a central contradiction between the Real, our own visceral being-in-the-world, and the Imaginary, an image that is given to us as initially alien from ourselves but that we nevertheless must continuously desire to become. Although, with the acquisition of language, we have new (symbolic) ways to refer to the mirror image as being "ours" and to ourselves as independent subjects more generally (in other words, we acquire what Lacan describes as the "*I*-function"), the drama of the mirror stage never ends. We continuously have to desire to assume an image of ourselves that would grant us the recognition and desire of the Other. Echoing the Lacanian mirror stage, men who perform Maasai warriorhood for tourists encounter this persona as something at first alien to themselves—at least in part. It may appear on postcards, in films, in the touristic fantasy, but it does not fully coincide with what they know. So, in becoming "morans of business," they seek to assume that image in ways that promise to elicit the recognition and desire of foreigners as well as their home communities (if only later, when they will have accessed money). This process is never complete; the desire of the other never guaranteed. But the quest to embody, fix, and stabilize the relation between the subject and the desired body image drives a dialectical process through which both subject and image are remade.

Understanding Samburu men's assumption of the moran body image as akin to the Lacanian mirror stage requires some clarification. First, encountering their brand image is certainly not the only way in which these men come into subjectivity. Nor is it one of the first moments of subjectivation in their lives. Nothing could be further from the truth. In Samburu District, domestic practices, kinship relations, schooling, humanitarian aid, circumcision ceremonies, and the customary institution of moranhood, among other things, play central roles in the making of masculine subjectivities, from early childhood through adulthood (Spencer 1965). One might even interpret Samburu modes of subjectivity as ontologically opposed to psychoanalytic universalisms (see, for example, Straight 2007). I posit instead that in a wider context of competing means of subjectivation, encountering one's brand image speaks of a particular drama of subjectivity that resonates with what Lacan described as the mirror stage. Rather than describing a universal psychic process, as some psychoanalysts claim, I approach this drama of subjectivity as having come to circulate worldwide as part of globalization and the ever-growing political economy of commodities and visual media. Second, it is important to avoid reducing the drama of the Lacanian mirror stage to a childhood phase of development.

For, as Lacan himself argues, though the drama of mirror stage begins to play out in early infancy, its central contradiction—the irreconcilability of the Real and the Imaginary forces of subjectivity—haunts subjects for the rest of their lives, even as the acquisition of language complicates things further (1977, 78–79). The very fact that Samburu I worked with refer to this image as "theirs," at times ethnicize it as "Maasai," or objectify it in economic transactions, troubles the developmental connotations of a prelinguistic mirror stage. In this sense, my analytic parallel aims to capture the generative contradictions of this mirror drama without its developmental psychological undertones. And, that being said, the life course is not irrelevant to my analysis. The desire of Samburu men to assume the moran body image, as we shall see, takes a different turn, for example, as they age and their bodies no longer correspond to the brand images of the youthful moran.

But why should we understand this process of assuming a body image as *branding*? Is the term merely an analytical import? Or is it how postcolonial subjects themselves understand and refer to the process of marketing their culture and identity? Or is it both? Branding, as both a linguistic signifier and as a process of value production, appears widely in Kenya today in relation to identities. It does so on different, segmentary scales: ethnic, pan-ethnic, regional, religious, and national. In March 2008, for example, the state launched Brand Kenya, a government organization whose scope is "to build a strong country brand that fosters national pride, patriotism, and earns global recognition and preference." According to the organization's web page, its board has "the responsibility of identifying and refining the key attributes of Kenya, that contribute positively to the image and reputation of the Nation." Indeed, the future of a national identity lies here in its ability to market its resources, like a corporation (see also Comaroff and Comaroff 2009, 122–36). In an attempt to combat colonial images of primitivity, among other things, the organization seeks to use the achievements of Kenyan intellectuals and images of modern cities and industry to brand the country. But, perhaps ironically, Brand Kenya's website also uses, on its homepage, an image of Maasai warriors dancing. This suggests that, primitivist as it may be, the image of Maasai warriors is too valuable to be renounced completely.

This is no doubt also the case for Maasai themselves who now explicitly approach both their image and their collective name as "brands" of their ethnic identity. In 2013, Maasai made international news when they announced that they will trademark their "brand." The Maasai Intellectual Property Initiative (MIPI), an organization based in Kenya, collaborated with Light Years IP, an international NGO, to copyright the name and the image of Maasai, estimating their brand value at $10 million per year. Isaac ole Tialolo, the chair of MIPI, told BBC: "We all know that we have been exploited by people who just come around, take our pictures and benefit from it."[3] Although it was not clear which Maasai would profit from the copyrighting process more specifically, what is relevant here is that people thought of their *identity* and *image*—the two inextricably linked—*as* a brand. But even when people did not actually use the word "brand," the logics of branding were already at work in relation to ethnicity. In Samburu District, the Maa-language radio station, Serian FM, brands itself through the logo of the warrior holding a spear; local honey producers label their jars with images of morans; and NGOs like Maasai Cricket Warriors gained international fame by adding a new twist—a colonial sport—to an otherwise older and globally recognizable image of the moran. Young men who belong to this organization play cricket dressed traditionally, while championing the abolition of female genital cutting and early marriage and promoting schooling and development in northern Kenya.

Few of my informants spoke to me of their performances at the beach or in hotels as a way of *branding*, though they often referred to the Maasai moran as "our brand." Nevertheless, the logics of branding—not as a *thing* but as a *process*—were already at work in the wider context of their performances and thus informed the ways they went about enacting this image. There were high stakes in embodying the moran brand image, for with it came the promise of money, wealth, and a respectable future. It is no surprise then that, in claiming a certain brand image, men I worked with spoke of it often as a "thing" they had embodied and owned all along. But, in reality, their brand was a quite uncertain thing, to be performed, claimed, and assumed, always with an outlook to the desire of tourists and its ability to produce cash.

A brand image then is not just any kind of image. It is an image invested with more transformative potential than other images—it congeals a more salient promise for happiness and fulfillment. In this sense, the drama of the Lacanian imaginary stops short of accounting for the intensity of desire that a brand image may generate. If anything, the brand image—its assumed ability to generate value almost magically—is more akin to Lacan's notion of the phallus. For Lacan (1985, 82, 84), the phallus represents a "privileged signifier" of "the desire of the Other." Rather than refer to the penis as such, the phallus is a thing one wants to have or to embody in order to attract the desire and recognition of the outer world (or, the social world—what Lacan calls the big Other). In such desire and recognition, one seeks self-affirmation and fulfillment. In this sense, "The phallus refers to plentitude; it is the signifier of the wholeness that we lack" (Sapur 1988, 16). Samburu men sought that plentitude in the wealth and well-being that their brand image promised. Meanwhile, for foreigners, as I argue elsewhere, the moran brand congealed another promise of wholeness: the transformative potential of partaking in the cultural difference of the other (Meiu 2011; 2017, 113–22). But like the moran brand image, the phallus is an ambiguous thing for Lacan. On the one hand, it promises "lending reality to the subject in the signifier" (Lacan 1985, 84). On the other hand, it remains elusive, "making unreal the relations to be signified" (84). In this sense, the phallus is also a fetish, one that—like the fetishism of the commodity (see, for example, Krips 1999)—has exceptional generative power.

The intense desire to embody, as it were, the brand image of the Maasai warrior—or, in other words, to become the phallus—transformed how Samburu men understood themselves in relation to the moran image and Maasai identity. For them, brand-making involved (re)establishing genealogical ties to Maasai and internalizing a sense of pan-Maa identity. Tourist advertisements, postcards, dance shows, and cultural villages almost always presented Samburu morans as Maasai and Samburu men also introduced themselves to tourists in this way. "Some tourists read about the Maasai and Samburu," Tiras, a young Samburu man told me, "and they know what's Samburu. They know what's Maasai. But most of them know us as Maasai." "Do you explain the difference?" I asked. "Sometimes yes, sometimes no," he said. "It's just better to say you are a Maasai. Or, maybe a Samburu-Maasai." While it was rare in the north for Samburu to identify with Maasai, Samburu who lived at the coast internalized a Maasai identity. They not only responded when locals called them Maasai but also referred to themselves as Maasai in conversations with other people. The claim of Samburu men to a Maasai identity represented, in part, a way of commensurating their cultural difference through a denominator with which foreign tourists and other Kenyans were more familiar (cf. Kasfir 2007, 295–97). At the same time, I suggest, the fact that tourists and other Kenyans recognized them as Maasai generated a pan-Maa identity and consciousness among Samburu in coastal towns.

"We have something called Maa," a Samburu elder in Mtwapa explained to me in English. "Call them Samburu, call them Maasai, call them Nchamus. Those are all of the universal name we call Maa." The identification of Samburu with Maasai, this informant suggested, was not a *mis*identification or switching of ethnic identities, but rather a form of *pan*-identification (cf. Kasfir 2007, 295–96). The discursive category of the Maa-speaking people to whom Samburu also belonged emerged throughout the twentieth century as linguists, anthropologists, and government officials classified the population of Kenya according to common ancestries, similarities of language and culture, and historical evidence. This does not mean that previously Samburu had not claimed such relatedness. They certainly have. But the terms of such claims were different: more focused on ties of descent and kinship between specific Samburu clans or lineages and those of Maasai proper and less on the comparative criteria of the social sciences. In tourism, however, Samburu claimed a more generic pan-Maa identity to speak of themselves as Maasai. "Let me tell you the truth about our history," offered Saitoti, a Samburu man I interviewed in the coastal town of Watamu in 2011: "The Samburu are just Maasai. But, long time ago, they separated. The Samburu stayed north, and the other Maasai went south, even into Tanzania. But the Samburu are just Maasai. . . . But, you see, the tourists don't want those Maasai from the south, because they have lost most of their culture. Us, Samburu, we still have the old Maasai culture. If you look at us and you look at them, you will see that they don't wear those beads around the neck like we do. That is the original culture. That is what tourists want to see."

For Saitoti, Maasainess can stand in for a pan-Maa identity of which the southern Maasai, or the Maasai proper are as much part as are Samburu and Chamus. Samburu men like Saitoti took the nominal index "Maasai" to represent at once the Maasai proper and the Maa-speaking people more generally. Here (through what Charles Sanders Pierce calls abduction syllogism), the descriptor of a part was taken to stand in for the whole. In this way, in the context of tourism, Samburu claimed both similitude *and* difference in relation to Maasai. First, by taking the more marketable subcategory of Maasai and substituting it for the category of the Maa-speaking people to which Samburu also belonged, they could legitimately claim Maasainess as one of their identities. Second, by claiming Maasainess as a pan-identity (and not a primary ethnic identity), they could also sustain their distinction from Maasai proper. According to Saitoti, Samburu were indeed the more original Maasai, with "the old Maasai culture" that "the tourists want to see."

In the process of identifying with the Maasai brand, Samburu migrants in tourism also anchored their identity more strongly in the visual appearance of the moran body. For Saitoti, the beads that morans wear around their necks are proof of the fact that their culture is more authentic than that of the Maasai. My other Samburu interlocutors at the coast also emphasized that "being Samburu" is about "being morans." In interviews I carried out in Mtwapa in 2008, I asked: "What does it mean for you to be a Samburu?" By implying an essentialist identity, the question inevitably called for an essentialist response. Interestingly, however, most of the answers I received invoked the moran, in one way or another. "Being Samburu," one man suggested, "is to keep this culture of the moran, with the red ochre [M: *lkaria*] and the long hair [M: *lmasi*]."

"It is about wearing these beads and feathers," another man explained point-ing to his moran attire. While, in Samburu District, moranhood had long been indexical of men's adherence to tradition (Holtzman 2009, 169), among men who participated in tourism, the visual icon of the moran adorned in colorful bodily decorations became emblematic of ethnicity in new ways. In tourist resorts, they all wore moran attire and introduced themselves to tourists and other Kenyans as "morans," regardless of whether they actually were in the age grade of moranhood or not. They performed "moran" dances, sold "moran" spears, and enjoyed the sexual freedom of "morans." Here then, the phallic imaginary of the Maasai warrior affixed collective identity to the body of the young man.

While men I worked with embraced this brand image enthusiastically, this was not an image of their own making—at least not entirely. Colonials, missionaries, and travelers have long used the image of the moran to invest a whole ethnic population with an excessive sexual drive (Meiu 2017, 47–56). Tourists themselves came to seek the sexuality of morans for its allegedly exotic nature. Here, then, the Lacanian phallus is suggestive in another regard: it speaks of a certain kind of reduction of identity to genitality, a reduction that concentrates the very possibility of a collective future onto the sexuality of the Maa warrior.

The phallic imaginary that characterizes the individual struggle of men seeking to embody the moran brand image is then also a collective struggle. Through claims such as "we are all Maasai" or "we are all morans," the brand image reorganizes, if only partially, the meanings of collective identity. And so, the collective and the individual come to depend on one another in new ways: it is only through the collective identity of the Maasai (or Samburu) that the body of a specific man can come to generate value, and it is through the bodies of their young men that the group can access resources. This then, as we shall see, also generates a set of conflicts over belonging, age, and gender among Samburu men in tourism.

EXCESS, EXCLUSION, AND ERASURE IN
ETHNO-EROTIC BRANDING

For Samburu men at the coast, "loyalty to the universal brand" meant loyalty to the marketable image of the young moran. This presupposed a set of excesses, exclusions, and erasures. First, the brand type excluded women from the onset. A few young Samburu women had joined their husbands or brothers on the coast. But most of them worked as house maids or sex workers and did not participate in tourism as such. If women joined men at dance performances, they remained mostly in the background. Second, the brand type presupposed erasing the social differences between different men, making them into tokens of the brand. This involved not only dressing up as morans, regardless, for example, of whether a man had gone to school or not, but also regardless of whether a particular man actually was part of the age grade of moranhood. Furthermore, even as men tried to erase generational hierarchies, aging bodies made for tokens that only poorly indexed the ideal brand type.

That all Samburu men were morans for purposes of business produced a set of contradictions and conflicts. The desire of elders to erase generational differences for purposes of tourist commodification collided with their attempts to exert authority as elders over younger men. I became aware of this issue following a conflict I witnessed in March 2011. On a Friday evening, a group of Samburu dancers went to perform at the Bamburi Beach Hotel. As the dancers waited in front of the hotel to be allowed to enter, a European woman approached Boniface, a moran of the Lkishami age set (initiated in 2005), asking to take a picture of him. After the woman left, Boniface called her, trying to sell her some beads. Lkeseyion, an elder of the Lkuroro age set (initiated in 1976, two age sets above Boniface), scolded Boniface for disturbing the tourist. Boniface turned to the elder and asked him rudely: "Is this the white of your mother? Or, why are you telling me what to do?" A fight ensued. Elders of the Lmooli (initiated in 1990) and Lkuroro age sets fought with the morans. The following evening, I joined the dancers at the Bahari Beach Hotel. Before entering the hotel for a dance performance, the leaders of the dance group, two junior elders, called for an emergency meeting in the bushes in front of the resort. The leaders had missed out on the performance of the previous night and asked to be told what had happened. After listening to both parties, one leader stood up to address the dancers: "Stop arguing over who is an elder and who is a moran!" he ordered with a violent gesture of his knobkerrie: "If you want to destroy our business, why don't you all go and work as watchmen? Here, in Mombasa, there is no difference between the Lkishami, the Lmooli, and the Lkuroro. If you want to call us all morans, call us all morans! If you want to call us all elders, call us elders! We are all morans. We are all elders. We are all the same."

This incident points to the perceived incompatibility of touristic warriorhood with Samburu age grade relations. As an elder and a ritual "firestick patron" (M: lpiroi) of the morans, Lkeseyion would have been entitled to scold Boniface for his behavior. In coastal resorts, elders like Lkeseyion oftentimes invoked their senior age grade status as a way to exert authority over morans. However, elders told me that coastal morans did not listen to them and explained the disobedience of morans as a result of their financial independence and of the poor morality of coastal areas. Meanwhile, young morans like Boniface laughed at elders like Lkeseyion, who proudly pretended to be morans two decades after they had become elders. They explained that they refused to accept their authority because, for them, these men did not set an example of respectability. To emphasize this point, morans on the coast very often used the phrasing: "There are no elders in Mombasa. All the elders are at home" (M: *Metii lpayeni Mombasa. Netii lpayeni pooki nkang*). According to the morans, men who aged at the coast were not elders, but neither were they morans as such. Instead, as a moran put it, they were "men who have forgotten that their time has passed" (for a more detailed discussion of this incident, see Meiu 2017, 238–40).

Indeed, elderly men did not have the same chances of success in tourism as younger men. The statement of the leader of the dancing group—"We are all the same"—occluded this reality in an attempt to produce what Chanock (2000, 26) calls a market-driven "loyalty to the universal brand." The brand of the moran presupposed, of course, an erasure of intergenerational antagonisms, if only temporarily, for the purposes of successful business. As men of different age sets dressed as morans to perform in hotels and sell artifacts at the beach, they developed a strong sense that what brought them together, day after day, night after night, was an ethnic identity that was anchored in the bodily appearance of the young, sexual moran. Despite intergenerational conflicts—or as a way to prevent them—these men came to understand themselves as part of a "culture of the moran, with the red ochre, and the long hair."

There are echoes here, again, of Lacan's turbulent processes of the imaginary, with the difference that a drama of subjectivity becomes also a drama of collectivity. Through the branding process, a social group must assume the body image of the young warrior as condition of its continued existence on the market. The Maasai warrior becomes the "symbolic matrix" for collective identity. This however generates both an awareness of a *lack*—an inability to fully produce oneself in one's brand image—and contradictions, such as those of age. Men engaged in ethno-erotic economies were aware that their individual possibilities of success depleted as they aged and their bodies no longer corresponded to marketable notions of sexual desirability. The brand type of the moran depended on brand tokens that were relatively young looking. Aware of their depleting youth, these men sought to speculate on how to produce wealth quickly. Riches that seemed easy to acquire when men were young appeared more and more out of reach as they aged. Younger men dismissively called these elders "beach-boy elders" (M: *lpayian oo bichboi*) to question their respectability (Meiu 2015). Typically, beach-boy elders never acquired any wealth or had "lost" their wealth drinking alcohol, gambling, or spending money on mistresses. They continued to live on the coast and returned to the beach in search of (further) life-transforming encounters with female tourists. But most of them only made ends meet by working as watchmen or begging money off younger men.

SECURING MARKETS: FAKE MORANS, CULTURAL PIRACY, AND ETHNIC ASSOCIATIONS

"The very first thing tourists ask when the planes land in Mombasa is: Where are the Maasai?" A district commissioner (DC) of Kenya's coastal region of Kilifi allegedly uttered these words in a public speech, sometime in the late 1990s. Jeffrey, a Samburu man in his fifties, quoted the DC's words for me one evening in April 2011. We were sitting in an alleyway, in front of the small room he rented in the town of Mtwapa, at the coast. He spoke to me about interethnic tensions that Maa-speaking migrants, like himself, faced while living there. Jeffrey had migrated to Mtwapa for the past twenty-five years. That evening, he proudly invoked what the DC had said to explain to me that "Maasai"—by which he meant all Maa-speakers, including Samburu—were highly beneficial to coastal tourism. That is how, according to Jeffrey, the DC had meant his statement. Following fights between men of the local Giriama ethnic group and Maasai and Samburu migrants, the DC had called a meeting in Kilifi. "The Giriama wanted to chase us away from the coast," Jeffrey remembered, "and that's how the fight started." He recalled the DC asked Giriama youths: "Why are you chasing away the Maasai? Don't you know that it is the Maasai that are bringing us business? It is the Maasai that tourists want to see. There is no need to chase these people away." Jeffrey paused, smiling. "You see? The DC understood this. He told the Giriama: 'The money you pocket, don't you see where it's coming from? You want to kill these people? Now, that food that is in your stomachs, do you really want to throw it up?" Quoting the DC, Jeffrey invoked a widespread belief in the country, according to which angering those who feed you is tantamount to poisoning the food you ingest. Instead, Jeffrey suggested, Giriama and other coastal people should be grateful to Maasai.

It is important to recall that for Samburu migrants at the coast, Maasainess was a form of pan-identity if we are to make sense of what they saw as instances of cultural theft, piracy, and fakery. In relation to non-Maa speakers, Samburu claimed cultural ownership of Maasainess and often fought collectively alongside Maasai proper against Kikuyu, Kamba, or Giriama young men who dressed

up as Maasai morans in order to do business in tourism. Indeed, some of these
men were quick to admit that there was more to be gained by performing the
image of the Maasai warrior than approaching tourists in any other way. In 2004,
Kenya's *Lifestyle* magazine observed how men of other ethnic groups "don't see
anything wrong with disguising themselves as Maasai moran[s] and using that
as a tool of trade to earn a modest living."[4] Voicing the opinion of a "genuine
moran," the article maintained that "those masquerading as *moran* are soiling
the Maasai culture and reputation." My Samburu informants held a similar
view. They were concerned, for example, about the growing number of cultural
villages that found it was cheaper to ask their coastal Digo and Giriama dancers
to dress up also as Maasai warriors and perform Maasai dances. "This is killing
our business," the leader of a Samburu dance group told me in Diani in 2011.

While there was little that Maasai and Samburu men could do about the
decisions of the managers of hotels and cultural villages, they were more likely
to challenge directly the "fake morans" they encountered along the beach. Saitoti recalled in Swahili how, one time, he had been among a group of Samburu
who threatened to beat a Giriama man at the beach in Watamu: "I told him to
take [the moran attire] off right away, or it will be a fight. I asked him: 'Why do
you wear these clothes if you are not a Maasai? Do you have no *culture* of your
own? Dress in your own *culture!*' I told him: 'I should not catch you dressed like
that or I will take you to the police.' This is *piracy*! They have their own *culture*.
Why do they steal ours? *Each person should eat from his own culture* [italicized
text in English]." Because in the context of tourism, culture was about bodily
garments and decorations, "fake morans" could easily "steal business" (S: *kuiba
biashara*) from the Samburu by dressing as morans. Asking the Giriama man
to strip his moran attire, Saitoti and his friends claimed ownership of a Maasai culture that was centrally indexed by the visual appearance of the moran.
Although, in Kenya, ownership of indigenous culture was not protected by
law as in other parts of the world (see Brown 2003), everyday engagements
of Samburu men with what they saw as instances of theft of culture already
invoked a popular use of the "language of jurisprudence" (Comaroff and Comaroff 2006, 24). The conviction of Samburu men that these were instances of
"piracy," and that they could cooperate with the police to prevent them, affirmed
their sense of ownership of a Maasai pan-identity. Meanwhile, Saitoti's sugges-
tion that "each person should eat from his own culture" occluded a historical
reality in which not all material expressions of ethnic identities carried value
for the tourist market. Samburu men knew this well and often allowed a few of
their Kikuyu, Kamba, or Giriama friends, who had asked for their permission,
to dress up as morans and sell handicrafts at the beach. When I asked Saitoti

why other groups did not perform their own culture to tourists, he responded: "Their culture is not marketable."

In short, for Samburu-Maasai, brand-making through narrative genealogies and the physical defense of ethnic boundaries against piracy and theft are not only conditions for cultural commodification but also sources of pan-ethnic identity and consciousness. As men seek to control who can and cannot market Maasai culture, they affirm their adherence to a pan-Maa identity and express a sense of Maasai collective consciousness. But the language ownership and the practices of exclusion that it legitimized are also forms of violence. They are meant to draw lines of ethnic difference between young men who otherwise are quite similar in that they struggle to build lives in a context of poverty. It was as a way to defend their "rights" to their Maasai cultural difference that some of these men also turned to the incorporation of ethnic identity through state-registered business organizations or so-called self-help groups.

In 1986, Samburu men who lived on the coast registered the Maasai Moran Cooperative Society (MMCS) with the Department of Cooperative Development of the Kenyan government.[5] Based in Mtwapa, MMCS represented the interests of its members with tourist businesses and state authorities, as well as supervised Samburu migrants, managed their finances, and offered them various benefits. MMCS capitalized on both the growing tourist market for Maasai culture and the rising numbers of Samburu male migrants to the coast. It acted as a gatekeeper for Samburu migrants in the tourist industry. Its leaders obtained contracts with hotels and cultural villages and offered migrants the possibility of participating in dance performances. While relatively few of these men were actual members of MMCS (by some accounts 150 in the 1980s), all of them had to collaborate with the organization in order to access tourist venues or obtain permits to sell handicrafts at the beach.

MMCS benefited in various ways from the income of Samburu migrants in tourism, and offered them various benefits in return. Hotels and cultural villages rarely paid the dancers, instead offering them fifteen minutes after their performance to sell their handicrafts to the tourists in the audience. Men who sold handicrafts during this time had to pay a commission (M and S: *ses*) of 10 to 20 percent to the organization. In addition, dancers also had to sell artifacts that belonged to the organization (usually, artisanal Maasai shields). Men who were in relationships with European women were often charged higher prices for beach permits and were asked to contribute higher amounts of money to the organization. In return, MMCS placed individual dancers on the performance schedule and offered them welfare benefits. Among these were small loans to help young men with start-up costs, money for health emergencies, and bus fares for urgent trips to their homes in Samburu District. The organization also offered banking services to migrants, who could deposit their income in its corporate account to produce interest and resist the temptation of spending while at the coast; nonmembers usually registered with MMCS at the beginning of every tourist season and claimed their savings and profits three months later. Meanwhile, MMCS members divided part of the corporate profits at the end of each tourist season and kept the rest of the money in the corporate account to be invested in a future collective tourist project.

Age set relations played an important role in the process of ethnic incorporation. From the beginning, MMCS not only branded itself through the image of the moran but was also founded exclusively by morans. All of its members were men of the Lkuroro age set who had been morans throughout the 1980s. In the 2000s, for example, men of younger age sets remembered MMCS as "the Society of the Lkuroro." As the Lkuroro had become junior elders and prepared to return to Samburu District to settle down, MMCS had enabled a few of them to save money in a collective fund. When MMCS finally dissolved in 1994, one elder told me, its members had accumulated KES 24 million (about $290,000), part of which they invested promptly in a piece of prime land on the north coast, by the ocean.[6]

As the number of migrants to the coast grew in the 1990s, the Lmooli age set of morans opened their own organizations. Four organizations now covered respectively different areas of the coast: the Samburu Moran Curio Dealer Association in Mtwapa; the Samburu Self-Help Group in Watamu; the Samburu Moran Traditional Dancers association in Diani; and the Samburu Traditional Maasai Morans, also in Diani. Unlike earlier welfare cooperative societies, these organizations were registered with the Ministry of Gender, Sport, Culture, and Social Services and were no longer subsidized by the government. Because, in the meantime, the number of Maasai migrants from Tanzania and, to a lesser extent, from southern Kenya also grew in tourist resorts, Samburu rebranded their associations as "Samburu" for purposes of further distinction. Yet the moran and the claim of the Samburu to a more authentic Maasainess remained important for purposes of branding.

The incorporation of ethnic identity at once produced new inequalities and regenerated a sense of collective ethnic identity. Unequal access to money and authority cut across the relations between young men and the beach-boy elders, the stakeholders of the ethnic organization, and the migrants on whom they relied. But at the same time, these men all claimed ownership of and adherence to a Samburu-Maasai identity that was centrally indexed through the figure of the moran. Furthermore, ethnic incorporation also represented an institutionalized mechanism through which elders tried to redirect the cash produced in coastal tourism—albeit in uneven ways—to the making of futures in Samburu District.

THE VIOLENCE OF A PHALLIC IMAGE

Among coastal residents, abject poverty, chronic unemployment, and the loss of land existed alongside the spectacular riches of business owners and the large landholdings of luxurious tourist resorts. Mijikena—a pan-ethnic category that includes the Giriama, Digo, Duruma, Chonyi, and others—understood themselves as historically marginalized by the richer, more affluent Swahili and Arabs and, since the 1960s, by the "upcountry people" (McIntosh 2009). The latter category refers mostly to labor migrants and migrant settlers of the Kikuyu, Kamba, and Luo ethnic groups, who bought land, owned businesses, and dominated the tourist economy and other sectors. Here, the autochthonous notion of the "coastal people" is a form of collective consciousness formed in opposition to outsiders, or upcountry people. The two categories most likely emerged in the first part of the twentieth century with the rise of labor migration to the coast from other regions of the country. Nepotism and tribalism, coastal leaders often argued, led these upcountry people to favor members of their own ethnic groups for employment in hotels or other business. As a local put it to the *Daily Nation* on September 27, 1997, "Local hotels [are] 'packed' with upcountry people, while Digos are given 'a raw deal.' . . . The Digos are not being involved in tourism although much of it is taking place on their land."

The coastal category of upcountry people works to erase differences between various ethnic groups (a process typical of ethnic identity in urban contexts [see Mitchell 1956]) and to occlude the socioeconomical inequalities that exist between various migrants in their places of origin. Let us recall that, upcountry, Samburu already occupied a marginal socioeconomic position relative to more dominant groups. Thus, for example, when coastal people accused upcountry people of exploiting them or alienating their resources, they saw Maasai and Samburu as responsible for coastal inequalities as Kikuyu, Kamba, and Luo. Yet, not unlike the vast majority of coastal youth, most Maasai and Samburu young men at the coast lived in poverty while waiting for life-transforming encounters with tourists. Why, then, were they targeted as part of coastal youths' uprisings against foreigners?

The Digo youth movement of 1997, known today as the Kaya Bombo, emerged as one of the numerous historical attempts to chase out upcountry people and establish majimboism, a kind of federalism that would grant the coast more power of self-determination. Between May and August 1997, local political leaders collaborated with traditional religious leaders to administer oaths (Digo: *kinu*) to over three hundred Digo youths and other coastal young men in Digo sacred forest sites known as *kaya*. It is noteworthy that this movement turned to ancestral rituals and military training to produce warriors of a different kind, mixing the styles of national army soldiers with those of the traditional Digo warriors of the old days. On August 13, 1997, these young men raided and burned down the Likoni police station, stealing rifles and ammunition. Then they began burning down houses, kiosks, shops, bars, restaurants, and vehicles belonging to migrants from upcountry. Throughout the following year, they launched over twenty-five violent attacks. On these occasions, they also circulated leaflets or painted messages on public walls that urged upcountry people to "return to their homes" and called on coastal people to reclaim their land. One such leaflet read: "The time has come for us original inhabitants of the Coast to claim what is rightly ours. We must remove these invaders from our land."[7]

On September 5, 1997, the Kaya Bombo attacked Shirlon Bar near Shelly Beach Hotel, where they encountered the Samburu dancers. Peter Lelenguia, who was depicted on the postcard I described in the beginning of this chapter, spoke to the journalists of the *Daily Nation* just before he died. He said that the "raiders" entered the bar and cut people with machetes. Then they burned down the bar. Samburu men I interviewed on the coast in 2008 and 2011 explained to me that on that day in 1997, Samburu were not targets of violence as such. The Kaya Bombo, they suggested, targeted the owners of Shelly Beach Hotel and the Shirlon Bar, who were Kikuyu. Unlike Kikuyu or Luo, very few Samburu owned land on the coast. Rather, as one informant put it, "the men were in the wrong place, at the wrong time."

I wish to offer a different reading of these events. While indeed few Maasai and Samburu owned land on the coast, they claimed relative monopoly over a cultural and sexual brand that was central to the tourist economy. Recall Jeffrey's words—it is, after all, the Maasai that tourists want to see. As Samburu men sought better to embody and claim ownership of the phallic image of the erotic moran, they sometimes resorted to acts of violence against coastal youths who sought to partake in the tourist economy. In the case of Samburu, loyalty to the brand image of the Maasai warrior involved violent exclusions of those youths. Hence, the latter more readily recognized Samburu (and Maasai) bodies as essentially Other and threatening. So, even though Samburu did not own local land or were not much involved in the formal labor market, their bodies and sexuality, when read through the phallic brand image, represented a form of mysterious capital that—being ethnically marked and marketed—others could not easily access.

In this context, interethnic violence cannot be reduced to either the manipulations of corrupt political leaders or simple conflict between predefined autochthons and foreigners. It is important instead to understand violence in relation to the phallic image of the Maasai brand, its almost spectral power to both lure subjects with promises of miraculous wealth and evade their attempts to ever fully attain or pin down its image. At some level, Samburu migrants and coastal young men had much in common. They all inhabited a context of rampant unemployment with uncertain speculative economies in which masculine respectability and the pursuit of social reproduction have come sharply into question. In this regard, more often than not, violence emerges at points of similarity rather than difference. For coastal youths, violence against Samburu was then, first of all, an attempt to disambiguate their difference against the backdrop of a socioeconomic predicament they all seemed to share: if we are all living in times of hardship and poverty, so the logic went, how come *they* can suddenly become wealthy and *we* cannot? But Samburu and other Maa-speaking migrants claimed exclusive rights over an image that, like the Lacanian phallus, promised more than it could deliver while also reorganizing subjective and collective life around itself—as a pursuit of its uncertain promises. The fact that this highly desired brand was itself uncertain, elusive, and alien to those who desired to embody it only intensified the force with which Samburu claimed it: they performed, incorporated, and at times defended it violently. For coastal youths, violence against Samburu was then also an expression of their desire to inhabit the plenitude and wholeness of wealth and full citizenship that the Maasai brand image promised to Maa-speakers, but not to them. There was, as such, a desire to become the phallus.

Sex and sexuality were central sites of uncertainty over social reproduction, relatedness, and belonging. Like the orgiastic sexuality of the witch (so well documented in classic Africanist ethnographies), in contemporary Kenya, the imagined sexualities of beach-boy elders, prostitutes, gays, lesbians, and others were held responsible—if to different extents—for the alleged failures of normative expectations of family, kinship, and reproduction. It is this very anxiety and ambiguity over sexuality, its power to yield cash instead of offspring, that plays out centrally in the materiality of violence as bodies are cut, castrated, and disfigured. In this sense too, the Kaya Bombo was also an attempt to pursue some sort of moral rehabilitation: it sought to produce a different kind of warrior, a different kind of masculinity, a different kind of pathway to the phallus—to the possibility to reposition oneself and one's community in relation to the state and to gain political plentitude and whole-ness, as it were.

I suggest that the indeterminacy of ethno-erotic branding—the neces-sity of its perpetual reiteration through creative performance and violent exclusions—intersects with collective anxieties and uncertainties over both belonging and social reproduction to give particular meaning to interethnic violence. Arjun Appadurai (1998, 906) argued that "the ethnic body [becomes] a theatre for the engagement of uncertainty under the special circumstances of globalization." Here, "violence can create a macabre form of certainty and can become a brutal technique (or folk discovery-procedure) about 'them' and, therefore, about 'us'" (909). Building on Appadurai's insight, I suggest that the cutting off of genitalia, the butchering of bodies deemed erotically desir-able, the crashing of heads, all of which are common in interethnic violence in coastal Kenya, represent such a macabre form of producing certainty—to reveal the essence of the commodity fetish, to expose that which seems threat-ening and dangerous and beyond comprehension. Here, again, the branding of ethnic sexuality is premised on and generates a constant potential for ethnic violence: both the violence of cultural ownership and exclusion involved in the production of the ethnic brand and the violence of a cultural logic of ethnic essences, essences often deemed sexual.

CONCLUSION

If the possibility of rapid enrichment attracted Samburu men to the coast, their chances of success in tourism seemed ridden with uncertainty. Migrants knew that relatively few of them would find foreign partners. They also knew that their chances of success decreased as they aged and became less attrac-tive to visitors—less fit, as it were, to perform youthful warriorhood. Hence, they tried constantly to craft new ways to improve their performances, to pin down and stabilize the concrete ways through which those performances could be converted into cash. Meanwhile, however, they also faced the challenges of living and working in a region to which they felt they did not belong and where interethnic tensions often led to violence. Several Samburu have died throughout the past few decades at the hands of coastal youth. But Maasai and Samburu migrants have also initiated violent attacks on "fake morans," men of other ethnic groups, including the coastal Digo and Giriama, who dress up as morans hoping to find European partners more easily. Interethnic violence is not merely a byproduct of a tourist market venerating Maasai morans but also an integral part of an economy of ethnic sexuality that brings belonging and social reproduction into question.

At the center of the dialectics between branding and belonging in Kenyan coastal tourism is another dialectical relationship: an open-ended dialectic between an identity anchored in body image and the desires, performances, and subjectivities of those who try to embody it as a condition of producing social and economic value. I understand this dialectic in light of what Lacan saw as the role of the imaginary for the subject in the mirror stage but also in terms of the desire of the subject to become the phallus. Here the constant attempt to assume an image that exists outside oneself produces all kinds of turbulences, contradictions, exclusions, and insufficiencies. Similarly, those who seek to fashion their identity through the image of the young warrior generate exclusions and conflicts along lines of gender, age, generation, and ethnicity. Some of these conflicts play out violently. Here, then, the meanings of violence cannot be reduced to a preexisting ethnicity, but must be understood in relation to the process of cultural branding, through which identity and belonging reemerge in new, albeit messy ways.

NOTES

1. Throughout this chapter, I use the abbreviations "S" and "M" to refer to words and phrases in the Swahili and Maa languages, respectively. Swahili is the national language of Kenya whereas Maa is the language of Samburu and Maasai. (Words and phrases included here are from the Samburu dialect of Maa.)

2. "Seeing the Sights," *Daily Nation*, June 19, 1980, 3.

3. Cordelia Hebblethwaite, "Brand Maasai: Why Nomads Might Trademark their Name," BBC, May 28, 2013, http://www.bbc.com/news/magazine-2261 7001.

4. Oscar Obonyo and Daniel Nyassy, "Ways of the Commercial Moran," [*Daily Nation*] *Lifestyle*, December 12, 2004, 2–3.

5. The development of cooperative societies was part of Kenya's national development plan since the 1960s. Dillon Mahoney (2017) argues that in the 1990s and 2000s, as tourism came to be controlled by private investors, the poor had to be removed from the scene. Consequently, government subsidies for cooperative societies were cut. In 1997, the government passed the "Cooperative Societies Act and Seasonal Paper" (No. 6), which, in a response characteristic to liberal market reforms, cut all subsidies to cooperative societies. Cooperative societies became "free enterprises" meant to compete with privately owned businesses (Mahoney 2017, 71–75).

6. Not all MMCS members agreed to invest their money in a collectively owned piece of coastal land for tourism. Some thought it was dangerous for "foreigners" like themselves to purchase land on the coast and preferred to invest their money in Samburu. Those who collectively purchased land in Mtwapa eventually sold it in 2013 and divided the money.

7. Quoted in *East African Standard*, August 26, 1997, 3.

REFERENCES

Appadurai, Arjun. 1998. "Dead Certainty: Ethnic Violence in the Era of Globalization." *Development and Change* 29:905–25.

Broch-Due, Vigdis. 2005. "Violence and Belonging: Analytical Reflections." In *Violence and Belonging: The Quest for Identity in Post-colonial Africa*, edited by Vigdis Broch-Due, 1–40. London: Routledge.

Brown, Michael F. 2003. *Who Owns Native Culture?* Cambridge, MA: Harvard University Press.

Bruner, Edward M., and Barbara Kirshenblatt-Gimblett. 1994. "Maasai on the Lawn: Tourist Realism in East Africa." *Cultural Anthropology* 9 (4): 435–70.

Chanock, Martin. 2000. "'Culture' and Human Rights: Orientalising, Occidentalising, and Authenticity." In *Beyond Rights Talk and Culture Talk: Comparative Essays on the Politics of Rights and Culture*, edited by Mahmood Mamdani, 15–36. New York: St. Martin's Press.

Comaroff, John L., and Jean Comaroff. 2006. "Law and Disorder in the Postcolony: An Introduction." In *Law and Disorder in the Postcolony*, edited by Jean Comaroff and Jean Comaroff, 1–56. Chicago: University of Chicago Press.

———. 2009. *Ethnicity, Inc.* Chicago: University of Chicago Press.

Cooper, Frederick. 1987. *On the African Waterfront: Urban Disorder and the Transformation of Work in Colonial Mombasa*. New Haven: Yale University Press.

Geschiere, Peter. 2009. *The Perils of Belonging: Autochthony, Citizenship, and Exclusion in Africa and Europe*. Chicago: University of Chicago Press.

Geschiere, Peter, and Birgit Meyer. 1998. "Globalization and Identity: Dialectics of Flow and Closure." *Development and Change* 29:601–15.

Holtzman, Jon. 2009. *Uncertain Tastes: Memory, Ambivalence, and the Politics of Eating in Samburu, Northern Kenya*. Berkeley: University of California Press.

Kasfir, Sidney L. 1999. "Samburu Souvenirs: Representations of a Land in Amber." In *Unpacking Culture: Art and Commodity in Colonial and Postcolonial Worlds*, edited by R. B. Phillips and C. B. Steiner, 67–83. Berkeley: University of California Press.

———. 2007. *African Art and the Colonial Encounter: Inventing a Global Commodity*. Bloomington: Indiana University Press.

KIPPRA (Kenya Institute for Public Policy Research and Analysis). 2013. *Kenya Economic Report 2013*. Nairobi: KIPPRA.

Krips, Henry. 1999. *Fetish: An Erotics of Culture*. Ithaca, NY: Cornell University Press.

Lacan, Jacques. 1977. *Ecrits: Selected Writings*. New York: Norton.

———. 1985. *Feminine Sexuality*. New York: Norton.

Lynch, Gabrielle. 2011. *I Say to You: Ethnic Politics and the Kalenjin in Kenya*. Chicago: University of Chicago Press.

Mahoney, Dillon. 2017. *The Art of Connection: Risk, Mobility, and the Crafting of Transparency in Coastal Kenya*. Berkeley: University of California Press.

Manning, Paul. 2010. "The Semiotics of Brand." *Annual Review of Anthropology* 39 (1): 33–49.

Mazzarella, William. 2003. *Shoveling Smoke: Advertising and Globalization in Contemporary India*. Durham, NC: Duke University Press.

McIntosh, Janet. 2009. *The Edge of Islam: Power, Personhood, and Ethnoreligious Boundaries on the Kenya Coast*. Durham, NC: Duke University Press.

Meiu, George Paul. 2011. "On Difference, Desire, and the Aesthetics of the Unexpected: 'The White Masai' in Kenyan Tourism." In *Great Expectations: Imagination and Anticipation in Tourism*, edited by J. Skinner and D. Theodossopoulos, 96–115. Oxford: Berghahn.

———. 2015. "'Beach-Boy Elders' and 'Young Big-Men': Subverting the Temporalities of Aging in Kenya's Ethno-erotic Economies." *Ethnos* 80 (4): 472–96.

———. 2017. *Ethno-erotic Economies: Sexuality, Money, and Belonging in Postcolonial Kenya*. Chicago: University of Chicago Press.

Mitchell, J. Clyde. 1956. *The Kalela Dance: Aspects of Social Relationships among Urban Africans in Northern Rhodesia*. Manchester: Manchester University Press.

Moore, Robert E. 2003. "From Genericide to Virtual Marketing: On 'Brand.'" *Language and Communication* 23:331–57.

Mwakikagile, Godfrey. 2001. *Ethnic Politics in Kenya and Nigeria*. Huntington, NY: Nova.

Nakassis, Constantine V. 2012. "Brand, Citationality, Performativity." *American Anthropologist* 114 (4): 624–38.

———. 2013. "Brands and Their Surfeits." *Cultural Anthropology* 28 (1): 111–26.

Oucho, John O. 2002. *Undercurrents of Ethnic Conflicts in Kenya*. Boston: Brill.

Sapur, Madan. 1988. *An Introductory Guide to Post-Structuralism and Postmodernism*. Athens: University of Georgia Press.

Schoss, Johanna H. 1995. "Beach Tours and Safari Visions: Relations of Production and the Production of 'Culture' in Malindi, Kenya." PhD diss., University of Chicago.

Simpson, George L. 1994. "On the Frontier of Empire: British Administration in Kenya's Northern Frontier District, 1905–1935." PhD diss., West Virginia University.

Spencer, Paul. 1965. *The Samburu: A Study of Gerontocracy.* London: Routledge.

Straight, Bilinda. 2007. *Miracles and Extraordinary Experience in Northern Kenya.* Philadelphia: University of Pennsylvania Press.

GEORGE PAUL MEIU is John and Ruth Hazel Associate Professor of the Social Sciences in the Department of Anthropology and the Department of African and African American Studies at Harvard University. He is author of *Ethno-erotic Economies: Sexuality, Money, and Belonging in Kenya.*

TWO

—⚏—

THE SCARCE AND THE SACRED

Managing Afterlives and Branding the Derivative in Post-Soviet Buddhism (Inc.)

TATIANA CHUDAKOVA

IN THE SUMMER OF 2017, the courtyard of the Rimpoche Bagsha Buddist Temple, one of the largest Buddhist temples in Ulan-Ude, acquired a new and somewhat surprising ritual object—so surprising, in fact, that it had made the local news. The new acquisition was the statue of a *buuza*, a traditional Buryat meat dumpling considered a staple of local cuisine (see fig. 2.1). The marble dumpling is technically located at the outside periphery of the temple's concentric spaces of worship. Yet the statue elicited mixed reactions from the local public—as well as from out-of-town tourists—ranging from delighted amusement to puzzled indignation. In an interview with the local news agency, the temple's administration explained its decision to install a culinary monument in terms of its religious symbolism: Buryat buuza traditionally sport thirty-three pinches, a number that is meant to represent thirty-three Buddhist deities. And in the everyday gestures of temple visitors, the buuza quickly became an object of a simple, tactile ritual activity—touching the sculpture, much as rubbing the fat tummy of an Arhat (the representation of a protector deity), quickly came to be associated with generating good luck, prosperity, and bodily well-being.

Oxana Olegovna, a long-term friend and informant who often took on herself the informal role of local guide for visitors to Buryatia, was critical of the sculpture, although not quite for the same reasons as the couple of out-of-town tourists from Western Russia that she was entertaining. For her, as for many other local voices commenting on the temple's decision to adopt the buuza, the problem with the sculpture was that it did not offer a visually accurate representation of this food's variant in the local cuisine. And indeed, the sculpture has a

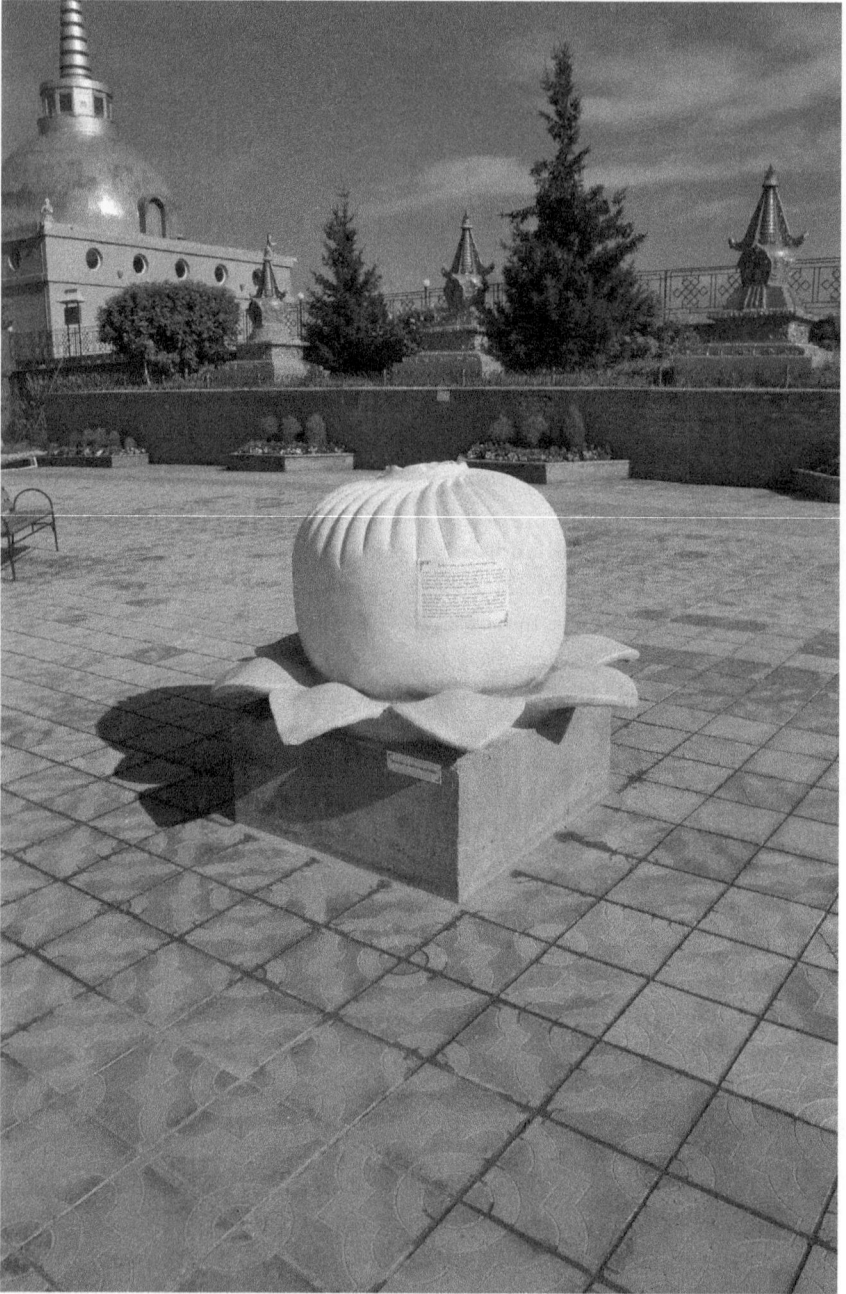

Fig. 2.1. Buuz Sculpture, "Rinpoche Bagsha" Buddhist Temple, Ulan-Ude, Buryatia, Russia. (Photo by the author.)

double identifier on the plaque next to it, where it is described as both a Buryat "buuza" and a Tibetan "momo." If the conflation seems like a mere technicality, it is important to understand that in the Buryat context, the ethnoidentifier that accompanies Buddhism—for example, the question of whether any given Buddhist temple is "staffed" by the Buryat Buddhist Sangha or by members of the refugee Tibetan community—is a contentious one, as is the question of Buddhism's cosmopolitan claims. By extension, collapsing a national Buryat dish with a national Tibetan one is not a politically neutral decision, in particular at a temple that since its inception in 2000 has long been associated with a distinctly ethnically Tibetan Buddhist practice and community.

In addition to offering its marble flank for the haptic generation of merit, the buuza sculpture affords other surfaces of friction. In particular, it dramatizes the competing interpretations of Buryat Buddhism and its expressions—architectural, ritual, aesthetic, and commercial—as both firmly part of everyday religious practice and as fully incorporated into Buryatia's tourist economy. The lines drawn between the ritual object and the commodity form or its referents become sites for the careful choreographing of different messages targeted to locals—often presumed to be approaching such spaces with the practical considerations and tastes of "parishioners"—and to outsiders, presumed to consume them as abstract "culture."

And indeed, for outsiders looking in—for example, for the tourists that Oxana Olegovna was introducing to the Buddhist temple and to Buryatia's particular tradition of Buddhism—the sculpture of the dumpling was either funny, or incoherent, a sign of inappropriate mixing of sacred and profane signifiers: a culinary dish propped on a lotus flower, with its rich significance in Buddhist iconography, squared poorly with their sensibilities that the religious space ought to be free of such prosaic intrusions. And in fact, one of Oxana Olegovna's out-of-town guests had a viscerally negative reaction to the sculpture, an early moment in what would eventually escalate into a hostile rejection of the Buddhist spaces Oxana Olegovna sought to present as, distinctly, the region's cultural heritage, open to "neutral" touristic consumptions. By contrast, for local actors, the association between the buuza and Buddhist temples is a long-standing one, in part because most temples include a *poznaya*—a café that offers traditional Buryat cuisine to temple visitors.

That Buddhism in Buryatia would be hitched to national cuisine, hitched, in turn, to the generation of merit *and* profit does not automatically cause a sense of dissonance locally. Instead, the negotiations over how such cohabitations ought to be interpreted offers a productive site for reflecting on the intersection between religion, notions of cosmological efficacy, and the production of ethnocommodities in Buddhist Siberia. Set in Buryatia, a semiautonomous ethnic minority republic of the Russian Federation located on the border with Mongolia, this chapter examines the different efforts, undertaken at multiple, and sometimes competing scales, to formulate a branded regional identity. The chapter moves from broader theoretical concerns over what constitutes the production of religiously tinged ethnocommodities in a place like Russia with its specific histories of state policies toward both ethnicity and religion to ethnographic examples centered on Buddhist medicine, which dramatize how the paradoxes of the ethnocommodity draw on and blur the lines between competing concepts of potency, both economic and otherwise.

In the context of present-day Russia examined here, branding ethnic, cultural, and religious distinction is a complicated political gambit for regional governments, all the more so since representational projects involved in the maintenance of tourist circuits are not so much a top-down affair: rather, tourism works as a site of hopeful, if often underdetermined, interpellation for a variety of local actors. In part, this is due to the Russian state's internally contradictory strategies for self-presentation. On the one hand, official state discourses emphasize Russia's multinational identity, extending the Soviet Union's claims to radical ethnic plurality inherited from Soviet nationalities policies, and, indeed, the assertion that the people of Russia are a multinational unity brought together by geography and historical processes is a core claim of the Constitution of the Russian Federation. On the other hand, present-day public political articulations in Russia construct the impression of a homogenous national and religious identity defined through Russia's supposed cultural opposition to the West (despite the country's economic espousal of neoliberalism since the 1990s), rooted specifically in Russian values, including Eastern Orthodoxy, social conservatism, the Russian language, and an unmarked and poorly defined ethnic "Russianness."[1]

In this political context, for regional governments and local businesses interested in articulating a distinct regional identity—often with the goal of turning it into a source of revenue for the region—transforming the culturally marked into a marketable good requires generating new discursive and representational strategies for aggregating ethnicity, culture, and religion into commodity forms available for consumption to private actors. And this while leaving them open to other kinds of interpretations and management, in particular on the part of the state. In this arrangement, cultural and historical difference must be consumable without becoming legible as ethnic nationalism or as claims to ethnonational sovereignty—in other words, it must operate without implicating a framework that counteracts the narrative of a historically unified state. Even so, such consumption cannot be seen to toggle into Russian chauvinism. As objects of multiple forms of consumption, ritually and therapeutically efficacious objects present a curious case. Their materialities move simultaneously and often rather messily across economies of merit and capital, and in so doing, they also reconfigure what is considered to be the ethnocommodity's possible field of efficacy and application.

"THE HEART OF RUSSIA IN ASIA" AND THE GEOPOLITICS OF BURYATIA'S BRAND

With its regional capital in the same time zone as Beijing, Buryatia's geographic, cultural, and religious distinctions from what is typically associated with Russia are part and parcel of local imaginaries of the region's future economic and social trajectories. Over the last decade, presenting Buryatia as a desirable tourist destination for both a domestic and an international market has been an active object of local administrative investment and public relations efforts. Developing tourism, however, is not only a state-mandated plan: it is also taken up at the edges of the professional tourist community, by individuals and institutions whose livelihoods are found in other economic spheres.

In 2007, the local Buryat government undertook an initiative to create a special commission in charge of brand-making—in time with the federal government's decision to turn part of Buryatia into a Special Economic Zone, with the goal of bolstering international tourism in the Russian Far East, developing Russia's domestic health resort industry, and improving the region's economic prospect (Sanzhin 2010). This federal rezoning echoed preexisting notions of what Buryatia had to offer to the state. Buryatia is considered one of Russia's top-ten most "dotational" regions, according to Russia's Ministry of Finances (2011)—which is to say, a region that relies on federal financial injections into its budget for its solvency and for the maintenance of its welfare provisioning (such as education, medicine, and social security), at the expense of other, donor regions. In the absence of large profit-generating industries, Buryatia's investment profile among the different provinces of the Russian Federation emphasizes the region's exotic remoteness and ecology, and hence its appropriateness for ecological, therapeutic, and, recently, ethnographic tourism.

When I asked my local interlocutors about the federal initiative's perceived success, I usually received responses that ranged from cautiously optimistic to sarcastically disparaging. The skeptical voices tended to focus on an infrastructure argument about the lack of easy and affordable transportation to and from the region and the quality of local lodging options that would likely turn away a Western tourist accustomed to greater creature comforts, as well as the seeming invisibility of Buryatia itself.

In 2008, Buryatia's then president Vladimir Nagovitsyn was pointing out that before the region could be turned into an attractive destination for investors and travelers, the administration ought to raise awareness of Buryatia's very existence. He argued that outside of Buryatia, most people still confused the region's administrative capital Ulan-Ude with Ulaanbaatar, the capital of Mongolia—an altogether different state. Indeed, in European, or Western, Russia, which typically refers to the territory to the west of the Ural Mountains, Siberia tends to be represented as a homogenous and sparsely populated expanse—a persistent frontier narrative that blends images of a resource annex with those of forced relocation from western parts of Russia and the Soviet Union—erasing, in the process, the presence of indigenous populations. And while some Siberian regions with large extractive industries are more visible in the media, Buryatia is typically classified as a generic "periphery" (*periferiya*).

While anthropology has classically critiqued center-periphery models for their inability to account for the complexity of cultural and economic circulations and flows (Appadurai 1996), it is worthwhile to reflect on how such models operate when they are locally taken to authoritatively describe current political and economic arrangements. Distinctions traced along a "center"/"periphery" (or "center"/"regions") axis are part of a colloquial geopolitical mythos, frequently invoked in everyday conversations to account for Russia's geography of internal differences and inequalities.[2] The actual political and fiscal organization of the Russian Federation is a complex matter, however, with multiple defined tiers of administrative and territorial units. One dimension of differentiation between regions is whether or not they derive their political identity from a particular ethnic group that inhabits them—such as Buryatia or Tatarstan (Busygina and Taukebaeva 2015)—with the caveat that there is no one-to-one correspondence between ethnic population and eponymous region and not all ethnic minorities have an associated territorial unit. One of the effects of this dichotomy is that identification is available laterally (regional identity that is distinct from Moscow) but not vertically.

The tendency to pin the center and periphery in a relationship of mutual confrontation also emerged in scholarly debates about Russia's possible territorial and political disintegration following the 1998 fiscal crisis. The possibility that the Russian Federation might cease to exist as a single entity was high on the agenda of political analysts both in the country and abroad—ethnonational separatist rhetoric, as well as the attempts by local administrations to institute regional currencies and economically isolate themselves from the rest of the country made the fracturing seem inevitable, a simple matter of time before Russia followed in the footsteps of the Soviet Union and ceased to exist as a single entity (see Alexseev 1999). That this did not happen is sometimes attributed to the rise of Putin's "strong state" in the early 2000s. For Russia's central government, balancing local elites' desire for autonomy with a promise of political allegiance to Moscow on the one hand while taking into consideration a region's economic solvency and bargaining power on the other involves some complicated political maneuvering that facilitates the entanglement between power and capital (Ross and Turovsky 2015; Sulakshin et al. 2013).

However reductive, the "center-regions" discourse in fact offers a productive heuristic for understanding the contexts in which ethnobranding efforts in Russia are taking place. What underpins it is a semiotic interplay between marked and unmarked poles of two mutually calibrated but nonetheless distinct axes (Waugh 1982): Muscovite identity opposed to undifferentiated provinciality and ethnic unmarked Russianness opposed to ethnically marked otherness. The precarious work of aligning these two sets of distinctions has, in recent years, consistently spilled out into aggressive nationalist rhetoric along the lines of slogans like "Russia for Russians."[3] It is not simply that Russia's public discourses normalize racist and xenophobic sentiments, although this is the case to a degree. But, more subtly, what characterizes the relationship of the ethnically marked to the ethnically unmarked in Russia is laminated over the opposition between center and periphery, which always risks a reversal of what comes to stand in for the abstract, general category.

Peripheries, margins, frontiers, and, more generally, places defined by their distance from recognizable centers are especially fertile ground for the proliferation of hybrid discourses that reflect on and recenter claims to global incorporation (Tsing 2005). For its part, Buryatia finds itself in a kind of gravitational relationship to several centers. These multiple spheres of influence are not necessarily delimited by predetermined state formations and national borders but span different kinds of geographic and social encompassments and claims to situatedness, including the pan-Buddhist world, a sense of pan-Mongol ethnicity that intersects in complex ways with the Eurasanism, as well as the more prosaic itineraries of pursuing education, work, and medical care.[4] Local debates about regional branding reflect the strategic toggling between ways in which belonging is articulated in Buryatia.

By the end of the first decade of the aughts, Buryatia's visibility had become less of a concern—but other issues came to the front. During a conference on the image of Russia and its regions taking place in Ulan-Ude in June 2010, the participants were lauding the relative success of promoting Buryatia's

association with Lake Baikal, a UNESCO World Heritage site while reaffirm-
ing the necessity of furthering the republic's attractiveness as a recreational
and ecological destination, in particular for domestic tourists. By then, several formulations for defining Buryatia's image had made their way into the
media. A description of Ulan-Ude as the "Heart of Asian Russia" became commonplace, and Buryatia itself was reframed as "the Gateway to Asia." During
the June conference, the new slogan proposed a reversal of sorts: Buryatia as
the "Heart of Russia in Asia."

Despite this proliferation of Buryatia's identification with Asia, some of the
conference participants cautioned that any brand development would be taking
place in the context of Russia's broader geopolitical reputation, which gave little
cause for optimism. Thus, for example, a Moscow-based political scientist suggested that Russia's image in neighboring China was of a "negative-disdainful
character." Another participant cited the yearly report by BBC's Globe-
Scan about the international popularity of different states to note that "Russia finds itself as the 5th country from the bottom of the list, outperforming
only Iran, Pakistan, Israel, and North Korea." And yet, developing a brand
that would distance Buryatia from Russia by aligning it more explicitly with
either neighboring China or Mongolia had its own perils. One of the local
experts on regional branding expressed his concerns that banking on Buryatia's
"otherness"—Buryatia as the Heart of Russia in Asia—drew attention to Buryatia's inherently ambiguous marginality: "The geopolitical question for the
Russian Federation is a sore point. The Far East is under threat of Sinification,
which is something that worries Russian geopolitical analysts. The fact that
Buryatia is part of the Mongol world within the R[ussian] F[ederation] is something that they feel ambivalent about: strong connections with Mongolia, Asia,
China, and Tibet give some analysts reason to talk about separatist tendencies
in Buryatia. To reduce these tensions, it would be correct to signal to the federal
government that we consider ourselves to be one of Russia's regions, that we
guarantee Russia's interests" (Kuzmin 2010).

These debates point to the complex politics that underpin Buryatia's
brand-making initiatives. In order to make Buryatia's distinctiveness legible to
tourists and investors, the ethnobrand references preexisting and long-standing
national discourses on Russia's own cultural and political liminality, as a bridge
between Europe and Asia (Bassin 1991). This self-presentation narrates the
state's geography as a matter of cultural gradients, where remoteness from
the implied centers in European Russia works as value added, which, in turn,
must be managed at the risk of being misinterpreted as political threat. In this
sense, the center/periphery imaginary to which these debates about branding

Buryatia speak reinscribe economic activity—the hoped-for arrival of tourists and investment capital into the region—within a politics of potential ethnonational secessionism.

While the overt orientalism of the slogan "Heart of Russia in Asia," which exploits the implicit opposition between a presumably European Russia and an undifferentiated Asia, might be simply a marketing strategy, it also delimits *what* can become an ethnocommodity in the region and influences what shape such ethnocommodities could take. Buryatia, as the Heart of Asia in Russia, offers an "Asian experience" to domestic tourists, without the inconvenience of visas, language barriers, and other hurdles associated with international travel. In this sense, it echoes a Soviet-era aesthetics of geographic and cultural imitation designed for internal consumption by a population that was severely restricted in its ability to travel (Gorsuch 2011). Similarly, Buryatia as the Gateway to Asia promises an "Asian experience" to an unmarked Russian subject, who is presumably ethnically and culturally European, hailing from one of Russia's western regions, and either unable or unwilling to travel beyond the state's borders. The invocation of Asia, while indeed making Buryatia more legible to a hypothetical Western consumer, simultaneously suggests that Buryat culture-as-commodity is the more accessible, knock-off version of an original (abstractly Asian) cultural essence.

The imagined audience of Buryatia's Asian brand is assumed to follow familiar itineraries: from west to east along the Trans-Siberian railroad, from Europe to Asia, from urban centers to provincial towns and Nature. These accountings of geographic space and connections simultaneously articulate with and reproduce specific national narratives. They both speak to a politics of political self-sufficiency and a fantasy of global economic uninvolvement and echo a frontier-oriented settler colonialism that gets glossed as the "conquest of Siberia."

Concomitantly, such anticipatory figurations of Buryatia's "potential for tourism" obscure the complex movements of people and things that already characterize this part of the world: movements *between* Siberian regions, such as Buryatia and the Sakha Republic (which bypasses western Russia entirely) or between Siberian and Far Eastern urban hubs, such as Novosibirsk and Vladivostok. They also obscure the trans-border traffic among Russia, Mongolia, and China in pursuit of trade, education, and employment and the religious migration along Buddhist pilgrimage routes (for the latter, see Bernstein 2013).

For its part, Buddhism has been successfully folded into the region's promotional self-presentation as one of its defining characteristics. Much of what was pointed out to me by my interlocutors as Buryatia's "Asian" architectural style derives from a combination of Buryat and Mongol Buddhist temple architecture, with distinctly curved roofs and color symbolism, and a more recent style of urban commercial buildings that consciously echo these features. In this way, not only are Buddhist aesthetics woven into the infrastructural armature of the market, they are also packaged as symbolic experiences to be consumed as part of tourist circuits. For example, tourist agencies in Ulan-Ude, the regional capital, actively weave Buddhism into their products, by offering to experience Pilgrimage Tours and Sacred Springs Journeys to domestic and foreign visitors.[5] However, this intersection between Buddhism and the market are neither accidental nor reducible to a commodity logics encroaching onto a religious domain. Rather, the ways in which Buddhism and markets speak to each other in Buryatia make them an especially productive terrain for reflecting on the unique ways in which ethnocommodities function.

BUDDHISM INC.

Entanglements between postsocialist religious revivals and markets have been widely documented both in Russia and elsewhere (Jasarevic 2012; Lindquist 2001, 2005). Although Buryatia is a multiconfessional region, the official Buddhist Sangha of Russia, based in Buryatia, has worked to consolidate the region's association with a Buddhist heritage and tradition. In recent years, it has also argued for the independent status of Buryat Buddhism, and hence its freedom from foreign influences or hierarchies. The Sangha, as the Buddhist organization with most claims to a state affiliation in Buryatia, functions as a consequential voice in both local, and to some extent national and international politics. Economically, much of the Sangha's activity is directed toward and informed by the market, and many of the schisms and upheavals the organization has undergone in the postsocialist period have had a distinctly economic dimension (Makhachkeev 2010).

While the political goals and visions of the regional administration and of the Sangha have not always aligned, both have actively promoted the sense that Buryat Buddhism is not only a religious and moral but also an economic force shaping the region—though, of course, its economic power is often made to speak back to its moral and ethical dimensions. On the one hand, banking on a local Buddhist heritage is risky business, in that Buddhism already operates as a cosmopolitan commodity in a global spiritual marketplace (Geary 2008; Saxer 2013). However, the labor of connecting Buryatia's image with a particular vision of Buddhism is not a coordinated endeavor but one in which many local organizations that are not directly affiliated with—or sometimes outright in competition with—the Sangha still feel compelled to participate. Instead, it is a nebulous and shifting assemblage of multiple actors, many of whom find themselves interpellated to participate in and respond to an already circulating discourse on what constitutes a region's value to an outside gaze. For example, the local traditional medicine hospital that became one of the focal sites of my fieldwork felt obligated to take on the role of tour guide for international colleagues, high-ranking patients, and visiting dignitaries who showed an interest in the activity of the medical institution. It therefore interspersed its more specific medical offerings with guided tours that incorporated a Buddhist temple visit and a trip to the history museum to view the collection of thanghka illustrations that constitute the Buryat copy of the Atlas of Tibetan Medicine.[6]

Nor is the process of ethnobranding limited to expert-led endeavors. Both local organizations and individuals frequently enter Buryatia's tourist economy as purveyors of free labor, and as themselves producers and promoters of a particular vision of Buryatia's image. These forms of participation are often framed as part of local cultural etiquette—as a sign of being "good hosts" (*gostepriimstvo*). Ferrying their visitors around Ulan-Ude or the countryside is a common way of passing the time with one's guests, and a practice that intersects with a long-standing Soviet-era tradition of amateur regional studies (*kraevedenie*) cultivated in school curricula and local museums. On the other hand, such excursions are also occasions for perpetuating exchange relationships with nonhuman others that inhabit Buryatia's landscape. In particular, travel across specific sacred sites (*oboo*), such as mountain passes or streams, demands donations to local place dwellers (*savdak*) as a token of safe passage. While tourists might be officially recruited in these actions—and making offerings is reframed as ethnographic information about local customs—the implications of not following proper etiquette toward the local spirits can have dire consequences for both outsiders and locals. In multiple conversations with my Buryat friends and interlocutors, explanations for car accidents and other unexpected fatalities were framed as a breach of proper comportment toward the *savdaki*. More often than not, if the accident involved tourists, ignorance of an oboo figured as the primary cause.

However, in the case of Buddhism in Buryatia, the cartographic imaginaries of what is and what is not worth showing go hand in glove with some top-down initiatives to promote certain aspects of Buryat Buddhism but not others. Not all temples are seen as worthy of outside visitors—and many of the Buddhist communes unaffiliated with the Sangha are not housed in architecturally distinct buildings that appropriately index Buryatia's Asianness. These occlusions in turn create a homogenous sense of Buryat Buddhism that does not reflect its internal fractures and tensions, which are quite important for local religious pursuits. More generally, because much of Buryatia's Buddhist architecture has been reconstructed (or constructed anew), save for a few notable temples, many members of Buryatia's Buddhist community express a sense of scarcity of authentic places of worship, though discussions of a temple's potential for aesthetic enjoyment, no matter its history, are quite prominent in local conversations about what counts as a properly sacred space. More generally, Buddhism in Buryatia often functions as a kind of double signifier, one that simultaneously operates as a space for the consumption of Buryat religious history and culture by outsiders, and one that figures in local exchanges centered on the generation of merit. But the relationship between the sacred and the mundane does not articulate a strict dualistic opposition, nor are the presupposed boundaries between religion-as-commodity and religion-as-lived-practice uncontested or self-evident. Much of that relationship—the question of where the mundanely economic ends, and where economic concerns begin to bear religious significance—is articulated through the idiom of scarcity.

SCARCE SACRALITIES

The competing senses of scarcity that arise at the site of encounter between Buddhism and neoliberal market logics in fact have long individual and collective histories that implicate the Soviet state. During my research in Buryatia in the late 2000s, queuing for hours to obtain sacred objects and services was a perfectly ordinary undertaking, despite the market's visible saturation with religious commodities. Buddhist lectures and empowerments regularly sold out, despite the long waits and prohibitive price tag. Ritual objects, from the mass-produced colored scarfs used for offerings in both Buddhist and Shamanic rites, to various amulets, prayer beads, incense burners, deity statuettes, thangka postcards, and dashboard prayer wheels crowded the shelves of temple gift shops and downtown art galleries. They also coexisted with other examples of national or ethnic arts and crafts, sold along Buryatia's tourist circuits, such that ritually efficacious objects and mass-produced tchotchkes aimed at tourists shared a messy, ambiguous boundary. Faced with the abundance of mass-produced religious kitsch, my Buryat interlocutors bemoaned a sense of scarcity of truly powerful objects and spiritual teachers—what a friend and local Buddhist scholar described to me as a "blessing deficit."

A particular incident might help illustrate the tensions between these contrasting experiences of excess and scarcity. The crowd in front of the Sampilov Art Museum snaked raggedly down the building's well-worn concrete steps, constantly threatening to spill beyond the temporary aluminum railings that attempted to contain it, and looped along the small street towards Ulan-Ude's pedestrian artery with its touristy cafes, clothing boutiques, and mobile phone stores. By 10:00 a.m., on a cool September morning in 2010, the line had swelled to several hundred people, but the museum's main doors remained closed. Uniformed policemen overlooked the crowd from the Soviet structure's elevated porch, occasionally wandering off to smoke a cigarette or make a phone call.

Such massive gatherings, unusual for the local art museum, are quite typical for Ulan-Ude's religious events. A section of the museum had been repurposed to house the sand mandala of "Otosho Bagsha,"[7] or the Medicine Buddha. The mandala, assembled over several days by six monks from Buryatia's largest Buddhist temple, became a site of worship for the local Buddhist community. Considered to be the temporary earthly manifestation of the Medicine Buddha's realm, the mandala also concentrated sacredness into its material substance. Upon its ritual deconstruction, the karmic benefit accumulated through its creation and worship would be released. The queue had formed because those desirous to obtain a small packet of sand from the soon-to-be-destroyed mandala far exceeded the museum workers' expectations. Upon seeing the line that had formed outside, the staff called in law enforcement in fear of a stampede.

As the scheduled time for distributing the sand came and went, people in the queue began to grumble that there wouldn't be enough for everyone anyway. Some countered that if one had paid their respects to Otosho Bagsha, they had already received the benefits the mandala bestowed. Unsurprisingly, such assurances did little to thin the queue. An older Buryat man standing in front of me turned around and joked loudly, to anyone in earshot: "And here you have it, our Soviet Buddhism. Like queuing for sausage."

From the perspective of creating a Buryat variant of Buddhism Inc., the mandala queue was irrational—an example of fetishism, in both its anthropological and Marxist senses. At the same time, the mandala reveals the Janus-like qualities of a cultural commodity produced for both internal and external consumption—or, rather, for a commodity that operates as a shifter, as *both* religiously and economically efficacious object. Its assembly and disassembly were advertised as a cultural event—something to draw in tourists and a general public, rather than worshippers—and its location in a museum space seemed to cement its availability to a secular audience. However, because the mandala to the Medicine Buddha addresses itself explicitly to corporeal, embodied hopes and desires, its audience engaged it as a site of worship—or, to be more specific, as a site of healing—and not as a museum exhibit.

The queue for the sand mandala, with its inherent contradictions—immaterial abundance of sacredness offset by a pedestrian experience of material scarcity—helps lay bare some of the productive tensions that characterize the commodification of religious and cultural practices in Siberia. If the ethnocommodity has the paradoxical tendency to resist the loss of aura suffered as the result of mass production or repetition more broadly, as John and Jean Comaroff (2009, 20) argue, the "blessing deficit" points us to a different way in which the "lossy" qualities of authenticity become reconfigured as sites for generating value. Here, scarcity is a *historical* condition with a long-embodied afterlife and long-term consequences for the people embedded in circuits of karmic merit and capital, which, in practice, are coarticulated. As religious distinction in Buryatia is being hitched to global ethnocommodity markets, it simultaneously enfolds these markets within the history of a distinctly postsocialist experience of Buddhism—with attention to what it might mean to recuperate and reenliven traditional religious practices at the peripheries of a *Pax Buddhica* in which Buryatia is often thought of as a marginal addendum, though with a different sense of marginality from the one articulated in the economic cartographies of the Russian state. The labor of keeping these circuits separate—and worrying at their junctures—is also what enables some ethnocommodities to accrue symbolic (and economic) value at the expense of others.

MAKING BURYAT-TIBETAN MEDICINE

It is not an accident that the queue, with its reanimated memories of a Soviet mundane, centered on questions of medicine and healing. Since the late 1980s, the regional administration has been invested in developing and promoting a local tradition of Buddhist medicine, locally known as simply "Tibetan medicine." The case of Tibetan medicine in Buryatia illustrates another problem at the intersection of ethnocommodities and imitation: the labor required to turn a cultural icon local, when it is already coopted by other, more recognizable, entities. Participants in projects of promoting local medical traditions frequently struggle with the suspicion that much of the culturally distinguishable features to which Buryatia might lay claim have already been claimed elsewhere. Debates around Tibetan medicine in Buryatia make these difficulties especially visible.

The official banquet, held in celebration of the conference "Development of Traditional Medicine in Russia," organized in Ulan-Ude by the East-West Medical Center in August 2010, was punctuated by an abundance of toasts. One such toast, delivered by a representative from Buryatia's Ministry of Health Protection, invoked one of the recalcitrant and seemingly trivial problems that had plagued the conference. Before moving forward to a greater institutionalization of Tibetan medicine in Buryatia and Russia more broadly, how should Tibetan medicine in Buryatia be identified? In a humorous proposal, he offered his own solution: "I have suggested that we call it the 'Tibeto-Indo-Perso-Greeko-Mongolian-Buryat medicine of Russia,' but I was told that this is too long and isn't catchy enough."

Scholarship on the globalization of traditional medicine has made several important points that challenge assumptions about the self-containment and homogeneity of different medical systems. Scholars of Asian medicines for example have pointed to the heterogeneity and plurality that results from the long histories of cultural borrowings and encounters at the intersections of trade routes, military conquests, colonial projects, and religious expansions, as well as to the contingent processes of formalization within therapeutic traditions that are internally plural (Scheid and MacPherson 2011; Pordié 2010). In other words, *traditional* medicines are never singular or homogeneous formations. Indeed, it was precisely this very point that the healthcare administrator cited earlier was wrestling with during his toast.

In addition to the hoary business of negotiating Buryatia's political affiliations, establishing a recognizable and distinctive image for the region encounters conceptual problems that have to do with claiming a cultural icon that is identifiably local rather than already coopted by other, more recognizable, entities. In Russia's vibrant domain of nonbiomedical, natural care, which includes a variety of institutions, therapeutic methodologies, and products, Tibetan medicine is only one of multiple therapeutic offerings identified as "traditional." Several conceptual contrasts operate in this field of therapeutic distinctions, where Eastern modalities of care frequently marked as "natural" are almost automatically opposed to Western approaches, equated to "modern" and essentially "synthetic" or "artificial" interventions. Within this therapeutic pantheon, the label "Tibetan medicine" simultaneously draws on an orientalist aesthetic of the "mysterious" East and references the internal diversity and "multinational" composition of the Russian Federation.

Establishing Tibetan medicine as a recognizably Buryat form of care depends on practices of scale- and place-making (Raffles 1999; Tsing 2005) that unsettle entrenched national center-periphery imaginaries. In recent years, Buryatia has unexpectedly found itself at the forefront of Russia's efforts to incorporate and formalize different forms of nonbiomedical healing, although the semiotics of regional self-presentation betray a constant slippage between Tibetan medicine as part of Buryatia's claims to a Buddhist heritage, and therefore its inclusion into a broader Buddhist world and its cooptation by the republic's health care system and scientific research centers as part of a more broadly defined "traditional" (and ethnic) knowledge and skill.[8]

Attempts to produce and stabilize the Buryatness of Tibetan medicine open up the question of what is identifiably Buryat in the first place. For example, one site of debate for local practitioners of Tibetan medicine is how to differentiate Tibetan medicine in Buryatia from its interpretation in neighboring Mongolia, which is understood locally to have a more authentic claim to a recognizable cultural identity. Medical practitioners who use Tibetan medicine (and traditional medicine more broadly) in their professional practice often wistfully mentioned to me Mongolia's ability to nationalize Buddhist medicine by making it *Mongolian*, on the model of TCM in China. Institutionalizing Buddhist medicine in Buryatia along the same national medicine model is patently impossible, in part because of the tenuous claims Buryatia might have to an authentic and uninterrupted medical tradition but, in greater part, because it would run up against Russia's multinational rhetoric.

Thus, for example, in 1998, when the founder of the East-West Medical Center gave a presentation of his work at the now disbanded State Scientific Research Institute of Traditional Treatment Methods in Moscow, the stated goals of his research were grappling with demonstrating that traditional medical practices in Buryatia were recognizably Tibetan. In recent years this concern has been reversed. Present-day administrators, scholars, and medical professionals are more concerned with demonstrating that Tibetan medicine in Buryatia is properly Buryat, and that it is therefore the legacy of a multinational Russian state. It is then unsurprising that the unwieldy problem of labeling Tibetan medicine in the region made it into the introductory address at the conference with which this section began. The speaker—the vice-minister of Healthcare and Social Development—began by drawing attention to this seemingly trivial issue: what should Tibetan medicine in Buryatia be called?

> Buryatia is the only region of the Russian Federation where in the culture for many centuries so called traditional Tibetan medicine is used. By the way, we call it different things. Some time back, I have proposed . . . to establish a unified term, and I proposed the term "Tibetan medicine of Buryatia" but it just won't take root. . . . In fact, there is a problem in identifying the medical system that concerns us. And, there are reasons to say that since the middle of the 17th century, on the territory of Siberia, Russia, Buryatia, this medicine lives and develops, and we can say that in the same way that there is Tibetan medicine, there is also Tibetan medicine of Buryatia.

This statement uniquely captures a conceptual paradox that informs much of the efforts at institutionalizing Tibetan medicine in the region. Tibetan medicine in Buryatia is caught between two imperatives, derived from the local administration's desire to articulate it as part of Buryatia's regional identity. On the one hand, in order to legitimately become part of Buryatia's national offerings to the Russian state, it must be presented as compatible with the state's healthcare objectives. Because of its legal status, or rather lack thereof, Tibetan medicine, insofar as it is to be used in Russia's official health sector, must lend itself to easy disassembly into alienated medical technologies—therapeutic modules recognizable within Russian mainstream public health categories. From the perspective of a modular and atomized view, different medical technologies cannot be overtly marked as culturally or ethnically specific, or at least they must be detached from their philosophical or conceptual underpinnings to be deployed discretely in clinical settings. On the other hand, the appeal of traditional medicine is derived from its claims to being a system—a total form of care. To reconcile these tensions, local scholarly voices have begun to argue that what makes Tibetan medicine distinctively Buryat is that it is not *singularly* Buryat. In other words, Tibetan medicine is presented as always already integrative, and especially so in Buryatia. If Buryat-Tibetan medicine is in reality an assemblage of different medical cultures and techniques—Russian, Mongolian, Persian, Greek, Indian, and so forth—then Buryatia's own perceived derivative hybridity has the potential of being reconfigured into a brandable feature—a sense of branding that also redefines what a center is, framing the region as a site of cultural and historical intersection rather than one of self-enclosed and historically continuous identity.

LIVING OUT SOVIET AFTERLIVES

The representational footwork in which Tibetan medicine in Buryatia is mired elides the everyday strategies of navigating local therapeutic geographies. The pharmaceuticals of Tibetan medicine, as well as its associated forms of knowledge and practice also enter Buryatia from elsewhere—from Tibet, India, and Italy, for example—as material substances and religious teachings, assumed to be easily deployable in a market already primed by local cultural and religious traditions. Quibbles over the authenticity and potency of different substances and practitioners with different loci of origin shape much of the conversation about local therapeutic geographies.

One of the more controversial sites of commercialization of Tibetan medicine was the local branch of the International Academy of Traditional Tibetan

Medicine, an organization that, as its name suggests, operates on a global scale, and has the dual purpose of teaching Tibetan medicine to those able to afford it, and to promote Tibetan medical culture more generally. ATTM's headquarters are located in Milan, Italy, but the organization has a presence throughout western and eastern Europe, the United States, India, Japan, and China. The Russian central office is located in Moscow, but in 2009 an offshoot opened in Ulan-Ude and quickly became a site of both concentrated interest and vitriolic controversy for the local Buddhist community. The Siberian office primarily specialized in inviting guest speakers to lecture on Tibetan medicine and screened the televised teachings of Dr. Nida Chenagtzang, the academy's founder, as well as organized meditation retreats for local patients interested in learning *yuthog nyingthig*, a *terma*[9] tantric practice associated with the Medicine Buddha.

The office's main administrator at the time, Ayur-lama, had big plans for expanding the organization: he hoped to organize a school of Tibetan medicine in the region with a fieldwork component that would monetize the labor of gathering medicinal herbs by making it part of an ecotour package for wealthy foreigners and Muscovites. In the meantime, his primary activity centered on putting together meditation retreats organized around yuthog nyingthig. And while Ayur-lama was perhaps not a particularly visible participant in Buryatia's more visibly mediated tourist economies, the fact that he operated at these circuits' fringes did not mean that he worked in obscurity, nor did it diminish his organization's economic impact for himself or others. The events organized by Ayur-lama were extremely well-attended and, at a steep individual cost, generated quite a bit of profit. My friends and acquaintances in the Tibetan medicine community read the signs of his economic activities of Ayur-lama's persona—commenting on dress, cars, homeownership, and other signs of wealth his activities afforded him.

In order to attract potential participants, Ayur-lama framed the benefits of learning the meditation techniques not in terms of accumulating favorable karma over multiple rebirths but by invoking their efficacies in this life. Rejuvenation and healing are believed to be byproducts of the systematic yuthog nyingthig practice. In fact, most tantric practices are associated with the acquisition of *sidhi* (Sanskrit)—paranormal or magical powers developed by the adept but thought to be distractions on the way to enlightenment. However, as far as Ayur-lama's marketing strategies were concerned, they made for a perfect advertisement campaign, since "rejuvenation" was an already intensely familiar product category in Russia, ranging from pharmaceuticals to various procedures associated with alternative and complementary medicine.

While my local interlocutors in the Tibetan medicine community critiqued Ayur-lama for what they felt was unscrupulous exploitation of a vulnerable population, the lectures that the organization put together were quite popular, despite high admission fees, and drew both practitioners and patients. One of their central appeals was the opportunity to expand one's therapeutic armamentarium with new medicinal formulas and techniques of medical preparation.[10] But in addition to these more material aspects of the craft of Tibetan medicine, for those who had learned the practice in a piecemeal fashion and without a formal teacher, the program promised a Buddhist empowerment at the end of the course. As in other tantric traditions of Buddhism, Tibetan medicine empowerments conveyed by a spiritual teacher authorize the student to undertake essential aspects of the craft. For example, the preparation of certain types of medicines, pulse divination, reading certain medical texts, and the meditative techniques associated with Tibetan medicine all require different empowerment levels. As it was explained to me, the empowerment is a ritual action where the teacher claims karmic responsibility for the student. Because the organizers explicitly monetized the empowerment component by charging higher admissions if one planned to stay until the end, participants quickly began to grumble about the improper intentions of the administration.

For his part, Ayur-lama saw no contradictions in the way he was weaving Buddhist teachings with market logics. In a sense, it is possible to see Ayur-lama as embracing and inhabiting the slippage between neoliberalism and a new age spiritualism: a rhetoric of self-perfection aimed at cultivating market success, and the cultivation of market success as a form of spiritual self-fashioning (Aldred 2000; Askegaard 2006; Farquhar 1996). However, such an interpretation would offer only a partial picture. In a conversation in 2010, Ayur-lama explained that money was simply the concentrated energy that one had expended to earn it. In other words, he argued, Buddhist protectors (*sakhyusan*[11]) actually consumed labor-power, and a high price tag was simply a way to pay respect to the Buddhist deities involved with one's practice. He felt irate with the financial reluctance of the attendees he had gathered, accusing them of being improper Buddhists, still plagued by a Soviet mentality of wanting to reap the benefits without (quite literally) working for it.

As much as he was a savvy businessman, interpreting Ayur-lama's actions and motivations purely through the lens of cynical profit-mongering would miss the more subtle ways in which Buddhism, markets, and the embodied histories of the Soviet state intertwine in Buryatia. Recent scholarship on Buryat and Mongol Buddhism has theorized the ways in which highly visible Buddhist bodies—in particular those of Buddhist monks and religious leaders—serve to anchor claims about sovereignty, national and religious encompassment, and the pleasures and perils of neoliberal market logics (Bernstein 2012, 2013; High 2013; Quijada 2012). Managing bodily and biographic instabilities wrought by postsocialist transformations transects and welds together religious and financial considerations and strategies. When I suggest that Soviet histories are embodied, I do not just mean that they are perpetuated in particularly resilient forms of bodily habitus, such as the sand mandala queue analyzed in this chapter. Rather, I argue that in Buryatia, Soviet biographic time has been subsumed into and reinterpreted through Buddhist logics of rebirth and karmic accumulation, which, in turn, are made to speak back to questions of financial circulation and economic solvency.

For those who, most of their lives, lived in what is often locally glossed as "Soviet times" or "the Soviet period," a personal history of a shortage of spiritual practice has very concrete and dire implications for the prospects of a good rebirth. In practice, it translates into an embodied temporality experienced as biological time running out. Referring to what one's life was like during socialism—which is to say, articulating continuities and discontinuities within a single lifespan—presents a comparable challenge to stringing together lifetimes and rebirths. During our conversation about reincarnation and what constitutes desirable rebirth, Bayar-lama, a talented thangkha painter in one of the city's temples, chuckled when I asked him, somewhat tongue in cheek, whether he knew what he had been in his previous life. "Of course I know. I was a photographer."

But for those of an older generation who do not have much of a chance at a second (postsocialist) life, what matters is a lifetime accumulation of favorable karma interrupted by political and historical events that does not bode well for future chances of a beneficial reincarnation. Older people are especially vulnerable in this calculus of time—"the grandmothers," as Ayur-lama affectionately yet somewhat patronizingly called the older women who were ready to brave hours of queuing to receive the material aspect of the blessing or empowerment—are terrified of getting permanently lost in "bardo," the intermediate state between reincarnations. It is in relation to this contingent finality that accumulating empowerments, blessings, and sacred objects becomes a way of trying to catch up to an ineluctable karmic calculus that does not make excuses for the accident of birth.

The activities and relative success of such religious organizations as ATTM in Buryatia might appear as confirmations of their successful adoption of a kind of global or cosmopolitan brand of Buddhism Inc. Unsettling this image of frictionless propagation of a perfectly translatable religious commodity, popular explanations about why ATTM had chosen Ulan-Ude that both organizers and participants offered invoked a logic of brand familiarity. Because there was already a local tradition of Tibetan medicine and Buddhism in Buryatia, less translational work would be needed to make the product desirable to the local population. However, both of these explanations fail to account for *how* such configurations of religion, self-improvement spirituality, and markets are in fact coopted into distinctly postsocialist Buddhist logics of managing historically fractured temporalities.

CONCLUSION

Anthropological scholarship on branding has noted that the brand's tendencies toward excesses and "surfeits" (Nakassis 2013)—manifested as the copy, the forgery, or the freestanding label to name a few—are both inherent to the semiotic processes through which brands come to be, and central to local regimes of social and economic value formation (Coombe 1998; Lemon 1998; Yurchak 2005; Vann 2006). Within these logics, the production of culture-as-commodity—and religion-as-commodity—is inevitably a recursive process that both depends on and puts into question such distinctions as "producer" and "consumer" (Comaroff and Comaroff 2009, 26; see also Mazzarella 2003; Manning 2010; Manning and Uplisashvili 2007). In this chapter, I have suggested that an additional dimension comes into play when the consumption of a religious commodity is thought of in simultaneously economic and ritually efficacious terms. As linguistic anthropologist Michael Lempert (2014) notes, mimesis needs not be strictly dyadic—or rather, such binaries as "authentic" and "inauthentic" are always a matter of specific semiotic optics and strategies. My point throughout this chapter has been that the production and circulation of ethnocommodities is not a matter of strategic toggling between frames—in Buryatia, Buddhist commodities (among them, Tibetan medicine), operate simultaneously in multiple circuits of economic and symbolic exchange. Claims regarding *which* regimes of circulation are primary become sites of contestation and social labor. In Buryatia, rather than transforming everything it touches into economic gain, an ethnobrand that mobilizes cultural uniqueness without making it politically perilous becomes, at different moments, a way of staking out a region's historical connections, a site for the articulation of cultural distinction, and an optic for the production of moral and symbolic worth. It also offers a meta-commentary on the nature of postsocialist change. It is to this last point that I would like to return here.

What makes the accusation of Sovietness such a productive metaphor in local discourses on the encounter between Buryat Buddhism and the market? The juxtaposition of banality and desirability appears to make religious commodities—whether empowerments or ritual objects—a site of reflection on the nature of (post)-Soviet life itself. By way of illustration, it may be helpful to go to one of the most widespread pejorative terms employed to describe former Soviet subjects, and the quality of Soviet existence. *Sovok* or *Sovkovyi*, substituted for *Sovetskiy*, is a play on words that transforms Soviet (council) into *sovok*—"dust-pan," "scoop," or "trowel." While some debates exist about the etymological origins of this neologism, what interests me here is that the pejorative connotation appears to be partially a function of the term's almost profane prosaicness. *Sovok* is a critique because it defines the Soviet experience as the constant coexistence between lofty utopian aesthetics and rhetorics and the dull tedium of everyday housekeeping. Perhaps ironically, in everyday parlance *Sovok* sometimes comes to stand in for petit bourgeois ambitions, values, and tastes. In my conversations with people from an older generation for whom queuing had been, and often still is, an integral part of the everyday economy of obtaining goods and services, certain objects were taken to be iconic of what it meant to live in Soviet times. They often invoked, with equal measure ironic amusement and puzzlement, a list of commodities remarkable for their banality yet no less passionately coveted: sausage, vodka, shoes, nylon stockings. It is these overtones of the Soviet scarce commodity as a uniquely profane fetish that helps people make sense of the local circuits of postsocialist Buddhism.

Yet, distinctions between proper and improper lives—ones that are too tarnished by Soviet histories, or by neoliberal market logics, for example—miss the more subtle ways of strategizing a living within and across lifetimes in postsocialist Buryatia. Attending to the accumulations of karmic benefit while running against the biological clock is part of a broader temporality of fractalized lifetimes that do not readily or obviously map onto particular life spans. Unsurprisingly, Ayur-lama was particularly sensitive to these internal biographic rifts. "In my past life as a good Soviet citizen," he joked, "I graduated from the pedagogical institute and did a stint as a physics teacher in Aginsk. Now, I teach Buddhism, but actually, knowing how to explain physics to a bunch of village kids is really helpful for it." I heard a variation of this story on a regular basis, from a variety of Buddhist practitioners, both Buryat and Russian. The uncomfortable suturing that helps maintain a coherent lifetime becomes a site for making historical and political arguments. For example, those critical of the leader of Buryatia's Buddhist Sangha, Dagba Ayusheev, frequently took his ready involvement in local politics as a testimony of the improper holdover of his Soviet (nonreligious) life on his new, postsocialist "incarnation" as a religious figure.

The liminal mixtures proliferated by the logics of the ethnocommodity, or of Buddhism Inc., have their own unique efficacies. The sand from the Otosho Bagsha mandala, for example, worked as a portable agent of the sacred, harnessing karmic benefit into the everyday. The packets of blessed sand could be incorporated into the walls of a house, hung from the rearview mirror of a car, or worn as amulets to heal the body and extend biological lifetimes. The practices of yuthog nyingthig that the controversial ATTM branch advertised to aging Buddhists, could help extend a lifetime where properly following the Dharma had been jeopardized by a state-imposed atheism. In the intimate interstices of everyday life, the commodified practices of Buryat Buddhism add time to "present-life" and thus, in the long run, maximize lifetimes of opportunity for bridging historical transitions, whether within this lifetime or the next.

NOTES

1. The concept of the "multinational state" (*multinatsional'noye gosudarstvo*) has been increasingly in tensions with recent rhetorics on the "Russian world" (*russkij mir*), used, notably, to justify the annexation of Crimea in March 2014 and subsequent involvement in Eastern Ukraine. Nevertheless, official assertions that ethnic or religious nationalism poses a threat to the very integrity of the state—including a threat to its most numerous ethnicity—is increasingly part of Vladimir Putin's political messages to the population.

2. For an argument that recuperates the "center-periphery" divide to characterize Russia's place in a global economy, as, primarily, an exporter of natural resources and hence a "resource annex" to other capitalist powers, see Kagarlitsky (2002, 27).

3. The slogan, recuperated in recent years to stand in for the political message of the nationalist parties, whose numbers were predicted to increase in the post-Bolotnaya January 2012 election fraud protests, was originally coined in 1905 by V. A. Gringmut, one of the main ideologues of Chernosotintsy, a Russian ultra-right nationalist movement active in the early 1900s. It should be noted that the epithet "Russian" was not used as an ethnonym at the time but instead as a reference to national affiliation.

4. In an account of the diplomatic relations between the Manchu and British empires at the end of the eighteenth century, James Hevia noted that rituals focused on the Manchu emperor's body produced relations of cosmological centering and distancing that did not result in permanent loci or configurations

of power (Hevia 2002). I find this insight helpful in considering the ways in which the political "center" is always a contingent and emergent category in Buryatia.

5. Buddhism is only one of the religions practiced in Buryatia—the others include Shamanism (Tengerism), Eastern Orthodoxy, and Old Believers (Staroobriadchestvo). Similar to Buddhism, shamanism has also made its way into the Buryatia's identity-making politics and branding initiatives (Quijada and Stephen 2015), as have Old Believers (Evstrop'eva 2013; Kirillov et al. 2014).

6. One of three existing copies of the atlas, which offers an illustrated guide to the Gyushi, the canonical manual of Tibetan medicine, was at the center of a controversy in the 1990s. Contestations over its appropriateness for secular circulation and display became a source of public outrage and vitriolic conflict between the regional government and the Sangha (Chudakova 2013; Makhachekeev 2010).

7. The Mongolian and Buryat name for Manla (Tibetan) or Bhaiṣajyaguru (Sanskrit).

8. There is a particular ethnic politics that centers on this question. While in theory, Buddhist practitioners in Buryatia often affirm that the selection of disciples for transmitting Buddhist knowledge and empowerments, medical or otherwise, should not be based on ethnicity but on the individual qualities of the prospective students, ethnically Russian practitioners of Tibetan medicine of an older generation, who began their apprenticeship either in the 1980s or the 1990s often complained that only very few authoritative Buddist practitioners who were ethnically Buryat would take on ethnic Russians as disciples. There is certainly a racial politics to Buddhism in Buryatia, although it is perhaps less pronounced now that the local Tibetan diasporic community is actively promoting the Westernization of Buddhism. In the domain of Tibetan medicine, however, these tensions seemed to me to not be particularly pronounced, as apprenticeship, collaboration, and treatment certainly happen across ethnic lines. There is perhaps a greater rift between ethnically Buryat Buddhist practitioners and the local Tibetan diaspora. This rift is expressed through a mutual critique by Buryat and Tibetan *emchi*, where Buryat practitioners might claim that the Tibetan diasporic presence is largely motivated by opportunities for financial profit, while the Tibetan practitioners claim that there is no such thing as Buryat Tibetan medicine and that Buryats have largely lost their therapeutic traditions.

9. *Gter ma (Tib)*, or "hidden treasure," is a teaching that was originally hidden and discovered at a later date. Yuthog nyingthig was created by Yuthok Yonten Gonpo the Younger (1126–1202), along with the Four Tantras, the canonical text of Tibetan medicine.

10. Many practitioners of Sowa Ripga in Buryatia make their own medicines and gather themselves the herbs, minerals, and animal products necessary for their production.

11. Or Dharampala (Sanskrit), wrathful deities that act as defenders of the dharma.

REFERENCES

Aldred, Lisa. 2000. "Plastic Shamans and Astroturf Sun Dances: New Age Commercialization of Native American Spirituality." *American Indian Quarterly* 24 (3): 329–52.

Alexseev, M. 1999. *Center-Periphery Conflict in Post-Soviet Russia: A Federation Imperiled.* New York: St. Martin's Press.

Appadurai, Arjun. 1996. *Modernity at Large: Cultural Dimensions of Globalization.* Minneapolis: University of Minnesota Press.

Askegaard, Søren. 2006. "Brands as a Global Ideoscape." In *Brand Culture,* edited by Jonathan Schroeder and Miriam Salzer-Mörling, 91–102. New York: Routledge.

Bassin, Mark. 1991. "Russia between Europe and Asia: The Ideological Construction of Geographical Space." *Slavic Review* 5 (1): 1–17.

Bernstein, Anya. 2012. "More Alive Than All the Living: Sovereign Bodies and Cosmic Politics in Buddhist Siberia." *Cultural Anthropology* 27 (2): 261–85.

———. 2013. *Religious Bodies Politic: Rituals of Sovereignty in Buryat Buddhism.* Chicago: University of Chicago Press.

Busygina, Irina Markovna, and Elmira Taukebaeva. 2015. "Federalizm Ili Unitarizm Kak Strategisheskii Vybor I Ego Posledstviia (sravnitel'nyi Analiz Rossii I Kazakhstana)" [Federalism or Unitarism as a Strategic Choice and Its Consequences (a Comparative Analysis of Russia and Kazakhstan)]. *Comparative Politics* 1 (18): 101.

Chudakova, Tatiana. 2013. *Recovering Health: Tibetan Medicine and Biocosmopolitics in Russia.* PhD diss. Chicago: University of Chicago, Division of the Social Sciences, Department of Anthropology.

Comaroff, John L., and Jean Comaroff. 2009. *Ethnicity, Inc.* Chicago: University of Chicago Press.

Coombe, Rosemary J. 1998. *The Cultural Life of Intellectual Properties: Authorship, Appropriation, and the Law.* Post-Contemporary Interventions. Durham, NC: Duke University Press, 1998.

Evstrop'eva, Oksana Vladimirovna. 2013. "Ethno-recreational Potential of the Baikal Region." *Geography and Natural Resources* 34 (1): 61–68.

Farquhar, Judith. 1996. "Market Magic: Getting Rich and Getting Personal in Medicine after Mao." *American Ethnologist* 23 (2): 239–57.

Geary, David. 2008. "Destination Enlightenment: Branding Buddhism and Spiritual Tourism in Bodhgaya, Bihar." *Anthropology Today* 24 (3): 11–14.

Gorsuch, Anne E. 2011. *All This Is Your World: Soviet Tourism at Home and Abroad after Stalin*. Oxford: Oxford University Press.

Hevia, James. 2002. *Cherishing Men from Afar: Qing Guest Rituals and the Macartney Embassy of 1793*. Durham, NC: Duke University Press.

High, Mette M. 2013. "Cosmologies of Freedom and Buddhist Self: Transformation in the Mongolian Gold Rush." *Journal of the Royal Anthropological Institute* 19 (4): 753–70.

Jasarevic, Larisa. 2012. "Pouring Out Postsocialist Fears: Practical Metaphysics of a Therapy at a Distance." *Comparative Studies in Society and History* 54 (4): 914–41.

Kagarlitsky, Boris. 2002. *Russia under Yeltsin and Putin: Neo-Liberal Autocracy*. London: Pluto Press.

Kirillov, Sergey, Natalia Sedova, Elena Vorobyevskaya, and Tatiana Zengina. 2014. "Problems and Prospects for Tourism Development in the Baikal Region, Russia." *14th SGEM GeoConference on Ecology, Economics, Education and Legislation* 2 (SGEM2014 Conference Proceedings, ISBN 978-619-7105-18-6/ISSN 1314-2704, June 19–25, 2014, vol. 2, 531–38).

Kuzmin, Andrey Vladimirovich. 2010. "Buryatia: Serdze Rossii v Azii" [Buryatia: The heart of Russia in Asia]. *Delovoy Mir Baikala* 6:1.

Lemon, Alaina. 1998. "'Your Eyes Are Green like Dollars': Counterfeit Cash, National Substance, and Currency Apartheid in 1990s Russia." *Cultural Anthropology* 13 (1): 22–55.

Lempert, Michael. 2014. "Imitation." *Annual Review of Anthropology* 43:379–95.

Lindquist, Galina. 2001. "The Culture of Charisma: Wielding Legitimacy in Contemporary Russian Healing." *Anthropology Today* 17 (2): 3–8.

———. 2005. *Conjuring Hope: Healing and Magic in Contemporary Russia*. Vol. 1. New York: Berghahn.

Makhachkeev, Aleksandr. 2010. *Portret Ierarkha: XXIV Pandito Khambo Lama Damba Ayusheev*. Ulan-Ude: NovaPrint.

Manning, Paul. 2010. "The Semiotics of Brand." *Annual Review of Anthropology* 39:33–49.

Manning, Paul, and Ann Uplisashvili. 2007. "'Our Beer': Ethnographic Brands in Postsocialist Georgia." *American Anthropologist* 109 (4): 626–41.

Mazzarella, William. 2003. *Shoveling Smoke: Advertising and Globalization in Contemporary India*. Durham, NC: Duke University Press.

Nakassis, Constantine V. 2013. "Brands and Their Surfeits." *Cultural Anthropology* 28 (1): 111–26.

Pordié, Laurent. 2010. "The Politics of Therapeutic Evaluation in Asian Medicine." *Economic and Political Weekly* 45 (18): 57–64.

Quijada, Justine Buck. 2012. "Soviet Science and post-Soviet Faith: Etigelov's Imperishable Body." *American Ethnologist* 39 (1): 138–54.

Quijada, Justine Buck, and Eric Stephen. 2015. "Performing 'Culture': Diverse Audiences at the International Shaman's Conference and Tailgan on Ol'khon Island." *Études Mongoles et Sibériennes, Centrasiatiques et Tibétaines* 46:1–21.

Raffles, Hugh. 1999. "'Local Theory': Nature and the Making of an Amazonian Place." *Cultural Anthropology* 14 (3): 323–60.

Ross, Cameron, and Rostislav Turovsky. 2015. "Centralized but Fragmented: The Regional Dimension of Russia's 'Party of Power.'" *Demokratizatsiya: The Journal of Post-Soviet Democratization* 23 (2): 205–23.

Sanzhin, Bato Bairovich. 2010. "Formirovanie I Razvitie Turisticheskogo Klastera v Respublike Buryatia Na Osnove Gosudarstvenno-Chastnogo Partnerstva" [The formation and development of the tourism cluster in the Republic Buryatia on the basis of a state-private partnership]. *Ekonomicheskoe Vozrozhdenie Rossii* 26 (4): 133–42.

Saxer, Martin. 2013. *Manufacturing Tibetan Medicine: The Creation of an Industry and the Moral Economy of Tibetanness.* Vol. 12. New York: Berghahn.

Scheid, Volker, and Hugh MacPherson. 2011. *Integrating East Asian Medicine into Contemporary Healthcare.* London: Elsevier Health Sciences.

Sulakshin, Stepan Stepanovich, Vladimir Nikolaevich Leksin, A. N. Shvecov, L. A. Rejmer, and A. S. Malchinov. 2013. *Regional'noe Izmerenie Gosudarstvennoj Jekonomicheskoj Politiki Rossii.* Moscow: Nauchnyi Expert.

Tsing, Anna Lowenhaupt. 2005. *Friction: An Ethnography of Global Connection.* Princeton, NJ: Princeton University Press.

Vann, Elizabeth F. 2006. "The Limits of Authenticity in Vietnamese Consumer Markets." *American Anthropologist* 108 (2): 286–96.

Yurchak, Alexei. 2005. *Everything Was Forever, until It Was No More: The Last Soviet Generation.* ACLS Humanities E-Book. Princeton, NJ: Princeton University Press.

Waugh, L. R. 1982. "Marked and Unmarked: A Choice between Unequals in Semiotic Structure." *Semiotica* 38 (3–4): 299–318.

Zhan, M. 2009. *Other-Worldly: Making Chinese Medicine through Transnational Frames.* Durham, NC: Duke University Press.

TATIANA CHUDAKOVA is Assistant Professor of Anthropology at Tufts University

THREE

ETHNICITY AS POTENTIAL

Abundance, Competition, and the Limits of Development in Andean Peru's Colca Valley

ERIC HIRSCH

DURING HOLY WEEK IN 2014, the public square of the Colca Valley town of Chivay became an exposition of Andean abundance. An image of free market competition in miniature, the expansive plaza was covered with stalls, each of which put an aspect of Collagua or Cabana ethnicity on display and on sale. The Collaguas and the Cabanas are the two indigenous ethnic groups that have populated this region of twenty linked communities in Peru's southern Andes since before Inca rule.[1] Peruvian tourists on their Holy Week vacations and international tourists had arrived to see Colca's traditions and dramatic land-scapes in real life, spending the week immersing themselves in the bucolic villages that populate the valley's steep hillsides. Here, commodification through staged competition was a mechanism of revitalizing identities that were, as of just a decade earlier, the subject of overt racism and long disparaged as counterproductive to economic growth.

The plaza was buzzing on the market's opening day. Stalls were filled with a plenitude of bright, colorful fabrics whose embroidered motifs marked their village of origin. Walking the plaza, I was overwhelmed by the pungent scents of roasting alpaca, pork belly, trout, and guinea pig meat and by the trumpet-and sousaphone-marked beats of the *Wititi* dance that a group of young people were performing in the plaza center.

Vendors from Colca's villages sold organic *maiz cabanita*, a highly in-demand breed of corn indigenous to the community of Cabanaconde; alpaca weavings with motifs unique to each village; off-the-beaten-path ecotourism experiences in a profusion of colorful brochures; and creative dishes centered on the valley's quinoa, potatoes, fruit, and protein-rich grains. These vendors underwent great

Fig. 3.1. Vendors and customers at the Holy Week fair, Peru. The two female vendors' sombreros are typical of Collagua (*left*) and Cabana (*center*) styles. (Photo by author.)

effort to attract visiting customers by drawing out the infinitesimal cultural differences between each community's local iteration of Collagua or Cabana ethnicity, in a place where these populations have been blended together for centuries (fig. 3.1).

This was not a typical market day in Chivay, which occurs on Mondays and Thursdays in a designated lot behind the plaza for vendors from throughout the valley to sell produce, electronics, traditional medicine, and clothing to other residents. Instead, the Holy Week fair was staged by Desco, a national nongovernmental organization (NGO).[2] Desco deployed the fifty entrepreneurs it was supporting to demonstrate to residents and visitors alike that the Colca Valley was not a poverty-stricken out-of-the-way place in need of aid, but a site of cultural abundance. It also invited other nonparticipant vendors, which it framed as "ethnic entrepreneurs" (DeHart 2010), to sell products rooted in Colca's two ethnicities. According to Desco, Colca's Collagua and Cabana ethnicities were key sources of the region's potential for growth and sustainability. Despite the apparent scarcity of food, money, education, and services that many of its subsistence and tenant farmers face, the Colca Valley's abundance in culture, knowledge, and other resources, once unleashed as part of a retooled development model, would soon obviate any need for external aid.

Desco's project fits a regional trend in Latin America in which entrepreneurs are tasked with performing ethnic identities in highly public competitive settings. The NGO's focus on Andean heritage and competitive entrepreneurship, instead of the direct distribution of services or monetary aid, is typical of neoliberal development projects around the world today. Yet recent ethnographies of "ethnic entrepreneurs" and "ethno-development" have tended to track projects whose ultimate goal was to alleviate poverty (DeHart 2010; Radcliffe 2015; West 2012). This chapter suggests that development in the Colca Valley has shifted from the work of poverty alleviation to something entirely different: the management of *already existing wealth*. Mirroring Peru's approach to its massive mining boom, such wealth manifests itself in the release of potential abundance in tradition, environmental knowledge, and what project staff would call "cultural resources," which includes expertise in gastronomy, agriculture, dance, and artisanship (Eric Hirsch, interview with Liliana Suni, proprietor of Hostal Sumac Wayra, July 2017, Yanque). Desco took the cultivation of these potentially profitable resources to be a new means of unleashing economic growth.

The Colca Valley cradles communities that development's policymakers opportunistically see as bursting with hidden wealth. Such wealth had the potential to render Colca development not only sustainable, but inexhaustible. In this chapter, I analyze the making and marking of ethnic development subjects, through staged competition, as a means of activating those subjects' potentially limitless wealth. I do this by describing how two contestants constructed success stories that were exemplary of Desco's vision. Their business success was atypical. Most entrepreneurs failed. But their self-realization narratives exemplify Desco's approach to ethnicity and indigeneity. Their work also illustrates a tension between two contradictory ideals: on the one hand, Desco's emphasis on transforming collective culture into ethnic "assets," "resources," and "potential" and, on the other hand, the fundamentally individualized framing for neoliberal entrepreneurship.

What happens when ethnicity becomes an inexhaustible resource in a place where rural ethnicity was previously associated with economic scarcity? How is Collagua and Cabana ethnicity converted into value under the sign of abundance? For development's subjects, what does it mean to individualize gain from a collectively shared ethnicity newly reframed as a site of untapped growth? What can we learn about the social effects of ethnicity's commodification from contexts in which ethnic markets emerge through the linked logics of staged competition, restrained financial investment, and hidden wealth?

I argue that ethnicity emerges here as an index of potential abundance, the result of a new paradigm of development whose mission it is to demonstrate that the Colca Valley is already a site of prosperity. This argument is not a claim that the practices, traditions, and expertise associated with Collagua and Cabana ethnicity are somehow "invented" (Hobsbawm 1983), "inauthentic," or not otherwise meaningful in Colca. Rather, I show how development workers deploy ethnicity as an alibi for not providing broader forms of economic support. For development workers and the municipal leaders they recruit to their projects, ethnicity is a fecund source of sustainable growth. The campaigns that sought to establish this idea headed by Desco and other organizations would reshape social life within Colca communities in important ways. Namely, the ability to tap into the expertise, history, and ancestral knowledge ethnicity afforded became a new type of skill, a form of individualized excellence. This chapter shows how a development institution focus on building skilled ethnic self-knowledge transforms subjectivities, creates new images of political respectability, refashions reciprocity structures, and reconfigures economic inequalities. I also highlight the limits of a strategy presented as the sole means of improving everyday life, without alternatives.

At the core of this strategy, contests were vital tools for framing ethnicity. The contest-based project I detail reframed ethnic subjects as purveyors of abundance through their capacity to mesh sensual displays of traditional expertise with explicitly declared distinctions between villages that together amounted to elaborate, colorful scenes. Out of their ethnic differences, Desco sought to craft a broad sense of economic dynamism.

In what follows, I discuss the rise of ethnicity as a development symbol by considering intervening institutions' point of departure as a presumed wealth in culture instead of poverty and scarcity. I then situate the discussion in the historical and political context of Andean Peru. Turning to the ethnographic core of the chapter, I outline Desco's youth entrepreneurship competition and delve into the distinct experiences of two winning entrepreneurs, Rogelio Taco Viza and Anacé Condori Palma. Analyzing their ethnopreneurial self-discovery narratives to demonstrate the project's idealized subjectivities, I unpack the components of their success in the context of a highly unequal economy in which Colca's ethnicities have become prized assets for a select few.

A third, contrasting ethnographic section then brings those experiences into relief. There, I recount the forced transformation away from entrepreneurship that Gerardo Huaracha and Luisa Cutipa, two elderly ethnic entrepreneurs, faced when a 5.2-magnitude earthquake destroyed their Collagua museum, the selling point for their live-in cultural tourism business, in August 2016. I conclude by addressing the implications of a paradigm that trains development's focus on abundance channeled through ethnic difference but does so without room for alternatives.

ETHNICITY AND SUSTAINABLE DEVELOPMENT: A CONCEPTUAL BACKGROUND

In his analysis of coastal Kenya's "ethno-erotic economies," George Paul Meiu (2015, 476) indicated that one result "of market liberalization in Africa and elsewhere, since the 1980s," is the fact that "many people with scarce material resources have capitalized on their ethnic difference and cultural identity." Here, Meiu—like other contributors to this volume—described an opposition between "scarce material resources" and ethnicity, which represents the potential abundance of a distinct category of "resource": history, expertise, tradition, and other characteristics of a shared heritage that, all over the world, have become sources of immense promise and, in some cases, profit when brought to sites of market exchange. This chapter interrogates that opposition between material scarcity and ethnicity's potential for framing resource abundance.

Material scarcity conceptually underlies contemporary development's twentieth-century origin as a means of peacetime political intervention. "Development" is thought to have begun after the Second World War with US president Harry S. Truman's "Four Point" speech and the postwar Marshall Plan (Rist 2008). In the second half of the century, poverty alleviation drove a new transnational circuit of state and nonstate actors committed to improving people's lives. Their rationales ranged from charity, ethics, and humanitarian intervention to disingenuous ploys to maintain a political hold on newly decolonized nations (Escobar 1995). Whether sincere or cynical, these interventions tended to be organized around the accepted fact of impoverishment in those nations, and the emerging notion that people had a fundamental right to be liberated from conditions of deprivation (Pogge 2007). The 1980s, 1990s, and 2000s also saw the rising trend of participatory and grassroots development schemes (Mosse 2005). Throughout development's seven-decade history, poverty was consistently framed as a manageable technical problem that aid could solve (Ferguson 1994; Li 2007).

A new way to solve this technical problem gained momentum globally as Peru embarked on its massive project of political and economic decentralization in the early 2000s, after years of inflation and internal armed conflict. Desco and other national NGOs and government projects decided to focus development aid less on communities and massive regional projects than on individuals. This entailed approaching the subject of development as not simply a needy pauper but, instead, as an entire person capable of improving his or her life by drawing together skills, connections, histories, productive traditions, and experiences. In other words, all individuals had potential human capital.

Barbara Cruikshank (1999) sees this idea as exemplary of neoliberal ideologies of "empowerment," a condition one is able to achieve upon realizing that economic and personal growth are not gifts from a state but achievements from within. In contexts of ethnicity-focused entrepreneurial development such as in Andean Peru, empowerment is individually achieved but at the same time, requires collective goods and interdependent networks. Empowerment discourses there draw heavily on ideas of identity, shared history, and self-realization as a subject's means of cultivating something that is completely, profoundly, and inalienably one's own, and then using that thing to improve one's lot through commodification. To empower an ethnic entrepreneur adequately, development workers saw their goal as configuring "neoliberal self-creation" (Freeman 2014, 2) while benefiting from the collective or corporate marketing of ethnicity. In this way, individual empowerment could also be extractive.

The three entrepreneurial trajectories featured in this chapter illustrate how subjects deployed their ethnicity as essential to their self-fashioning projects, with each competing to show their worth as an entrepreneur, "neoliberalism's heroic actor" (Freeman 2014, 17). These projects ultimately led to economic success for a very few. Rogelio and Anacé were atypical; I feature them here because Desco staff idealized them as entrepreneurial ethnic subjects. As of 2018, about 50 percent of Desco's fifty participants were still engaged in the business they had started in 2014; no more than five of those participants saw actual profits, and all bore some debt to at least one of the region's microcredit agencies. But Desco's primary goal was not so much to increase well-being as to whet a local appetite for the promise of success through entrepreneurship. The three entrepreneurial stories featured here illustrate that knowing oneself and one's culture became an "entrepreneurial project" of self-realization in terms of the economic assets that ethnicity has the potential to yield (2014, 3).[3] To understand how entrepreneurship became the goal of self-fashioning, and how self-knowledge became an entrepreneurial project, I turn to a brief discussion of development in Peru's Andes.

THE FRUITS OF ETHNIC DIFFERENCE
IN THE PERUVIAN ANDES

The Colca Valley's main ethnic groups, the Collaguas and the Cabanas, have a long history of interethnic mixing. In much of the valley, they are at present indistinguishable communities. The Collaguas historically clustered in the eastern part of the valley; that group's indigenous charter myth narrates the physical emergence of the first Collaguas from a volcano called Collaguata (Eric Hirsch, interview with Natalio Huayhua, agriculturalist and co-proprietor of the Hostal Bella Flor, February 2014, Yanque). The Cabanas have historically occupied the western portion of the valley, in settlements near the present-day community of Cabanaconde; their own charter myth describes their emergence from a second volcano, Hualca Hualca (Elson and Covey 2006).

While centuries of mixing and intraregional migration have rendered these groups largely culturally indistinguishable today, development projects like that of Desco urged their participants to make as many micro-distinctions as they could between Collagua and Cabana, seeking to fix fluid categories. To these programs, maximizing marketable differences was essential to potentiating economic growth.

Territorialized ethnic distinctions were especially encouraged between villages, for example with the historic Yanque-Collaguas group being uniquely affiliated with what is today the village of Yanque, the Lari-Collaguas with the village of Lari, and the Cabanas with the village of Cabanaconde. Further distinctions were rendered through women's sombreros typical of the Collaguas (a flat straw hat) and the Cabanas (a curved, colorful hat [see fig. 3.1]). Complex embroidery and textile patterns could vary widely between villages, but motifs of flowers and birds in bright blues, yellows, and reds were identified with Collagua weaving, and dense smaller multicolored vines and plants classically characterized Cabana design. There is also the regionally shared Wititi dance, whose steps are particular to each village. The version of the Wititi dance from the Colca village of Yanque was recognized in 2015 by UNESCO as a symbol of intangible cultural heritage (UNESCO 2015).

Therein lies the distinction between indigeneity and ethnicity most important to the Colca Valley: while Andean *indigeneity* frames its broad history, Collagua and Cabana *ethnicities* afford a means of wringing immense value out of infinitesimal difference. Because Desco and other institutions see ethnicity to be so fecund with potential value, those institutions believe that ethnic entrepreneurial subjects need only minimal external aid to discover their most productive, empowered selves. The fabric that sells in a Holy Week market stall and the choreographed Wititi version receiving UNESCO recognition are the physical manifestations of ethnicity that development projects like Desco framed as something with unrivaled power to enrich the region. Also, part of this entrepreneurial self-fashioning is a flourishing immaterial ethnicity that connects individuals with a passion for continuing ancestral traditions. For example, upon winning UNESCO's recognition of the Wititi, a young costumed dancer offered UNESCO's videographer this testimony about what it means to embody his Collagua ethnicity: "Looking at the dance, I think one looks and feels the music and the body moves by itself, and everything we have in our roots, in our ancestors, emerges" (UNESCO 2015).

Ethnic micro-distinctions have over the last decade been elaborately highlighted and choreographed in the Colca Valley. By contrast, competitions have long been essential to Andean ritual and economic life. As the indigenous Andean agricultural-ritual calendar meshed with the colonial timeline of Catholic patron saint festivals, patronage relationships under Spanish rule between colonial and creole settlers and Andean residents birthed the tradition of engaging wealthy sponsors in competition to create spectacular village patron saint festivals. Throughout much of the twentieth century, regional markets and expositions in Colca, as elsewhere in Peru (De la Cadena 2000), would feature similar forms of competition.

Today, festival sponsorship by the village's wealthier indigenous-identifying peasants persists as an important way to accumulate prestige within a Colca Valley village, although many people I met decided to take themselves out of the cycle of fiesta reciprocity because they believed the costs had become prohibitively expensive. Within those ritual activities, the theme of competition frequently appears in beauty pageants, athletic tournaments, dance, gastronomy, animal girth contests, and other events. As in other regions of Latin America, competitions brought communities together around displays of traditional expressive performance (Faudree 2013; Wroblewski 2014).

The first decade of the 2000s saw that Andean familiarity with friendly competition coopted into a deliberate program of cost-saving, decentralized neoliberal development (Wiener Fresco 2007). Development programs like the Ministry of Agriculture and Irrigation's Sierra Sur Project saw competitive fairs as productive models for new development projects in their capacity to showcase local expertise and local resources. Since Sierra Sur's first contests in 2005, competitions helped train Colcans as ethnopreneurial subjects, teaching them that ethnicity was an asset that could be cultivated.

The initial fruits of ethnic difference, and their role in making the Colca Valley an emerging hotspot for tourism and organic food and gastronomy investments, were borne alongside Peru's aggregate economic prosperity in recent years. Colca is a place where, as some experts argued, extreme poverty has been eliminated (Fuentes 2011; Eric Hirsch, interview with Leni Delgado, Arequipa regional director of the Sierra Sur Development Project, July 2012, Ichupampa). The region's poverty indicators have seen a rapid decrease since the mid-1990s, after the Desco NGO and an array of financial institutions sought to open this frontier space to the national and global economy (Eric Hirsch, interview with Aquilino Mejía, former local office coordinator for Desco in Chivay, January 2015, Arequipa). This change, however, is hardly due to the presence of small-scale development programs promoting individual entrepreneurs. Improving poverty indicators owe themselves much more significantly to other factors. Peru's two-decade-long mining boom is widely cited to be at the root of unevenly rising incomes across the country. A number of Colca men are involved in Peru's mining economy, trading their consistent presence at home with more robust wages. The Peruvian government has also invested extensively in its new national brand, Marca Perú, which advertises Peru to travelers, foodies, and experts as a site of culture and treasure (García 2013). Locally, the tourism economy is expanding too, which means that more tourists, tourism agencies, and wealth are circulating through the Colca Valley than ever before, even if most tourism profits remain in the hands of large agencies based in the nearby city of Arequipa or abroad. Those aggregate improvements built on the foundation of President Alberto Fujimori's (1990–2000) mass provision of electrical, hydraulic, and educational infrastructure for the rural Andes.

Other perspectives on the Colca Valley economy add nuance to aggregate growth indicators. Testimonies from village leaders I interviewed in a 2017 focus group disputed claims that extreme poverty has been eliminated. A white paper prepared for the 2015–18 Arequipa regional government also identified a high nonextreme poverty rate in Caylloma Province, where Colca is located, at 42.3 percent (Zegarra López 2015, 8). A study undertaken by Desco-based researchers (unrelated to the project I go on to address) highlights Colca's dramatic inequalities of income, employment, literacy, and education even among its majority of agriculturalists and day laborers (Cárdenas et al., 2014). Colca's villages are sites of inequality and relative poverty. Ethnicity-based entrepreneurship, then, is in practice less a way of dynamizing the region than a means for a select few to profit from it. Desco's immediate aim was more to propagate the promise of ethnic entrepreneurship and the individualized self-discipline it required than to create economic growth. Its intervention was effecting personal transformations for those capable of modeling development with identity.

By 2010, Peru's aggregate economic improvement offered the region's development agencies an opportunity to reframe Colcan development as chiefly a means of managing abundance, namely, the region's projected abundance in cultural capital. Given the Andes-wide adoption of the competition as a development tool, initiatives have used competitions to engage local actors in the collective goal of job creation; in learning the strategies of entrepreneurship; and especially, in getting to know themselves as ethnic subjects.

CREATING YOUNG ETHNIC ENTREPRENEURS: THE DESCO COMPETITION

Chivay's bustling Holy Week fair represented, for the Desco NGO, the culmination of an eighteen-month investment in fifty young entrepreneurs between the ages of eighteen and twenty-nine. Desco's project was called "Development of Young Entrepreneurs and the Generation of Self-Employment in Caylloma Province, Arequipa." The project was primarily focused on job creation (Desco 2012). To fund it, Desco won its own competitive investment from the Peruvian Ministry of Labor's National Fund for Labor Capacity Building and the Promotion of Employment (Fondoempleo).

Each participant in the Holy Week fair had won financial capacity building from the NGO. The top-performing twenty participants also won physical seed capital for their proposals to commodify some dimension of their Collagua or Cabana ethnicity. Contestants could not win by framing themselves as poor people in need of aid, as staff and participants would emphasize. Rather, they presented themselves as already empowered people capable of creating jobs and wealth by bringing their culture to the market as a source of sustainable plenty.

A crucial characteristic of Desco's investment was its limited amount. The actual investment transferred to each of its twenty winners was 3,650 soles ($1,128.44 in 2014), awarded exclusively in the form of physical assets like sewing machines or ovens. That investment was paired with extensive pedagogical support via regular capacity-building seminars and business site audits.

The project used small amounts of money to make big things happen. Desco sought to convey that the smaller the amount of outside money invested, the greater the opportunity a participant would have to make his or her own personal financial investments, thus learning a core value of entrepreneurship. As one Agriculture Ministry report on a prior contest suggests, cultivating entrepreneurs through competition required minimal resources to bring about returns, as long as it was paired with sufficient technical knowledge transfer and cultural and affective validation (Wiener Fresco 2007).

To find its participants, the NGO held a competition for investment in villages throughout the valley in early 2013. Initially, nearly four hundred Colcans sought entry into the project, competing for twenty seed capital awards and thirty more places in the project that did not come with seed capital but did involve the same access to regular entrepreneurial advising and capacity building.

Here is how the competition unfolded, according to Desco's initial project proposal (Desco 2012) and corroborated by interviews I recorded with staff and participants. Both stages were structured like start-up pitch competitions. First came the village-level competition. In each Colca village, contestants would face a panel of interviewers, most of whom were entrepreneurship specialists working as consultants for the NGO; in most cases at least one member of the panel was employed by the municipality. Contestants would present their business plans and answer a round of judges' questions.

Then, contestants who advanced to the second stage would travel to the region's two largest towns: Chivay, the regional capital, for those located in Colca's eastern villages, and Cabanaconde, for those in the west. There, a smaller pool of participants was selected through an additional round of interviews. Three professionals made up this next selection panel: a "psychologist with knowledge of the region and [of] the characteristics of young entrepreneurs"; an expert in business planning; and a municipal representative engaged in fomenting local development who was not a Desco employee (Desco 2012, 37).

To be a contender, each participant had to present a viable business plan. This meant, in part, being able to speak as an expert on the characteristics of one's own ethnicity, which the eventual winners were able to deploy as they made the case for why their village was special within the region and therefore marketable. Desco representatives rigorously inventoried the specific characteristics of village-based ethnic groups, rendering the contest a process of deliberate self-fashioning that for each contestant forged membership in a group "whose identity is its difference" (Spivak 1988, 285).

Viability as a competitor also meant beginning the development contest with a visible baseline level of human capital, at least some secondary education or financial literacy, familiarity with what it means to be an entrepreneur, and in most cases, the ability either to coinvest their own capital or to handle a loan. Put another way, competitors had to bring something to the table that would articulate their position, not so much as a poor development beneficiary seeking to improve their lot, but instead, as a future job creator: a potential source of the rich but inert knowledge, skill, and culture afforded by ethnicity but in need of activation or conversion. These competitions that began Desco's intervention served as the first step in that conversion: they were encounters that transformed potential and promise into the plans, arrangements, and actions that would constitute participants' new identities as ethnic entrepreneurs. Two of Desco's seed capital winners exemplified this transformation: guinea pig farmer Rogelio Taco Viza and chef Anacé Condori Palma.

MULTIPLYING ETHNICITY WITH GUINEA PIGS: ROGELIO

In January 2013, Rogelio heard the call from the loudspeaker that sits atop the village of Lari's municipality building. The municipal secretary announced that Desco was holding a contest to participate in a new project to invest in local entrepreneurs. Rogelio, twenty years old at the time, had grown up in Lari with a subsistence farming family. He was generous with his smile and would prove quick to ingratiate himself with Desco's visiting professionals. Rogelio kept his hair buzzed and when he was not wearing tattered T-shirts caked with mud while tending to his guinea pigs, he often dressed in a blazer and black wing-tipped shoes. Over the course of the program's eighteen-month run, Rogelio's gregariousness would translate to entrepreneurial and political success, as well as the occasional critique that he was *pura boca* (all talk), making ambitious promises with sometimes inconsistent follow-through. In 2017, Rogelio explained to me how he initially became interested in operating a business:

> I was going to focus on fish farming, but it became clear to me that there would be more of an opportunity in caring for guinea pigs. I was looking for an adequate place to care for trout, to build my fish farm, but there was nothing nearby. So, calculating my costs, I would have needed to put a great deal of investment into caring for trout so far away. So, I decided that I would work with guinea pigs. I began with a small group, an artisanal-scale group, fifteen guinea pigs that my mother gave me as a gift. Then I was caring for the fifteen guinea pigs from August, September, October, November, December, and in January, the Desco project started. I competed. (Eric Hirsch, interview with Rogelio Taco Viza, June 2017, Lari)

In Rogelio's emergence as a business-savvy young person, promoting his own ethnicity was not initially a central goal. However, he quickly learned that guinea pigs would be an easier base on which to grow a business than farmed trout, due to both their lower costs and their marketable symbolism. Guinea

pigs had the power to represent a locally specific Lari-Collagua ethnicity and
build a Colca-area brand in a way that trout could not. This made Rogelio
especially attractive to Desco.

Rogelio's proposal was a business breeding and selling live guinea pigs, for
which he would build a barn on land that his family owned in Lari. It exemplified a neoliberal abundance ensured through entrepreneurial drive and disciplined management. Guinea pigs reproduced readily and could subsist on an
inexpensive, relatively plentiful supply of alfalfa grasses. Rogelio's enterprise
was called "El Aposento" (the chamber). Of nearly four hundred competitors,
Rogelio was one of the twenty contestants to win seed capital in the amount of
3,650 soles. He then spent nearly a year ignoring his business plan, aside from
his attendance at the required workshops and meetings with staff that occurred
about once every two months.

However, by the end of 2013, when I joined Desco staff members Liliana Suni
and Fabiola Dapino on a site visit to his base of operations in Lari, Rogelio was
building an expansive and expensive new barn, putting Desco's seed capital
investment to work. In the course of his construction, he found that seed capital
to be insufficient. He took out an additional credit in the amount of 7,925 soles
(about $2,291), which would be the first of several loans that would increase in
size as his business expanded. When I first interviewed him in 2014, Rogelio
told me that he was in the process of repaying credit to the financier PrestaPerú,
with confidence that he would have no problem making his payments.

In March 2014, Rogelio declared his newly expanded facility open for business. This was expertly timed for the project audit by Fernando Gonzalo, Desco's project supervisor at Fondoempleo. At his grand opening ceremony for the
new barn building, Rogelio's Desco advisor Fabiola Dapino broke open a bottle
of rum tied to the barn's lintel. Rogelio then took the floor, narrating his start in
the program as one of its least promising contestants. With Desco's investment,
in his narration, he was able to mature from a reckless twenty-year-old to one
of the region's most successful guinea pig vendors.

During Fernando Gonzalo's audit visit, the group of evaluators and participants gathered in Lari for the inspections enjoyed a large midday meal of
guinea pigs that Rogelio donated. Raquel, another winning Lari participant
who was also serving as a village council member (*regidora*), and several other
women came to the kitchen in the municipality and worked all morning to
incorporate methods and ingredients into the meal that would mark it as particularly Lari-Collagua for Fernando, thickly frying the meat and serving it
whole along with locally grown *peruanita* potatoes. They also served Coca Cola,
a nonalcoholic sign of professional conviviality and an implicit reference to the

high numbers of Pentecostals, Evangelicals, and Seventh Day Adventists in Lari, who cannot drink alcohol. The resulting dish epitomized culinary abundance with a plate of plump guinea pig, piles of fried potatoes, and a salad of local carrots, beets, greens, and tomatoes. Development workers and project participants alike were uncomfortably full by the end of lunch.

Rogelio would later tell me the story of his conversion into an entrepreneurial subject that Desco's initial contest and ongoing audits facilitated. This was not only a conversion to a particular kind of economic discipline, built on his potential to activate elements of a revitalized regional Lari-Collagua ethnicity by selling Lari-Collagua-branded guinea pigs. His conversion was also literally religious: he had converted from a teenager who spent his free time drinking in urban *discotecas* to a member of Colca's growing community of Evangelical Christians. Discussing his personal growth in our October 2014 and June 2017 interviews, his life history narrative traced the arc of a religious conversion:

> I had a lot of knowledge potential, I was the mayor of my high school, and I got good grades in university. But one detail, the kind of peer pressure that I began to live with in Arequipa with the other young people, well it wasn't a good influence for me because this was a shock to me. I had always lived with my mom, my dad [in Lari], then they leave me like this to live alone with my brothers and sisters [in Arequipa], so I begin to mess around like a libertine. And this wasn't good for me. So that's unfortunately a bad decision I made that led to me dropping out of my studies. Because of this, I came to Lari, and began to set up my businesses. (Eric Hirsch, interview with Rogelio Taco Viza, June 2017, Lari)

Winning a top-twenty spot in the Desco contest, along with his Evangelical conversion, marked Rogelio's turnaround. In a 2014 interview, shortly after the Desco program ended, he described the NGO's investment as small, but still "an incentive." Rogelio said, "It animated me to build more. And when I bought materials with the seed capital and added them to what I already had in the house, this also motivated me. As I knew, I had to put in my part to achieve this. [Desco's investment] helped me a lot. This project helped a lot. It has been a great blessing" (Eric Hirsch, interview with Rogelio Taco Viza, October 2014, Chivay). He echoed this sentiment in 2017: "If it hadn't been for these capacity-building sessions," Rogelio said, "I would never have opened up to the idea of becoming an entrepreneur" (Eric Hirsch, interview with Rogelio Taco, June 2017, Lari).

From his start as immature and unfocused, Rogelio's narrative of self-realized progress ends with his aspiration to become the top producer in the region. Crucially, his is more a story of individual transformation that builds on a revalorized ethnicity than a story of collectively shared ethnicity revalorized through talented entrepreneurship.

I witnessed an example of Rogelio's conversion into a clever businessman in October 2014. Rogelio invited me to join him for business errands in Arequipa.[4] This city is Peru's second most populous with about one million inhabitants. It is a three-hour bus trip from Chivay. While there, Rogelio planned to meet with a lawyer to formalize his enterprise and then to purchase guinea pig studs from one of his vendors.

He invited me to join him for the latter task. We found his vendor, who kept stacks of guinea pig cages in an urban rooftop pen. Our visit demonstrated Rogelio's ability to perform an expert entrepreneurial discipline. He rigorously inspected the living conditions of the studs he planned to buy. He was particularly proud of his ability to negotiate with the vendor and to choose studs in a way that would increase the variety of colors and types of guinea pig that he would be able to brand to fellow villagers as appropriate for the animal size, shape, and color to which they were accustomed. He had in mind the growing supply of tourist restaurants, but also, the upcoming fiesta calendar, which in many villages meant an annual meal that featured whole guinea pigs.

People in Colca tended to serve guinea pig only rarely for select holidays and honored guests. That is changing given tourists' and outsiders' interest in guinea pig meat, which is now widely associated with indigenous Andean cuisine (García 2013). Rogelio sells guinea pigs directly to restaurants, with several high-profit contracts in Chivay. He has immense success in the region in branding guinea pigs as both ethnically distinctive and "completely ecological" (Eric Hirsch, interview with Rogelio Taco Viza, October 2014, Chivay). By the end of 2014, Rogelio achieved his goal, becoming one of the highest-selling breeders in the valley.

Colca's local cultural tourism boom meant that demand for guinea pigs has been on the rise there in recent years. By the time Rogelio began his enterprise, nearly every restaurant that sought to capitalize on tourism in the valley was beginning to include guinea pig on its menu. Rogelio was quick to enter the game: "that's where I sell," he said, suggesting that Chivay's larger tourist restaurants provided him a great deal of profit.

This animal is now central to an emerging sense of Andean ethnic culinary plenitude, in which the Peruvian food boom has become the latest panacea for economic growth, at once "a marketing campaign" and "a development plan: Peruvian cuisine will bring Peruvians together, and open the world to Peru" (García 2013, 506). In addition to Rogelio's abundant production, the Colca

Valley region has responded to the global guinea pig craze with *Míster Cuy* (or "Mr. Guinea Pig") pageants, which involve competitions in girth, hair, breed, costume, and other categories that splice community breeding practices with distinctive manifestations of animal and human beauty articulated through traditional embroidery.

Beyond the rapidly multiplying, ethnically associated commodity that was the guinea pig, Rogelio's Andean upbringing also afforded him access to a distinct kind of local resource abundance: a profusion of goodwill channeled through a tradition of reciprocal labor. Desco entrepreneurship specialist Fabiola Dapino sought low-cost ways to build on the NGO's small investment. Rogelio brought to her attention the principle of *ayni*, a system of ongoing reciprocal exchange between individuals used throughout the Andes, and *faenas*, local communal work parties for large municipal projects that also function according to a logic of reciprocity (Gelles 2000; Wiener Fresco 2007). In Rogelio's words: "You know how we do it? First, one day we all help me. Another day, we all help someone else. We all help, all of the guys. That's ayni. Mutual aid" (Eric Hirsch, interview with Rogelio Taco Viza, October 2014, Chivay).

During the project's final months, the group used ayni to aid one participant, Mayde, in the construction of her own guinea pig barn in one month and assisted another participant named Miguel Iván assemble his museum of Andean sombreros (which he called "the National Identity Card of the Incas") in the next. Reciprocity layered communal bonds into economic lives, meshing an ideology of entrepreneurial competition with the idea that abundance also comes from strengthening social connections and cultivating in oneself the drive to reciprocate.

Engaging these principles would squeeze value for individual entrepreneurs out of Lari-Collagua ethnic identity. Fabiola sought to resuscitate these reciprocity traditions for local neoliberal entrepreneurship. Uncanny fits with Desco's logic of small financial investments paired with affective validation, ayni practice, and faena work parties only cost the entrepreneurs their time and effort and the NGO nothing, yet promised to increase profits and strengthen their business network. By resuscitating this Andean tradition, entrepreneurs could cooperate in a way that could theoretically benefit all program participants. Of course, reciprocity, especially as a supplement to entrepreneurial capitalism, does not redistribute wealth or unmake the new inequalities that emerge between a highly competitive entrepreneur and a less successful one. But it does build the promise of entrepreneurship into recognizable local logics.

Rogelio's atypical success would eventually lead him into politics. "Thanks to that Desco capacitation," Rogelio said, "thanks to my being an entrepreneur also, [Lari residents] chose me to serve as a representative of my district as a *regidor* [village council member]. So, like this I am opening little by little, thanks to that beginning I had" (Eric Hirsch, interview with Rogelio Taco Viza, June 2017, Lari).

In 2017, he received a certificate from an International Labor Organization workshop in Lima to become a facilitator for developing new young entrepreneurs, with the idea that he will promulgate the gospel of entrepreneurship. His experience as an entrepreneur and politician illustrates how an ethnicity-focused investment did not so much unleash local possibilities as configure them.

ENTREPRENEURIAL ETHNICITY AND FAMILY: ANACÉ

Across the valley, in the bustling regional capital of Chivay, Ana Carol "Anacé" Condori Palma broke into sobs as she expressed her gratitude to the Desco staff (whom I accompanied) who had come to Kaypi ("here" in Quechua), her restaurant and crafts shop, to celebrate its opening day. She made *Perú libres*, a variation of the *Cuba libre* made with pisco instead of rum. We toasted the new restaurant and paid our ritual respects by pouring several drops out of our shot glasses onto the earthen floor.

Anacé's restaurant was located behind her artisan shop. It was decorated with both Collagua and Cabana motifs. Both types of sombreros, white Collagua straw and colorful Cabana cloth, adorned the bar. Shawls with embroidered bands featuring the Collagua motifs of colorful birds and flowers by Chivay's artisan group served as curtains. The room's adobe walls were painted a dark red, allowing this restaurant to present a contrast to Chivay's other new tourist restaurants with walls of cement and whose floors were decorated with aspirational white tile.

Chivay itself had seen something of an ethnic revival over the previous several years. As the provincial capital and Colca's most populous town with some six thousand inhabitants, Chivay was historically a space of exchange between Collaguas, Cabanas, other Quechua- and Aymara-speaking Andean ethnicities, and mestizx Peruvians. The 2010–14 term of provincial mayor Élmer Cáceres Llica saw major changes to Chivay's appearance. He redecorated the brutalist facade of Chivay's municipality building with stone and straw in the Collagua style and had a row of statues of *camilis* (masked male ritual dancers) and of men and women dressed to demonstrate the distinctions between Collagua and Cabana fashion placed on pedestals along one of the town's walking paths. Featured among the statues dressed in the Collagua farming outfit of canvas pants and vest, and holding a rope for wrangling cattle, was the famous face of Ciro Castillo, a tourist from Lima who generated news and gossip after he perished falling into the canyon in 2011.

Anacé stumbled on her restaurant business in a fashion that idealized both a classically neoliberal savvy flexibility (Freeman 2014) and Desco's vision of an entrepreneurship that created returns on tiny investments in ethnic opulence. As she recounted to me, she was awarded her initial seed capital to run an artisan shop, and then her plans changed:

> They told us that we would be more highly valued [in the Desco contest] if we already owned a business. And I already had the artisan shop. And I was the only one who competed who was running an artisan shop. I already had my store. But it wasn't here, I had it in another place. By where the Ciro statue is, there, but the rent was really high. I ended up doing well, but it took a lot of sacrifice, I had to work a lot, to pay the rent, but then, this is my in-laws' house, my husband's parents. So all we had to do here was clean it up and now we're here. I normally work with guides, and I pay them a commission so that they bring me people. Right. Sometimes they don't bring me people, though, because we are far away, we're not in the center. (Eric Hirsch, interview with Anacé Condori Palma, April 2014, Chivay)

Her expansion from a small gift shop and embroidery studio into a combined tourist artisan shop and restaurant, which turned out to be significantly more profitable, showed her tactical ability to understand and meet local demand. Ethnicity underlay both businesses as a core marketing strategy. Chivay was home to a veritable glut of artisan-made Collagua and Cabana goods. Demand for food unique to those ethnic groups, however, was high, given the national gastronomic boom and the limited local supply of tourist restaurants. Anacé found a food market niche between those extremes, catering her restaurant toward middle-class Peruvian technocrats from Andean cities like Arequipa and the frugal international backpacker class. She sprinkled a Collagua flavor from her native Colca village of Madrigal that manifested itself in the *platos típicos* (typical dishes) of fried Colca River trout, white corn soup, and *lomo saltado* (sautéed beef) with alpaca meat replacing the beef used for this dish elsewhere in Peru.

Anacé bubbled with enthusiasm. She seemed to be at her most comfortable when multitasking. At the NGO's training sessions, she took on the role of group leader, frequently offering her input and ideas. During a capacity-building session, Anacé proposed creating a Desco youth district: a set of stores lined up next to one another along the same street in Chivay, each belonging to a young ethnic entrepreneur enrolled in the project. That way, they could easily help each other, saving money by sharing expenses and engaging in reciprocal physical labor as they did in Lari. This would also afford Desco's ethnic entrepreneurs a place where people would know to come seek out goods that competitive NGO support authorized as ethnically Collagua. Due to the entrepreneurship project's brief eighteen-month period, whose brevity its participants heavily criticized, the NGO was unable to create such a district. But staff members made clear to Anacé that she was thinking exactly like an entrepreneur should.

Anacé told me in our interviews in 2014 and 2017 that despite Desco professionals' enthusiasm for her entrepreneurial drive, her husband did not support her interest in business. She is a mother of two, and if her husband had his way, she would have stayed home to watch the children and tend to the house they share with his parents, even if that made the family poorer. Anacé "pay[s] him no mind" and suggested that despite her going against his preference, their family life was stable, for he only spent brief periods of time at home. Exhibiting a fundamental challenge of postcolonial intersectionality (Radcliffe 2015) as a rural Andean woman negotiating between male power and the promise of ethnic entrepreneurship brought in by a Lima-based NGO, Anacé said, "I want to feel developed as a woman also, and I want to work, because I like it and I want to contribute to our income, but my husband doesn't like that idea" (Eric Hirsch, interview with Anacé Condori Palma, April 2014, Chivay).

In 2014, he left a job as a traveling fiesta musician for more lucrative work in a distant mine, a common occupation for men in the valley. By 2017, he was back, reluctantly assisting Anacé with kitchen tasks in her increasingly profitable restaurant. Yet the tensions between their views of appropriate gender roles continued, an unintended social effect of Desco's support for ethnic entrepreneurs.

Anacé hopes one day to grow the restaurant business to a point at which all she needs to do is administer it and pay staff chefs, without needing to work nearly as hard to maintain its daily operations (Eric Hirsch, interview with Anacé Condori Palma, April 2014, Chivay). As of our 2017 conversation, though, her ambitions appeared only to be growing. She seeks to expand her clientele and, like Rogelio, plans to run for provincial office in a future municipal election.

What of Desco's nonexemplary program participants? Hundreds of young people left the program's initial contest having failed to prove their ability to balance ethnicity with entrepreneurship. Even among the winners of seed capital and pedagogical support, though, there also existed great variation. Fabiola confessed to me that in her several years of experience with entrepreneurial development projects, she found that only a small percentage of participants were ever likely to see long-term, postintervention success (Eric Hirsch, interview with Fabiola Dapino, Desco Youth Entrepreneurship Expert, April 2014, Chivay).

One participant named Zineyda planned and catered parties. She did not win seed capital. She told me that instead, the NGO offered her "moral support" (Eric Hirsch, interview with Zineyda, December 2013, Chivay). Fabiola would constantly suggest that Desco's support was more about affective than material investment. "We can't do anything more if you don't help us help you," she told a group of participants. In other words, the true transformation that unleashed ethnic entrepreneurship had to come from within. It was Desco's job simply to give participants the technical training that was required for branding one's business, formalizing it, and pitching Collagua and Cabana ethnicity as an asset and as something desirable.

Anacé, Rogelio, and the forty-eight other Desco participants gathered for the Holy Week fair in April 2014 to demonstrate their progress two months before the program's end. The fair demonstrated the ways development has shifted from a focus on poverty alleviation to a technical effort to manage an already existing abundance, and that ethnicity was taken to be the source and the substance of that abundance. However, abundance was also rooted in indebtedness, and in intensifying local inequalities. The profusion of booths and brands at the fair pointed to the widely perceived promise of Colca's burgeoning "ethnicity industry" (Comaroff and Comaroff 2009, 16). It took place on a holiday week when thousands of cultural and religious tourists flocked to Colca for its famed Easter rituals and its impressive landscapes freshly green from the rainy season.

The fair was a colorful bonanza of goods that belied Colca's former depiction as an out-of-the-way place at Peru's *últimas esquinas* (last corners; Eric Hirsch, interview with Plinio Trelles Mamani, Director of the Fondesurco Microcredit NGO, July 2014, Chivay; Eric Hirsch, interview with Zacarías Ocsa, local tour guide, January 2015, Chivay), where communities suffer profound economic and ecological scarcity. Notable here were the diverse brands. Each participating entrepreneur was tasked with marketing his or her business, choosing a unique logo that suggested a balance between local motifs and a transnational language of merchandising and "commodity images" (Mazzarella 2003). By capitalizing on ethnicity rooted in village locality, and on a broader distinction between the unique ethnic offerings of the Colca Valley region and Peru as a whole, Desco staff and participants sought to deploy ethnic abundance to render Colca a vibrant tourist destination. Erasing the stark inequalities between

Desco's most and least profitable participants, at the fair, all had to take part in the enactment of Colca as a site whose abundance overwhelmed the senses.

ETHNOPRENEURSHIP DESTROYED:
GERARDO AND LUISA

Gerardo Huaracha and Luisa Cutipa de Huaracha are an elderly couple in the Colca Valley village of Yanque, where several pre-Inca Collagua settlements remain standing. Their house was well known in Yanque as the site of a museum and archive, filled with old *q'eros* (pots), weavings, Andean Catholic relics from colonial religious festivals, agricultural cultivation tools like the *chakitaklla* (foot plow), documents, and other preserved representations of Collagua livelihood collected by Gerardo's ancestors since at least the nineteenth century. The museum was located in the oldest stand-alone structure on their property. It was built with adobe and stones in 1892, and topped with a thick layer of packed yellow straw, in the fashion of many traditional buildings throughout the valley. Its walls featured old paintings of flowers and birds, a frequently visible motif in Collagua art and embroidery.

Until 2010, this was an amateur archive. But with the help of a variety of NGOs and other entities invested in Andean cultural revalorization, Gerardo and Luisa transformed their museum into a tourist attraction. They also used it as a thematic anchor for their small tourism business by hosting tourists in two rooms they constructed for guests in the early 2000s, naming their business the Uyu Uyu Museum House.[5] A placard that hung outside of their home indicated the enterprise's recent institutional development sponsors, Desco and the provincial government of Navarre in Spain. Gerardo and Luisa were at the forefront of Yanque's movement to support and promote live-in *turismo vivencial* (cultural tourism). They were founding members of the Yanque Ayllus, a consortium of turismo vivencial enterprises composed of several families in the village. In 2012, they were invited to a national workshop on cultural tourism sponsored by an agency in Peru's Ministry of Foreign Trade and Tourism called Rural Community Tourism, which flew them to the city of Trujillo on Peru's northern coast. There, the museum won second place nationally for a museum collection focused on local cultural history, conveyed on a sleek triangular glass plaque that Gerardo placed at the center of the museum display.

Their success came to an abrupt halt late at night on August 15, 2016, when a shallow 5.4-magnitude earthquake whose epicenter was in Yanque wrought havoc on the village. It toppled scores of buildings. Three residents and one tourist died. The museum's fragile adobe walls did not hold; it was reduced to rubble.

Gerardo and Luisa were not rendered penniless by this earthquake. Their shared economic livelihood was somewhat diversified. For Yanque, they were relatively prosperous in land, crops, and livestock. However, Gerardo was seventy-eight years old, and Luisa was eighty-one. Ongoing agricultural labor was an increasing difficulty for them. Luisa had such difficulty moving that leaving the house was a hardship. They banked on the promise that the historic Collagua ethnicity to which they had direct, material access could become a reliable source of income. But their abundance in ethnically identified objects housed within a locally typical adobe building depended, ironically, on architecture that was both customary and physically fragile. Its destruction revealed a paradigm of development that did not leave alternatives once ethnicity ceased to be an option for generating income.

Worse, they had invested significant amounts of their limited nonagricultural income in the museum. It would now be extremely difficult to repay the credit they had taken out to purchase furniture and marketing materials, in an effort to grow the museum's clientele. Although Gerardo was able to save and store some of the relics in the collection, the museum building was completely destroyed. Vague promises from regional and national authorities to "rebuild Colca" (as Arequipa regional president Yamila Osorio put it) have so far failed to yield any action (Eric Hirsch, interview with Patricio Ccaza Mendoza, Lari resident and former Desco project participant, June 2017, Lari).

Yanque's earthquake illustrates the limits of ethnicity's promise as a basis for individualized entrepreneurship. When an Andean ethnicity's most potent material symbols are destroyed due to Andean seismic activity, villagers lose access to potential income and instead find themselves in a condition of scarcity that was no longer supposed to exist in the Colca Valley. The pathways Gerardo, Luisa, and others in Yanque forge next may offer clues about how to move beyond a myopically entrepreneurial approach to revalorizing ethnicity. For now, it is clear that the earthquake laid bare the stakes of an approach to which there is no alternative.

CONCLUSION

The scenes in which Colca's ethnic entrepreneurial identities are created and destroyed tell us a great deal about the making of model subjects in an era when neoliberal projects and sustainable fixes are being extended, consolidated, and fundamentally tested. This chapter has sought to explain how individualized entrepreneurship engages the inexhaustible resource that is collective ethnicity to potentialize growth. It found that a select few of Desco's exemplary entrepreneurs saw success and achieved local fame; nearly all went into debt; and two elderly entrepreneurs lost their new source of income as the result of an earthquake.

What do these processes tell us about the ways "collective consciousness of cultural likeness is rendered sensible" and valuable in the market (Comaroff and Comaroff 2009, 38)? Why is it that, as John and Jean Comaroff suggest in *Ethnicity, Inc.*, cultural tourism "seldom yields what it seems to promise" (9)?

The answer, I have argued here, allows us to extend their analysis into spaces of perceived potential resource abundance, broadly defined, that rests on a sense of economic and ecological stability that cannot always be assumed. The three narratives featured here also illustrate the implications of deploying ethnicity as the sole option for improving one's situation. Development has shifted from a focus on poverty alleviation to a technical effort to manage an already existing but hidden wealth. Ethnicity was taken to be the source and the substance of potential abundance. It grounded elaborate competitions through which organizations like Desco would deliberately hone and choreograph an ideal subjectivity.

Rogelio and Anacé were Desco's model figures, its development champions, from the initial moment of winning a place in the contest's twenty top performers to their ability to keep their enterprises alive after the project ended. Desco's campaign entirely reshaped their social lives, justifying spiritual choices (in Rogelio's case), reconfiguring family dynamics (in Anacé's case), and launching both into the regional political arena. Yet their current success is fragile, as Gerardo and Luisa's counterexample illustrates. Entrepreneurship, in startup culture and NGO-based empowerment alike, entails failure (Eric Hirsch, interview with Fabiola Dapino, April 2014, Chivay). Starting a business is being conveyed to eager participants as, in Desco capacity-building consultant Antonio Rojas's words, "the only way out" of difficult life circumstances. Thus, places like Colca are perpetually emerging, full of promise, but still the site of only a select few exemplary success stories.

Of course, post-Truman development aid has always engaged both material support and the affective and semiotic effort to remake subjects through various forms of incentivizing, training, and behavioral modification. I would suggest that ethnicity-focused development in today's Colca Valley is unprecedented in its ratio of investment size to the empowerment its ambitious practitioners expected to achieve. It is also unusual more locally in that the Collagua and Cabana ethnicities are understood among technocratic institutions as pathways to the accumulation of capital when that promise has yet to be borne out in the long term.

However, given the lack of alternatives in the projects that NGOs and state-affiliated institutions have brought to Colca in recent years, many Colcans were open to benefiting from any project that could offer them some kind of investment. In the follow-up interviews I recorded in 2017 with former project participants, most of them called for Desco to renew its entrepreneurship investments, despite its disappointments. Gerardo and Luisa did not share this view. But others made this call because the effort from institutions to deploy ethnicity as a source of potential abundance in capital, resources, and access runs against a broader trend of state disinvestment. Despite the sometimes-oppressive conditions of such projects, and despite the risks of betting on allegedly hidden wealth, investment in ethnic entrepreneurial self-actualization established itself as a rare remaining form of external support.

NOTES

1. The Colca Valley is a region in the southern Andes, located some 160 kilometers north of Arequipa, Peru's second-most-populous city. It consists of twenty village communities whose population counts range from four hundred to six thousand.

2. Desco, the Center for Studies and Promotion of Development, is a national nongovernmental organization in Peru and the longest-serving civil society organization in the Colca Valley. Its staff first arrived in Chivay in 1985.

3. Similarly, Comaroff and Comaroff (2009, 37) note that "ethnic identity, by contrast to race, may manifest itself primarily in expressive culture, in collective practices and products. . . . But it also betokens a unique, innate substance, a substance that inhabits individuals and communities alike, a substance that congeals in 'traditional' objects and activities and expertise."

4. I elaborate on this trip with a distinct analytical framework in Hirsch and Jones 2019.

5. Uyu Uyu is the name of the precolonial settlement that preceded present-day Yanque.

REFERENCES

Cárdenas, Pamela, Rodolfo Marquina, and Jaime Paredes. 2014. "La desigualdad en la provincial de Caylloma-Valle del Colca, Arequipa." *Perú Hoy*. Lima: Desco.

Comaroff, John L., and Jean Comaroff. 2009. *Ethnicity, Inc.* Chicago: University of Chicago Press.

Cruikshank, Barbara. 1999. *The Will to Empower: Democratic Citizens and Other Subjects*. Ithaca, NY: Cornell University Press.

DeHart, Monica C. 2010. *Ethnic Entrepreneurs: Identity and Development Politics in Latin America*. Stanford: Stanford University Press.

De la Cadena, Marisol. 2000. *Indigenous Mestizos: The Politics of Race and Culture in Cuzco, Peru, 1919–1991*. Durham, NC: Duke University Press.

Desco (Center for the Study and Promotion of Development). 2012. "Development of Young Entrepreneurs and the Generation of Self-Employment in Caylloma Province, Arequipa." Institutional Project Proposal to Fondoempleo.

Elson, Christina M., and R. Alan Covey, eds. 2006. *Intermediate Elites in Pre-Columbian States and Empires*. Tucson: University of Arizona Press.

Escobar, Arturo. 1995. *Encountering Development: The Making and Unmaking of the Third World*. Princeton, NJ: Princeton University Press.

Faudree, Paja. 2013. *Singing for the Dead: The Politics of Indigenous Revival in Mexico*. Durham, NC: Duke University Press.

Ferguson, James. 1994. *The Anti-Politics Machine: "Development," Depoliticization, and Bureaucratic Power in Lesotho*. Minneapolis: University of Minnesota Press.

Freeman, Carla. 2014. *Entrepreneurial Selves: Neoliberal Respectability and the Making of a Caribbean Middle Class*. Durham, NC: Duke University Press.

Fuentes, Julio. 2011. "Análasis del Microcrédito en el Ámbito Rural (Colca)." Internal report, Caja Nuestra Gente, Chivay, Peru.

García, María Elena. 2013. "The Taste of Conquest: Colonialism, Cosmopolitics, and the Dark Side of Peru's Gastronomic Boom." *Journal of Latin American and Caribbean Anthropology* 18 (3): 505–24.

Gelles, Paul H. 2000. *Water and Power in Highland Peru: The Cultural Politics of Irrigation*. New Brunswick, NJ: Rutgers University Press.

Hirsch, Eric, and Kyle Jones. 2019. "Hip Hop and Guinea Pigs: Contextualizing the Urban Andes." In *The Andean World*, edited by Linda J. Seligmann and Kathleen S. Fine-Dare, 555–70. London: Routledge.

Hobsbawm, Eric. 1983. "Introduction: Inventing Traditions." In *The Invention of Tradition*, edited by Eric Hobsbawm and Terence Ranger, 1–14. Cambridge: Cambridge University Press.

Li, Tania Murray. 2007. *The Will to Improve: Governmentality, Development, and the Practice of Politics*. Durham, NC: Duke University Press.

Mazzarella, William T. S. 2003. *Shoveling Smoke: Advertising and Globalization in Contemporary India*. Durham, NC: Duke University Press.

Meiu, George Paul. 2015. "'Beach-Boy Elders' and 'Young Big-Men': Subverting the Temporalities of Ageing in Kenya's Ethno-erotic Economies." *Ethnos* 80 (4): 472–96.

Mosse, David. 2005. *Cultivating Development: An Ethnography of Aid Policy and Practice*. London: Pluto Press.

Pogge, Thomas. 2007. "Severe Poverty as a Human Rights Violation." In *Freedom from Poverty as a Human Right: Who Owes What to the Very Poor?*, edited by Thomas Pogge, 11–54. Oxford: Oxford University Press.

Radcliffe, Sarah A. 2015. *Dilemmas of Difference: Indigenous Women and the Limits of Postcolonial Development Policy*. Durham, NC: Duke University Press.

Rist, Gilbert. 2008. *The History of Development: From Western Origins to Global Faith*. 3rd ed. Translated by Patrick Camiller. London: Zed.

Spivak, Gayatri Chakravorty. 1988. "Can the Subaltern Speak?" In *Marxism and the Interpretation of Culture*, edited by Cary Nelson and Lawrence Grossberg, 271–313. Urbana: University of Illinois Press.

UNESCO. 2015. "La danza del Wititi del valle del Colca." Accessed March 8, 2016. http://www.unesco.org/culture/ich/es/RL/la-danza-del-wititi-del-valle-del -colca-01056.

West, Paige. 2012. *From Modern Production to Imagined Primitive: The World of Coffee from Papua New Guinea*. Durham, NC: Duke University Press.

Wiener Fresco, Hugo. 2007. "La experiencia del Huchuy Ayni de Huancavelica." Lima: Instituto Nacional de Recursos Naturales.

Wroblewski, Michael. 2014. "Public Indigeneity, Language Revitalization, and Intercultural Planning in a Native Amazonian Beauty Pageant." *American Anthropologist* 116 (1): 65–80.

Zegarra López, Jorge. 2015. "Arequipa: El Desarrollo Productivo como Respuesta a la Pobreza." *CIES Report*. Lima: Consorcio de Investigación Económica y Social.

ERIC HIRSCH is Assistant Professor of Environmental Studies at Franklin & Marshall College.

FOUR

—ᘉ—

WARRIORS, INCORPORATED

The Militarization of Fijian Identity in the Era of Neoliberal Warfare

SIMON MAY

IT IS PROBABLY NOT AN exaggeration to say that every Fijian knows someone in the military. The Republic of Fiji Military Forces has 3,500 active soldiers and at least 6,000 reservists. Approximately 1,500 Fijians are currently serving in the British army, and between 2,000 and 4,000 more work as private military contractors around the world. In fact, most Fijians I talked to during my fieldwork knew not one but several people in the military and knew many, many more who were actively trying to enlist. In 2002, when the British army came to Fiji looking for 200 recruits, over 10,000 young Fijian men showed up to be interviewed. In 2005, when the local subsidiary of private military logistics firm Meridian Services Agency sought to fill positions on military bases in Iraq and Kuwait, upward of 15,000 Fijians applied. Such figures are remarkable, but especially so for a Pacific island nation-state of only 850,000 people. In 2008, a United Nations report on the involvement of private military forces in violent conflicts around the world identified Fiji as a major source of recruits for the global private military industry (United Nations Human Rights Council 2008).

The outsourcing of warfare is clearly big business in Fiji. For example, in 2003, as part of Operation ICE (Iraqi Currency Exchange), one of the single largest private military operations in recent years, a UK-based private military firm hired five hundred Fijians to help guard and transport Iraq's newly printed post–Saddam Hussein banknotes from Baghdad airport to the Central Bank of Iraq. Between 2006 and 2012, over one thousand Fijians a year left Fiji to take up work as private security contractors in the Middle East alone (Kanemasu and Molnar 2017), and since then Fijians have worked globally in a range of private military positions, from bodyguards in Afghanistan to oil pipeline guards in Nigeria. Most recently, forty-two Fijian former police and military officers were hired to provide security at Australia's erstwhile immigration detention center on Manus Island when it reverted to the control of Papua New Guinea (*Fiji Times*, October 29, 2017). Doug Brooks, president of the International Stability Operations Association, a US-based lobbying group for private military and security corporations, calls Fiji "a vital part of the industry" (*New York Times*, October 30, 2007).

It is an industry, however, that is inherently perilous, like few others. In its various forms—with the British army, in UN peacekeeping missions, and as private military contractors—overseas military service has claimed a lot of Fijian lives. Eight Fijians in the British army were killed over the course of the wars in Iraq and Afghanistan. Fifty-nine Republic of Fiji Military Forces soldiers have been killed during UN peacekeeping missions since 1978. And according to the website Coalition Casualty Count, at least nineteen Fijian private military contractors have been killed in Iraq alone since 2003.[1] Nevertheless, thousands of Fijian men continue to seek employment in overseas military service.

How can we explain the "vital" position of Fiji—a Pacific island nation-state of fewer than one million people—in the emerging global industry of outsourced military force? What accounts for the disproportionate role of Fijians in the neoliberal privatization of warfare? Why, when military service is so inherently dangerous, do thousands of young Fijians continue to apply for military jobs overseas, seemingly without concern for how many of their fellows are killed? And why are Fijian soldiers and private military workers drawn exclusively from the indigenous Fijian population, when almost half of the population of Fiji are Indo-Fijians, the descendants of indentured Indian plantation workers brought to Fiji by the British in the nineteenth century?

Drawing on Jean and John Comaroff's *Ethnicity, Inc.* (2009), I argue that, in the context of an expanding global market for private military power, indigenous Fijians have successfully mobilized militarized forms of their own ethnic and cultural distinctiveness as both "a means of self-construction and a source of material sustenance" (2009, 19). I show that many Fijians seek to promulgate the notion that they are a "fighting people" in order to secure positions for themselves within the global supply chains of outsourced warfare and thereby provide materially for themselves, their families, and their kin. In the burgeoning global market for privatized military labor, aspects of Fijian culture and history—particularly those traditionally associated with warfare and masculinity—are being revalued and thereby transformed, such that what had been "marks of otherness" (2009, 30) have become more akin to the trademarks of a new global military-ethnic brand: "Warriors, Inc."

Crucially, I show that Fiji's central position in the global private military industry is an effect of the lead role taken by the Fijian state in the production, distribution, and exchange of the Fijian warrior-soldier, the self-essentialized ethnocommodity at the heart of Warriors, Inc. I argue that the postcolonial state's monetization of the national military presaged the large-scale outsourcing of military labor that decades later would become the modus operandi of the global private military industry. I argue that in doing so the Fijian state initiated innovative processes of ethnic self-commodification and incorporation, anticipating the practices that would later become characteristic of what Comaroff and Comaroff (2009) have called "Ethnicity, Inc."

THE INCORPORATION OF WARRIORHOOD

The neoliberal turn of the late twentieth century—characterized by the extension of market logics, techniques, and metrics into spheres of human existence previously considered qualitatively distinct from the market—has transformed military power. The intrusion of neoliberal logics into the domain of warfare—opening up new spaces for capital—has broken down the previously fixed "public monopoly of the military profession" (Singer 2008, 8). By the early 1990s, private firms, often with intentionally vague names like Unity Resources Group and referring to themselves as "risk management consultants," were offering consumers a wide range of military and security services. Since then, the outsourcing of warfare has grown exponentially, with the US-led invasions of Afghanistan in 2001 and Iraq in 2003 precipitating a full-scale boom. With most UN and NATO allies unwilling to join the "coalition of the willing," the US had to resort to a "coalition of the billing," turning to private military firms to fill the gaps in their forces. One private military firm alone became the sixth-largest contributor of soldiers to the invasion of Iraq.[2] By 2008, the private military industry had an estimated annual revenue of $100 billion (Singer 2008, 78).

Fiji might be a key player in this multibillion-dollar global industry, but it would be hard to tell that from the nondescript building in Suva, the capital city, outside which I was standing one morning in 2009. Except for the polished brass plaque beside the door that read, "Global Solutions, Inc.," it was identical to the other small, nondescript buildings with which it shared a side street in downtown Suva. Standing there, it was hard to believe that from an office in this anonymous building—and from three or four others like it elsewhere in

Fiji—thousands of Fijian men (and some women) were sent across the globe to work as bodyguards, military drivers, and countless other positions within the burgeoning private military forces of the world.

I was there to meet Major Jone Sikeli, a former officer in the Republic of Fiji Military Forces (RFMF) who was now, as founder and director of Global Solutions, Inc., one of Fiji's most successful recruiters for the global private military industry. Major Sikeli started Global Solutions, Inc., soon after retiring from the RFMF. As he was at pains to make clear, his company is not itself a provider of private military services. Rather, he explained, it is a recruitment company contracted by private military firms, mostly based in the UK, to fill their vacant positions with qualified applicants, for which Global Solutions, Inc., earns a fee. But it was not only about the money, he said. He may have retired from the RFMF, but he was still serving Fiji, he said, by helping Fijians find good work outside the country:

> [I help] alleviate the unemployment here and create employment there for both our men and women. I've personally sent more than 500 over. But a lot more have been here, looking. A thousand, looking for the jobs. Could be more. There's no work here. Of course they want these jobs. And also, they like, they savour, to go overseas, to go and work overseas. If you want to recruit some Fijians overseas to work, their first reaction is "I'll go!" Never mind what's over there, they don't know what's happening in England, in Iraq, they don't know. "I want to go there!" You will not have any problem recruiting here, for any job overseas. Picking apples, fishing, military, they'll go!

But why, I asked him, did so many private military firms, most of whom were UK- and US-based, come all the way to Fiji to recruit? Surely, I asked, it was not just because of high local unemployment?

> It's because we Fijians have a reputation for being good soldiers. Yes. First because, in our village setup, we are taught to obey the elders from there. So that is inbuilt in a person. To respect, to obey, people in authority. Because once you have that it's easy to obey orders, because in the military you have to learn to obey. But also because of the warrior spirit. We have that. In the village setup they're called *bati*, the warriors, you know? For a chief, he's got his own people, they are the people who go and fight for the chief. And they are warriors in their own right. And that is in us. We just know. We react. We don't always show it, but when the instinct comes in, we fight, to protect whoever. If the chief is not there, it will be our commanding officer. Instinct. We react. It's natural. That's the right word for it, natural. That's why they come to recruit here. Our people are tailor-made for this profession.

The particularities of Fijian culture, values, and a supposedly innate "warrior spirit," these are the means by which Fijians set themselves apart in the global market for outsourced military labor. It is this cultural distinctiveness that finds full incorporation—quite literally—in Global Solutions, Inc. Major Sikeli's entire business—being a middleman, a broker, between private military firms and individual Fijians—as well as the business of several other militarized Fijian "ethno-preneurs" (Comaroff and Comaroff 2009, 50–51) is predicated on the incorporation of continuity: the continuity between "traditional" forms of Fijian warriorhood and contemporary professional soldiering. Essentially, Global Solutions, Inc., trades in self-essentialization, marketing Fijians as "natural" warrior-soldiers to the overseas consumers of outsourced military force. In these processes of self-essentialization and commodification, Global Solutions, Inc., is not alone.

"being a soldier is in our blood"

Whenever I asked young Fijian men why they wanted to be soldiers, the first answer was always, of course, money. Youth unemployment is high in Fiji (19 percent in 2016, according to the World Bank), and many young Fijian men despair of finding a job, even with a university education. But very often, they would add some variation of what became to me a common refrain: "And because being a soldier is in our blood." This claim was often accompanied by an almost resigned shrug, as if no statement could be more self-evidently true and thus no career-path more predetermined. "We are born soldiers," my Fijian interlocutors would tell me, time and again.

As Comaroff and Comaroff (2009, 15) note, empowerment in the postcolony connotes "privileged access to markets, money, and material enrichment." "In the case of ethnic groups," they add, "it is frankly associated with finding something essentially their own and theirs alone, something of their essence, to sell. In other words, a brand." With high unemployment and few options for young people at home, many Fijians have become invested—some, quite literally—in branding themselves as "born soldiers," mobilizing traditional Fijian notions of warriorhood in a process of self-commodification oriented toward securing privileged access to the emerging global market for outsourced military labor. During my fieldwork, almost every conversation I had about military service—with Fijians who were serving, had served, or merely aspired to serve—invariably involved the invocation of a Fijian tradition of warriorhood: we are soldiers now because we have always been warriors.

In creating this striking articulation between contemporary military labor and traditional notions of warriorhood, Fijians are drawing explicitly on aspects of their shared culture and history. The archaeological record, material culture, oral narratives, the Fijian language, early European accounts, and the very categories of Fijian social order all suggest that warfare has long been an important aspect of Fijian society (Teaiwa 2005; Halapua 2003; Sahlins 2004; Tippett n.d.). The politics of precolonial Fiji were characterized by conflicts between rival chiefs, conflicts that often involved organized violence between representative groups of warriors and, sometimes, large-scale pitched battles involving thousands (Clunie [1977] 2003). First contact with European traders precipitated a rapid and terrible intensification of Fijian warfare (Sahlins 2005), such that European missionary accounts of Fiji at this time were often dominated by descriptions of Fijian warriors and warfare. It is this history of indigenous warfare from which Fijians draw today as they seek to gain access to the global market for military labor.

It is not only history from which Fijians draw, but the categories of Fijian social structure itself. Classical Fijian social structure categorizes persons and social units hierarchically in relation to a chief and conceives of these social/cosmological distinctions as constitutive of (or perhaps more accurately constituted by) a complementary division of labor, whereby certain social units and the individuals they encompass are associated with the roles necessary for the ordered reproduction of existence. As Hocart noted, Fijian social units, particularly *mataqali* (clans), "owe their rank to the fact that in the cosmic ritual different parts have to be taken by different families" ([1936] 1970, 182). Some mataqali are defined by their role as fishermen; others, by their role as heralds. And some, the bati, are defined by their traditional role as the "teeth" of the chief, vassal clans that inhabit the margins of chiefly territories and thus formed the warrior vanguard of chiefly armies. Certain Fijians, in other words, are able to mobilize the traditional role performed by their *mataqali* in Fiji's socio-cosmological order to claim a personal aptitude for soldiering.

For example, when I spoke with Inoke, a private military contractor home on leave from his work in Iraq, he explained that his ability to do the job came from "something inside me." Inoke began working in the private military industry in 2003, when the United Nations put out a tender looking for personal protection officers (bodyguards) to work in Iraq. A recruiter in Fiji circulated the details, and Inoke, who was in the RFMF at the time, signed up. In Iraq he was on-call twenty-four hours a day, seven days a week, for four weeks at a time. He had been involved in several firefights, had guarded top UN diplomats, and was paid USD $10,000 a month. I asked him how he handled such a dangerous job. He replied: "My own approach is, I don't have that fear. Or I keep it out of my mind, because I've made a commitment to the job. So, I feel calm. And that's important, because it makes you good at the job. I don't have as much fear as other people. The Americans I work with are afraid of everything and everyone! They view everyone as a threat, which is counterproductive. But that's something inside me, to stay calm. That comes from being bati." And in addition to this, Inoke told me that he was particularly good at being a bodyguard, providing close personal protection to dignitaries and government officials, because he was a particular type of bati: "I'm not just bati, I'm *bati leka*, you know what that means? It means those closest to the chief, the warriors closest to him. *Bati balavu*, those are the ones further out. We've inherited that, from the generations. We're good at this job. We don't have to be taught it, we just do it, and we are strong enough to do it."

This was not the only time that I heard this particular claim. In fact, on several occasions I was told that all of the specialist bodyguard positions in the Republic of Fiji Military Forces were filled by men who came from mataqali that were bati leka, like Inoke. This idea, that their position in the sociocosmological landscape of Fiji transmits to certain Fijians a legacy of warriorhood—and that it is this legacy that shapes their supposed aptitude for contemporary soldiering—is a common feature of how these Fijians often talk about themselves. When asked by a BBC journalist to explain what it meant to be bati, a Fijian man responded: "If you are *bati*, the genes will come through you.... If you are on the street, you will become a street fighter. If in warfare, you will be the best warrior ever. That's your destination."[3]

By such warrior discourse is Fijian overseas military service effectively naturalized. Through it, Fijian military labor is disarticulated from such material concerns as employment and money and is instead represented as a contemporary manifestation of a specifically Fijian cultural/biological inheritance, a predisposition to violence so powerful that it supposedly determines the life course of Fijians who belong to such bati mataqali.

However, this discourse of inherited warriorhood is not the exclusive privilege of Fijian men who are bati. During my fieldwork, I met comparatively few Fijian men who were bati, and yet many felt able to lay claim to a shared history of warriorhood. Historically, all Fijian men, irrespective of clan membership, were expected to fight during times of warfare, such that "a Fijian army was essentially coextensive with the entire able-bodied adult male population of the society" (Carneiro 1990, 195).

Thus while some Fijian men might be able to base their claims on clan position, potentially all Fijian men are able to draw from a shared history of warriorhood. As one Fijian man told me, when showing me a picture he had drawn
of a Fijian soldier in modern military uniform standing next to a precolonial
Fijian warrior wearing traditional garb: "This shows the modern Fijian warrior and the other more traditional warrior standing shoulder to shoulder. The
intention is to show that Fijians have a tradition of fighting since generations
and that they value their traditions." In other words, the image represented
not two distinct figures but rather one figure—the Fijian warrior—in different
historical manifestations. For many Fijians, such a continuity exists between
the warrior of precolonial Fiji and the Fijian soldier of today that serving in
the military—even a foreign military—can be imagined and represented as
an unproblematic expression of traditional Fijian values, culture, and history.

The idea that Fijians are naturally predisposed to warfare—and that they
are, therefore, ideal recruits for military forces both local and global, both public and private—seemed almost to be taken for granted in Fiji. Almost, but not
quite. Because while everywhere these claims were accompanied by natural-
izing references to history and blood, culture and ethnicity, the notion that
Fijians are, as they would say, "a fighting people" never seemed to become a fully
naturalized part of what Gramsci (1971, 324) called hegemony, that disjointed
composite of received assumptions and dispositions that constitute the "taken
for granted" of any given social group. Indeed, if we take Gramsci's concept of
hegemony to refer to what Comaroff and Comaroff have called the "constructs
and conventions that have come to be shared and naturalized throughout a
political community," the claim that Fijians are "natural soldiers" seemed never
to fully enter the domain of the hegemonic. While many Fijians seemed to
accept it as self-evidentially true, the claim never achieved the "mute" character
of hegemony "at its most effective" (1991, 24). In fact, in many instances during
my fieldwork it seemed to actually *demand* explicit assertion, almost as if my
interlocutors were trying to convince me—or themselves—of its truth.

This tendency to explicitly reiterate a claim seemingly taken for granted
reveals, I suggest, the extent to which these statements might best be analyzed through the framework of ethnicity, inc. (Comaroff and Comaroff 2009).
These utterances are not taken-for-granted truisms, nor are they hyperbolic
boasts. Rather they are, I suggest, the slogans by which a new ethnocommodity is advertised to the world. They are the discursive means by which this
ethnocommodity—the Fijian warrior-soldier—is marketed by Fijians themselves, in the context of a rapidly expanding global market for outsourced
military force.

If "being a soldier is in our blood" is an advertising slogan, the overall business strategy that guides it might best be described as empowerment through self-essentialization (Comaroff and Comaroff 2009, 15). Many Fijians are invested—some, like Major Sikeli, quite literally—in representing themselves as warrior-soldiers, such that the figure of the Fijian warrior exists now as a kind of brand icon of what I have been calling Warriors, Inc., circulating in both local and global contexts, oriented toward the burgeoning market for private military power. Through its mobilization, Fijians secure the "savage slot" (see Trouillot 2003) in the supply chains of outsourced warfare. And as we shall see below, their success in commodifying aspects of their own history and their cultural distinctiveness in this way reciprocally feeds back into a reproduction of a particular form of what Fijians call *vaka i taukei*, "the Fijian way of life," that set of values, practices, orientations, and assumptions on which this entire process of Fijian ethnocommodification is predicated.

MILITARY MONEY AND SOCIAL (RE)PRODUCTION

Given the high levels of unemployment in Fiji, overseas military labor provides an invaluable source of income by which individual Fijians and their families meet their immediate needs and live materially more comfortable lives. Most of this money flows back to Fiji in the form of remittances and most of that to rural parts of Fiji. Indeed, the amount of money flowing back to rural villages in Fiji from overseas soldiers has resulted in the proliferation of mini bank branches opening in parts of Fiji previously underserved by the banking industry as Australian- and New Zealand–based banking corporations seek access to these new cash flows.

But whether in rural or urban Fiji, military money has particular effects, not least of which is the reproduction of the cultural distinctiveness on which the success of Fijians in the global market for military labor is itself based. To understand why Fijians use military money in the ways that they do, and how military money has the effects that it does, we must place their local investments in economic, cultural, and social contexts. On a pragmatic level, the almost exclusively local mobilization of Fijian military money can be explained by the relatively low cost of living in Fiji—especially in rural villages—as well as the advantageous exchange-rates between the Fiji Dollar and the foreign currencies in which overseas soldiers are paid. While the money Fijians soldiers earn abroad might not fund a salubrious lifestyle in London or Berlin, in Fiji these soldiers are able to leverage favorable exchanges rates to transform their pay into significant and life-changing amounts of local currency. Even relatively "entry-level" positions—a Private in the British army, for example—earn more money, when converted into Fiji dollars, than many mid-ranking civil servants in Fiji. As one former soldier told me: "You'd have to be a headmaster at a big school in Fiji to earn as much as I was on!"

This relative value must be placed in the wider economic context of Fiji, specifically the chronic scarcity of employment opportunities for young people. In his analysis of the Fijian garment industry, Donovan Storey (2006, 217) estimated that while new formal sector jobs in Fiji number around two thousand annually, the number of new entrants into the labor market each year is approximately seventeen thousand. No wonder that a father of two soldiers serving abroad described military service to me as "the best overseas employment scheme for Fiji."

One of the most notable aspects of Fijian overseas military labor is the way in which money sent by soldiers to their families in Fiji enters into a moral economy characterized by mutuality and reciprocity. For example, the sending of remittances home by Fijian military laborers working overseas is structured by what Sahlins has called a "kin ethics" (1962, 204), an expectation, indeed an obligation, that Fijians reciprocate care and support for those who cared for and supported them in their youth. For Fijian men, this obligation is compounded by the expectation, common across Oceania (see, for example, Elliston 2004; Tengan 2002), that it should be men who provide materially for their families. As such, overseas military labor allows Fijian men to meet both their traditional obligation to reciprocate care to their kin, and the gendered expectation that "proper Fijian men" provide materially for their families. In fact, many of my interlocutors claimed that the main reason Fijian men became overseas military laborers was to be able to support their families and kin.

Beyond allowing individual Fijian men to meet their obligations to reciprocate care and materially support their families and kin, military money sent back to Fiji also helps the families of soldiers meet—and even exceed—their own wider obligations. For example, remittances give the families of soldiers the material ability to accede to *kerekere* requests, quasi-formal appeals for material aid that one receives from and can make to one's kin, requests structured by an implied but vital mutuality. Military money flowing back to Fiji from Fijian soldiers allows their families accede to such kerekere requests, an ability that can have important social effects. Being able to graciously accede to a kerekere request tends to raise the esteem in which the giver is held (Sahlins 1962, 210), and thus families of overseas military workers, being able to more readily participate in kerekere exchanges as givers, thereby secure for themselves considerable social prestige.

Beyond the relatively quotidian appeals for aid that characterize the practice of kerekere, military money also allows the families of soldiers to fulfill, or even exceed, their obligations to contribute to higher-order ceremonial exchanges. In Fiji, important life-stage events like births, marriages, and funerals are marked by forms of ceremonial exchange characterized by the mobilization and redistribution of often large amounts of collective wealth (see, for example, Turner 1987; Hocart [1936] 1970; Sahlins 1962; Rutz 1978). Families and kin groups are expected to contribute to such exchanges, and in recent years, cash contributions have become an increasingly common means of meeting these expectations. Semi, a private security contractor, was telling me about patrolling the streets of Baghdad, when the conversation turned to money:

> The money is good. But maybe not so much when you see how dangerous the job is, you know? [laughs] But I mean, it's good money. So that's a lot, for us. I've bought some land, back on Gau, built a home there. And it helps us with our, you know, our traditional obligations? You have to contribute to things in the village. Funerals. Marriages. Births. A lot of things like that, you have to contribute. Your family has to. You probably don't ever experience anything like that where you are from, because you have no culture over there, right? [laughs] But we have that culture. So I'm sending money back and that helps my family.

The money remitted to Fiji by overseas military workers thereby enters into the local moral economy via the forms of ceremonial exchange by which Fijian social relations are constituted. Sometimes families contribute cash, but sometimes the cash is exchanged for ceremonial forms of value, with woven *voivoi* mats and even *tabua* sperm whale teeth available in the many pawn shops of Suva. Whether by using money remitted home by overseas military workers to make large cash contributions or by using pawn shops to convert remitted military money into traditional forms of ceremonial wealth, the families of overseas soldiers are able to fulfill, and very often to exceed, their expected contribution to these collective forms of exchange.

Similarly, the flow of military money back to Fiji facilitates the participation of soldiers' families in ceremonies characterized by expensive redistributive *magiti* feasts and *yau* presentations, such as the traditional *tevutevu* bride-wealth ceremonies, forms of redistribution of which only chiefly families were formerly capable. Military money increasingly allows nonchiefly families to engage in forms of ceremonial exchange that were formerly beyond their reach socially and economically. As with kerekere, engaging in such high-level redistributive exchanges—often in excess of expectations—allows these families to construct for themselves new positions in the social and economic hierarchy of Fiji that would never have been possible otherwise.

In sum, many of the constitutive aspects of vaka i taukei—such as the expectation that men provide materially for their families and kin and that social units contribute to the forms of material exchange by which social relations are constituted—are being reproduced, transformed, and extended by Fijian participation in the global market for private military force. It is precisely this success and, crucially, the fact that it is predicated on traditional forms of Fijian masculinity that are inextricable from vaka i taukei, that encourages other Fijian men to invest in the processes of militarized self-essentialization and ethnocommodification that define Warriors, Inc.

In fact, during my fieldwork I noticed that it was often young men who were not yet in the military who were the most invested in reproducing the commodification of the Fijian warrior-soldier, precisely because they could see how successful current Fijian soldiers were in "being Fijian" in valued and relatively normative ways. It was very often these young men, prospective transnational military laborers, and their families who were most vociferous about the truth of the claim that "being a soldier is in our blood." The reason these prospective recruits engaged in such discourses and practices of self-commodification was clear: they saw that Fijian soldiers, by occupying a contemporary form of a traditional role, were successfully able to provide materially for their families and kin and, further, were thereby able to facilitate the reproduction of Fijian cultural distinctiveness. As a result, an increasing number of young Fijian men, seeking to emulate these social and economic successes, became invested in representing themselves as natural "warrior-soldiers." So much so that, for many young Fijian men, the figure of the Fijian warrior-soldier appears to be displacing other ways of being Fijian.

THE STATE AS MILITARY ETHNOPRENEUR

It is not only soldiers and their families, or even the ethnopreneur middlemen like Major Sikeli, who are invested in and make capital from Warriors, Inc. The Fijian state itself is one of its leading investors and beneficiaries. In fact, as I will show, Warriors, Inc., has its roots at state level, and the Fijian state has long taken the lead in facilitating Fijian involvement in, and promoting Fijians as, overseas military labor. Fundamentally, if we want to understand how it is that Fiji, a Pacific archipelago with a population of 850,000, plays such a disproportionately massive role in the ongoing neoliberal privatization of military power, we must take the state into account as a key actor in the production, distribution, and exchange of the ethnocommodity—the Fijian warrior-soldier—that is at the heart of Warriors, Inc.

Of crucial importance, I argue, was the decision made by the Fijian government in 1978, eight years after independence from Britain, to expand RFMF beyond all proportion in order to send soldiers abroad on UN peacekeeping missions. As a result, Fiji has contributed more personnel to UN peacekeeping missions, per capita, than any other member state (*The Diplomat*, September 27, 2018). Over twenty-five thousand Fijian soldiers have served in UN peacekeeping missions in Angola, Bosnia and Herzegovina, Cambodia, Croatia, Darfur, Iraq, Kosovo, Lebanon, Liberia, Sinai, Namibia, Rwanda, Somalia, South Sudan, and Timor-Leste (Firth and Fraenkel 2009, 119).

As the United Nations has no standing military or police forces of its own, the enforcement of its resolutions and its peacekeeping missions rely on contributions of soldiers and equipment from member states, for which the United Nations reimburses the contributing governments. In March 1978, following Israel's invasion of Lebanon, the UN Security Council established the United Nations Interim Force in Lebanon (UNIFIL), and member states were asked to contribute soldiers and equipment to the peacekeeping force. In June 1978, the Fijian government responded to the UN request by sending a battalion of soldiers to join the UNIFIL mission, a move that required expanding the RFMF—which had comprised only 200 soldiers when the British left in 1970—to 1,300.

What was supposed to be a temporary, one-year engagement quickly became virtually permanent, with Fijian soldiers stationed in Lebanon continuously from 1978 to 2002 and then again from 2015 to 2018. In 1982, the Second Fiji Infantry Battalion was formed for the express purpose of contributing to the UN peacekeeping mission in Sinai, expanding the size of the RFMF again, from 1,300 to 1,800. When Fiji's role in the Sinai mission was expanded in 1986, so too was the size of RFMF, to 2,200. With the RFMF's ongoing involvement in UN peacekeeping missions overseas, the size of Fiji's military force has continued to increase and is currently 3,500 active and 6,000 reserve personnel.

Not only has the size of the RFMF expanded in order to be able to contribute large numbers of soldiers to UN peacekeeping missions, but its entire structure has also been reorganized to that end. Two of the three regular army battalions that compose the RFMF are now permanently based overseas: the First Battalion has been deployed on UN peacekeeping missions permanently since it was formed in 1978, first in Lebanon, and since 2002 in Iraq and Sudan. In 1982, the Second Battalion, which had been a Fiji-based territorial force, was converted into regular army unit and has been permanently deployed in Sinai ever since. The final regular army unit, the Third Battalion, is based in Fiji and is the largest of the three units, tasked with home defense. However, its other main responsibility is to train fresh troops for deployment overseas with the First and Second Battalions. With two of the RFMF's three regular army units now permanently based overseas and the third responsible for supplying new soldiers to the overseas battalions, in effect the RFMF has been completely restructured for the express purpose of outsourcing soldiers to UN peacekeeping missions overseas.

Those peacekeeping missions have brought a lot of money to Fiji: over $300 million since 1978 (Firth and Fraenkel 2009, 119). In effect, the expansion and reorganization of the Republic of Fiji Military Forces constituted the reimagining of the national military as a commercial enterprise, generating revenue and stimulating employment through the outsourcing of Fijian soldiers to the United Nations, for which the United Nations reimburses Fiji at the current rate of $1,428 per soldier, per month (a significant amount in a country where, according to the World Bank, the annual gross national income per capita is less than $5,000). "'We made a conscious decision to create an army bigger than we need to generate foreign currency,' said Lieutenant Colonel Mosese Tikoitoga, 46, senior officer in the RFMF and a former UN peacekeeper. 'Our economy has no choice but to build armies, and it's a good business. There are few other foreign investments. If we didn't do this, our people would be in the street creating havoc" (*New York Times*, October 30, 2007). At least a decade before the emergence of the private military industry, therefore, the Fijian state had seized on the commercial potential of supplying outsourced military force to overseas clients, effectively transforming the Republic of Fiji Military Forces into the world's first dedicated producer and supplier of offshore military personnel.

But if the expansion of the RFMF was, at least in part, the economic strategy of a cash-strapped postcolonial state, why was it chosen over some of the perhaps more obvious and straightforward alternatives, such as expanding the country's already existing sugar industry, or investing in the emerging tourism industry? After all, the military of Fiji was miniscule at the time, and expanding it in order to supply soldiers to the United Nations would have required significant up-front investment in new military infrastructure—training, housing, equipment, and so on—and the United Nations only reimburses troop contributing countries for costs incurred during deployment, not before (Coleman 2014, 21).

Furthermore, if the "commercialization" of the Republic of Fiji Military Forces really was about generating revenue for the state, why does UN peacekeeping seem to have contributed no significant amount of money to either the Treasury of Fiji or to the RFMF itself (*The Diplomat*, September 27 2018)? Since beginning UN peacekeeping, the RFMF has almost always overspent its ever-increasing annual budget—approximately $40 million in 2016.[4] In fact, supplying soldiers to the United Nations may actually be costing the Fijian state money: a 2014 report on the financing of UN peacekeeping missions found that the monthly cost incurred by troop contributing countries was $1,536 per deployed soldier and $1,762 if predeployment expenses were included (Coleman 2014, 16), well below even the current UN reimbursement rate of $1,428. It is perhaps no surprise, then, that Fiji's Permanent Representative to the United Nations, Ambassador Peter Thomson, was quoted at the time as saying: "It is completely unreasonable that the UN System expects troop contributing countries to subsidize the UN peacekeeping budget through an outdated and inadequate troop cost reimbursement rate which national pay scales have long since overtaken."[5]

If the Fijian state is not actually "making money" from its outsourcing of soldiers to the United Nations, then the attempt to commercialize the Republic of Fiji Military Forces would appear to have been a financial failure. And so, the questions remain: Why was this particular "economic strategy" seized on in the first place? And why, when it seems not to have enriched the institutions of the state, does UN military service continue to be a key aspect of Fijian state policy? Two important details may suggest an answer: the first is that, even though the money the RFMF receives from the United Nations is not enough to cover its costs, it still disburses almost the entirety of that money to the individual soldiers who serve as UN peacekeepers; the second is that the RFMF is almost exclusively made up of indigenous Fijian men.

I argue that for Fiji's indigenous political and military elites, outsourcing soldiers to the United Nations was not about generating revenue for the state as a whole, or even for the RFMF as an institution, but was instead a means to redistribute wealth exclusively to the indigenous Fijian community. The monetization of the RFMF challenged perceived Indo-Fijian control over the national economy while simultaneously encouraging indigenous Fijian economic activity in ways that did not threaten—but in fact emphasized—the supposed social and cultural distinctions between indigenous Fijians (communal, brave, self-sacrificing warriors) and Indo-Fijians (individualist, self-interested, and unsuited to warfare). In so doing, it shored up the system of tradition on which chiefly prerogative depended and fostered a relation of mutuality—a relation constituted, as Fijian social relations generally are, by exchange and the redistribution of wealth—between RFMF soldiers and their commanding officers. The long-term effect of the RFMF's monetization was to permanently fix the articulation between contemporary soldiering and indigenous Fijian identity, to entrench the military as the dominant institution of the Fijian state and, eventually, to place Fiji at the heart of the global private military industry.

In postcolonial Fiji of the 1970s and '80s, the prevailing sense was that, though indigenous Fijians controlled the institutions of the state—their paramountcy having been guaranteed by the structures of government and law bequeathed to Fiji by the British on independence—the national economy was increasingly dominated by Indo-Fijians (Kelly 1988; Gillion 1977; Rakuita 2007). With Indo-Fijians also having recently overtaken indigenous Fijians as the majority of the population, indigenous resentment over their economic and demographic position was stoked by nativist politicians like Sakiasi Butadroka, who claimed that indigenous Fijians were "a severely disadvantaged group, marginalized in the professions, commerce, and public life, [who] would disappear into political insignificance unless corrective action was taken" (Lal 1992, 235).

But what corrective action to take? There was much hand-wringing—among Fijian chiefs, foreign NGOs, and development academics—over how best to improve the economic position of indigenous Fijians. Essentialist explanations for Indo-Fijian economic dominance focused on their supposed "individualism," often glossed as "selfishness" or even "greed" by indigenous Fijian chauvinists (see, for example, Ravuvu 1988, 57). In contrast, the "communalism" of indigenous Fijian society was often cited to explain their relative lack of economic progress (see, for example, Nayacakalou 1975). The prevailing assumption was that the modern, entrepreneurial, market-based economic activity that supposedly came naturally to Indo-Fijians was incompatible with, and would be corrosive to, traditional Fijian culture and society, characterized as it was by a commitment to traditional communal values, to the good of the social unit to which one belonged, and to one's chiefs. Many in the Fijian elite were anxious about how to improve the economic position of indigenous Fijians in ways that would not undermine the communal ways of life—vaka i taukei—that constituted Fijian cultural distinctiveness (see, for example, Ganilau, quoted in Lal 1992, 207). Crucially, Fijian chiefs, even though they were facing increasing calls from their people to facilitate more engagement with the cash economy, had long been wary of anything that might loosen the communal ties of reciprocity and obligation on which their positions depended.

In this context of interethnic tension and socioeconomic anxiety, the decision to commercialize the Republic of Fiji Military Forces, from which Indo-Fijians have long been de facto excluded (see Kelly and Kaplan 2001, 64–81), essentially created a new sector of the economy, one that would be the exclusive preserve of indigenous Fijians, involving a form of economic activity that not only did not contradict or undermine "traditional Fijian communal values" but actually built on and reinforced them. The military is the preeminent "communal" institution of modernity after all, and for Fijians its ranks and duties mirror Fijian social hierarchies and obligations. And, of course, soldiering resonates with the valorized figure of the traditional masculine Fijian warrior, a resonance that deepened as military service increasingly came to occupy a central position in indigenous Fijian society.

The money flowing from the United Nations to RFMF soldiers—$300 million since 1978—meant that indigenous Fijian men did not have to "become like Indians," as the saying was, to engage in significant cash-generating economic activity, but could instead secure their material well-being, as well as that of their families and their kin, while reaffirming their commitment to "indigenous Fijian values" (and accruing significant international prestige in recognition of their peacekeeping services). It meant that the political paramountcy of indigenous Fijians was no longer tethered to a national economy almost entirely dependent on industries dominated by Indo-Fijians—the sugar industry and, later, the garment industry and service sectors. Instead, the outsourcing of indigenous Fijian soldiers began to displace, or at least challenge, the central position of those industries in the national economy.

Finally, the RFMF's transformation into a supplier of military labor to the United Nations has fostered a particularly durable and characteristically Fijian relation between rank-and-file soldiers and the military high command. The regular (non-UN) rate of pay for RFMF soldiers is so low that Fijians in the British army (who are paid much better in comparison) refer to them by the pejorative term ".50 cents," because, as one told me, "that's how much money they have to rub together!" After 1978, therefore, the economic livelihood of RFMF soldiers (and their kin) came increasingly to depend on the lucrative UN peacekeeping missions facilitated by their commanding officers.

In a sense, the relation between soldiers and officers became "value-added," structured as much by the redistribution of wealth as by military rank. In this, the relation between the RFMF's high command and its rank-and-file soldiers replicates the traditional relation between Fijian chiefs and commoners: commoners are obligated to perform service in tribute to their chiefs, whose ascribed positions of authority carry with them the expectation that they reciprocally redistribute wealth from the chiefly fund to those commoners. We might just as easily be talking about RFMF soldiers and officers when we say that the relation between Fijian commoners and chiefs is constituted by exchange and structured by rank, in which commoners perform service for chiefs, while chiefs, "by fulfilling their role in ceremonial exchange, bring general prosperity" (Turner 1992, 291). By identifying the commercial potential of overseas military service, and thereby appropriating to themselves the redistributive abilities of Fijian chiefs, the high command of the RFMF have forged a bond between themselves and the rank-and-file characterized by relations of loyalty and mutuality that far exceed the norms of military discipline.

Expanded in both size and power beyond all proportion, the Republic of Fiji Military Forces has become the preeminent institution of the Fijian state, known for jealously guarding its role as the protector of indigenous Fijian interests. The RFMF has been involved in four coups d'état in the decades since independence, all but the most recent in 2006 seen as explicit attempts to shore up indigenous Fijian political paramountcy.

The aftereffect of this political-economic strategy—the ethnically exclusive outsourcing of military force to the United Nations—has been the opening up of Fiji to private military firms (PMFs). The private military industry requires a pool of available trained military personnel from which it can draw its employees (a reserve army of military labor, to paraphrase Marx). A large pool of highly trained, highly experienced but unemployed or underemployed soldiers is precisely what makes Fiji a prime target for the recruiting agents of the emerging private military industry. When Fiji's role in the UNIFIL mission first ended in 2002, RFMF soldiers leaving Lebanon were concerned for their futures: "On arrival in Fiji they were demobilized and what eventually happened was that overnight we had a glut of highly skilled, highly trained soldiers doing nothing, despite being skilled in military duties. Members of one reserve battalion were give security duties at Morris Hedstrom supermarkets, but at the end of the day the soldiers realized that what they were being paid was not enough compared to what payment they could demand using their skills. Many of them opted to join security companies, securing work contracts in Iraq and Kuwait."[6] The "overproduction" of soldiers is one of the key conditions of existence from the private military industry, and in Fiji's case, the soldiers that had been had "overproduced" were made even more valuable to private military firms by the fact that they already had experience in the "overseas market." The decades-long centrality of overseas UN military service to the Fijian state and the RFMF is, therefore, the historical condition of possibility for private military recruitment in Fiji. Expanding the RFMF beyond proportion meant that private military firms were necessarily going to be drawn to recruit in Fiji, especially during any interruption to the demand from the United Nations (as almost happened after the 2006 military coup, when Australia lobbied the United Nations to stop using Fijian soldiers as peacekeepers).

With the social and political position of the Republic of Fiji Military Forces to a large degree dependent on keeping rank-and-file soldiers on its side by facilitating—or at the very least not blocking—their access to lucrative overseas postings, many in Fiji believe that the RFMF does whatever possible to make sure that its soldiers are able to take up easily positions with private military firms. When I was doing my fieldwork, for example, it was generally assumed by people I talked to that the state was allowing RFMF reservists, and perhaps even currently serving regular soldiers, to temporarily absent themselves from their RFMF responsibilities in order to take up overseas contracts with PMFs (even though this would be in direct violation of Fiji's constitution). In fact, one Fijian contractor I talked to explicitly told me that he'd resigned from the RFMF in order to take up a position with a private military firm in Afghanistan, though he also said he would have no problem leaving that job "if the army called me back to Fiji," suggesting at the very least some sense of ongoing obligation to, and perhaps contact with, the RFMF. There were even rumors (though during my fieldwork these were voiced much less frequently, and always with a significant degree of circumspection) that the RFMF received a "finder's fee" for each serving soldier it released to private military service.

There seems to be considerable confusion, in Fiji and in the international media, about the degree of direct involvement the Republic of Fiji Military Forces has in the private military industry. In a New Zealand Herald article about the operation of private military contractors in Fiji, for example, RFMF lieutenant colonel Mosese Tikoitoga, was described as the military's "private-army sales liaison." This designation implies that the RFMF is actively and directly involved in funneling its soldiers into private military contractor roles. But can this really be so, or is the designation a misleading gloss on the lieutenant colonel's actual role? (The RFMF command structure does not list a "private-army sales liaison" position but does include a director of peace support operations, as well as a deployable force directorate, whose role includes "develop[ing] Standard Operating Procedure to support Peace Keeping Operations" and "develop[ing] and enhance[ing] United Nations partnership"[7]).

The confusion and murkiness swirling around the outsourcing of military labor in Fiji, and especially around the degree of direct state involvement in the private military industry, is evident even in how Fijian military contractors themselves conceive of their work. For example, in my interview with Inoke, he started off by saying that "the UN had put out a tender for security personnel, and Fiji put in a bid and won." Was he really suggesting that the RFMF had bid on, and won, a commercial contract to provide security services? Is it possible, or even plausible, that the United Nations would award a commercial contract for security services to a nation-state military? The very fact that such questions can even be asked is suggestive of the murky ambiguity and confusion that characterizes the private military industry generally, and the Fijian state's involvement in it specifically.

If currently serving and reserve soldiers are so easily able to sign contracts with private military firms and the Fijian state appears to be facilitating—perhaps even organizing and benefiting from—private military contracting, then where does the line between the private military industry and the Fijian state lie? There are even more sensational examples of this blurring of lines. In the UN report on Fijian involvement in the private military industry, one informant claims that three Fiji government ministers are actively involved in running private military firms. Elsewhere, especially in the Fijian media, it has been noted that the RFMF has direct connections to Homelink Security Services, a Fijian PMF that has been awarded lucrative state contracts to provide security to the port of Suva and, most recently, to the three main public hospitals in Fiji (Firth and Fraenkel 2009, 129). In 2010, Homelink was ordered by Prime Minister Frank Bainimarama, former commander of the RFMF and leader of the 2006 military coup, to secure the Fiji Water bottling plant in the midst of a disagreement between the company and his government (Robertson 2017, 266).

To some degree, then, there is a spectrum of claims that circulate about the relation between the Fijian state and the private military industry: at one end of the spectrum, the claim is that the RFMF allows soldiers to take up positions with PMFs but doesn't benefit beyond the "good will" it receives from its soldiers for not blocking their access to such lucrative contracts. At the other end of the spectrum, the claim is that institutions/agents of the state are themselves directly involved in the private military industry, either by funneling soldiers to foreign military contractors for a fee or by running private military firms themselves.

In part, the difficulty in distinguishing fact from fiction when it comes to analyzing the Fijian state's role in facilitating the recruitment activities of private military firms can be explained, I suggest, by the similarities between the ostensibly public practice of outsourcing Fijian military labor to the United Nations and the ostensibly private practice of outsourcing Fijian military labor to PMFs (many of whom, coincidentally, are contracted by the United Nations to provide security services to its dignitaries). In effect, the two practices are virtually indistinguishable. The Fijian state has long treated UN peacekeeping missions like commercial operations, after all. Perhaps it is not surprising that when it comes to discussing the outsourcing of military labor in Fiji, the line between state and private actors is often impossible to distinguish.

Though it is difficult to say for certain which of the claims about Fijian state involvement in the private military industry are true, what can be said at the very least is that the Fijian state—having initiated Warriors, Inc., by transforming the RFMF into a producer and supplier of outsourced military power to the United Nations—seems to make very little effort to stop private military firms from recruiting in Fiji. The UN report on the use of mercenaries[8] notes that the Fiji government "may not wish to discourage persons from working in the field of security abroad, due to unemployment conditions in Fiji and the amount of remittances which these individuals can send to their families, who often live in rural areas of the country" (United Nations Human Rights Council 2008). And in 2005, Fiji's then minister for labor, Kenneth Zinck, was quoted in the *Fiji Times* as saying, "The Government knows that more men are leaving for Kuwait and Iraq and it is a good thing, because it is providing employment for the unemployed. This is one solution to the increasing unemployment rate in the country today." By some estimates, overseas military labor (i.e., Fijians working in the private military industry, the British army, and with the Fiji Military Forces in UN peacekeeping missions) is now Fiji's third-largest source of foreign revenue (Narsey 2009). Crucially, the increasing centrality of overseas military service to the Fijian state is mirrored in the increasing centrality of Fiji to the private military industry: as private military firms depend on the availability of trained personnel, Fiji's ongoing overproduction of such personnel enables the ongoing privatization of military force worldwide.

The role of state institutions in promoting Fiji as an offshore reserve army of military labor—first directly to the United Nations, and now perhaps more indirectly to the global private military industry—makes it clear that this is not merely an ad hoc attempt by a few opportunistic individual Fijians to market themselves or their fellows as warrior-soldiers. Rather, this is the organized, large-scale production, distribution, and exchange of an ethnocommodity, and Warriors, Inc., constitutes the efforts of an ethnopreneurial state to transform "marks of otherness . . . from devalued tokens of difference into scarce, desirable commodities" (Comaroff and Comaroff 2009, 30). Note the irony of identifying the Fijian state an ethnopreneur: "Warriors, Inc.," I suggest, is an innovative, entrepreneurial state scheme, predicated on and initiated to defend the supposedly anti-modern, anti-entrepreneurial culture of indigenous Fijians.

I argue, too, that the Fijian state was a pioneer of ethnicity, inc., anticipating in 1978 the commodification, monetization, and incorporation of ethnic specificity that would only later become ethnicity, inc.'s defining characteristics. As the Fijian state presaged the outsourcing of military force decades before the rise of the private military industry, so too, I suggest, did it anticipate some of the forms of self-commodification and ethnoincorporation that would come to characterize ethnicity, inc.

In bringing the ethnocommodity produced by Warriors, Inc., to the global market for private military force, I argue that the Fijian state asserts a market-based sovereignty grounded in and reproductive of indigenous Fijian ethnic specificity. In seeking to secure the economic sovereignty of indigenous Fijians by trading in indigenous Fijian identity, Warriors, Inc., constitutes, therefore, a form of economic self-determination that is predicated on an articulation between the concreteness of ethnicity and the abstraction of the market, in direct contradiction to the supposed incompatibility of the two. I suggest that, since 1978, the Fijian state has been mobilizing the constitutive processes of capitalist modernity—commodification, monetization, incorporation—to successfully defend the cultural specificity to which those processes are supposedly corrosive. The state's ongoing role in the production, distribution, and exchange of the Fijian warrior-soldier has had the effect not of dissolving the concrete particularity of Fijian ethnicity, but of distilling it, fixing its essence ever more concretely at the site of articulation between the warrior and the solider, between tradition and modernity, situating a very particular form of Fijian identity ever more forcefully at the heart of both the Fijian state, and the global private military industry.

CONCLUSION

From the ethnopreneurial institutions of the Fijian state, to the canny ethno-brokers like Major Sikeli, to the young Fijian men aspiring to secure positions in the global market of military labor by claiming that "being a soldier is in our blood," Fijian ethnicity is "becoming more corporate, more commodified, more implicated than ever before in the economics of everyday life" (Comaroff and Comaroff 2009, 1). Looking for a competitive edge in the burgeoning global market for private military force, Fijians are their own "ethno-commodities," performing themselves "in such a way as to make their indigeneity legible to the consumer of otherness," (Comaroff and Comaroff 2009, 142). In this they have been remarkable successful.

Every instance of Fijian involvement in overseas military labor, in UN peacekeeping, in the British army, or in the private military industry, seems to reproduce the notion that Fijians are natural warriors, from whom good soldiers can easily be recruited. Even the United Nations begins its report on mercenaries by noting that "Fiji has an established tradition of well-trained, disciplined and highly skilled military and security personnel, who perform security functions in various capacities worldwide" (United Nations Human Rights Council 2008). The prevalence of this discourse suggests that the marketing campaign behind the militarized ethnocommodification of indigenous Fijian identity has been a success.

The success of the militarized ethnocommodity of indigenous Fijian identity worldwide also underlines a crucial aspect of ethnocommodification generally: circulation. Exchange is the fundamental predicate of the commodity form; only when it has been brought to the market to be exchanged with another can a use value be transformed into value (Marx 1992). Paradoxically, however, the mass circulation of a commodity is often assumed to degrade its "aura," such that while exchange is a predicate of value, circulation is corrosive to it. However, as Comaroff and Comaroff note, ethnicity—the raw material of the ethnocommodity—is not depleted by mass circulation. To the contrary, "mass circulation reaffirms ethnicity [such that] greater supply entails greater demand" (2009, 20).

As such, the success of Warriors, Inc., is both predicated on and reproduced by the circulation of thousands of Fijian men, engaging in overseas military service, which constitutes the condition of possibility of the ongoing reproduction of their own selves as ethnocommodities. Their value as ethnocommodities depends on this circulation, without which their ethnic and cultural distinctiveness would remain in the form use-value alone. Militarized transnational migration, then, both produces and is produced by the continued circulation of the Fijian warrior-soldier.

The ethnocommodity of the Fijian warrior-soldier circulates in another, perhaps more important regime of value: it circulates locally, for the producers of ethnocommodities are also their consumers (Comaroff and Comaroff 2009, 26). For all money's fungibility, the trace of the warrior-soldier ethnocommodity exists in Fiji in the culturally specific forms of social action that its global circulation makes possible. And this is the key to the success of Warriors, Inc. It does not matter whether foreign military recruiters actually believe they are enlisting naturally proficient soldiers. Few of them do, incidentally. Rather, what matters is that indigenous Fijians themselves continue to invest their hopes for a better future, for themselves, their families, and their kin, in the figure of the warrior-soldier. In so doing, they render overseas military service—to themselves—not merely thinkable, but desirable. It is this desirability, finally, that makes Fiji such an effective recruiting ground for private military firms, guaranteeing as it does a surfeit of potential recruits. In a sense, therefore, the most loyal consumers of the ethnocommodity at the heart of Warriors, Inc., are Fijians themselves.

NOTES

1. Michael White, Iraq Coalition Casualty Count, March 20, 2014, https://web.archive.org/web/20140320113321/http://icasualties.org/Iraq/Contractors.aspx.

2. Peter W. Singer, "Warriors for Hire in Iraq," Brookings Institution, April 15, 2004, https://www.brookings.edu/articles/warriors-for-hire-in-iraq/.

3. Nicola Fell, "Fijians Take on Dangerous Iraq Roles," BBC News, March 15, 2007, http://news.bbc.co.uk/2/hi/asia-pacific/6449075.stm.

4. Fijian Government, Archive Budget 2016, April 18, 2019, https://www.fiji.gov.fj/Budget/2016.aspx.

5. Fijian Government, "Fiji Envoy Reaffirms Peacekeeping Commitment to Global Community," February 25, 2014, https://www.fiji.gov.fj/Media-Center/Press-Releases/FIJI-ENVOY-REAFFIRMS-PEACEKEEPING-COMMITMENT-TO-GL.aspx.

6. Nic Maclellan, "Fiji, the War in Iraq, and the Privatisation of Pacific Island Security," APSNet Policy Forum, April 06, 2006, https://nautilus.org/apsnet/0611a-maclellan-html/.

7. Republic of Fiji Military Forces, RFMF HQ Composition, April 17, 2019, http://www.rfmf.mil.fj/rfmf-hq-composition/.

8. The irony here, of course, is that the United Nations is one of the leading employers of Fijian private security contractors around the world.

REFERENCES

Carneiro, Robert L. 1990. "Chiefdom-level Warfare as Exemplified in Fiji and the Cauca Valley." In *The Anthropology of War*, edited by J. Haas, 190–211. Cambridge: Cambridge University Press.

Clunie, Fergus. (1977) 2003. *Fijian Weapons and Warfare*. Suva: Fiji Museum.

Coleman, Katharina P. 2014. *The Political Economy of UN Peacekeeping: Incentivizing Effective Participation*. New York: International Peace Institute.

Comaroff, Jean, and John L. Comaroff. 1991. *Of Revelation and Revolution*. Vol. 1, *Christianity, Colonialism, and Consciousness in South Africa*. Chicago: University of Chicago Press.

Comaroff, John L., and Jean Comaroff. 2009. *Ethnicity, Inc.* Chicago: University of Chicago Press.

Elliston, Deborah A. 2004. "A Passion for the Nation: Masculinity, Modernity, and Nationalist Struggle." *American Ethnologist* 31 (4): 606–30.

Firth, S., and J. Fraenkel. 2009. "The Fiji Military and Ethno-nationalism: Analyzing the Paradox." In *The 2006 Military Takeover in Fiji: A Coup to End All Coups?*, edited by S. Firth, J. Fraenkel, and B. Lal, 117–37. Canberra: ANU Press.

Gillion, K. L. 1977. *The Fiji Indians: Challenge to European Dominance, 1920–1946.* Canberra: ANU Press.

Gramsci, A. 1971. *Selections from the Prison Notebooks.* New York: International Publishers.

Halapua, Winston. 2003. *Tradition, Lotu, and Militarism in Fiji.* Suva: Fiji Institute of Applied Sciences.

Hocart, A. M. (1936) 1970. *Kings and Councilors: An Essay in the Comparative Anatomy of Human Society.* Chicago: University of Chicago Press.

Kanemasu, Yoko, and Gyozo Molnar. 2017. "Private Military and Security Labour Migration: The Case of Fiji." *International Migration* 55 (4): 154–69.

Kelly, John D. 1988. "Fiji Indians and Political Discourse in Fiji: from the Pacific Romance to the Coups." *Journal of Historical Sociology* 1 (4): 399–422.

Kelly, John D., and Martha Kaplan. 2001. *Represented Communities: Fiji and World Decolonization.* Chicago: University of Chicago Press.

Lal, B. 1992. *Broken Waves: A History of the Fiji Islands in the Twentieth Century.* Honolulu: University of Hawai'i Press.

Marx, Karl. 1992. *Capital.* Vol.1, *A Critique of Political Economy.* London: Penguin Classics.

Narsey, W. 2009. "PICTA, PACER Plus, Labour Mobility and PIC Development: What Are Our Options?" Delivered at the Regional Symposium on Population and Development: Accellerating the ICPD Programme of Action, UNFPA and USP. AusAID Lecture Theater.

Nayacakalou, R. R. 1975. *Leadership in Fiji.* Suva: University of the South Pacific.

Rakuita, T. 2007. *Living by Bread Alone: Contemporary Challenges Associated with Identity and Belongingness in Fiji.* Suva: Ecumenical Centre for Research Education and Advocacy.

Ravuvu, A. 1988. *Development or Dependence: The Pattern of Change in a Fijian Village.* Suva: University of the South Pacific.

Robertson, R. 2017. *The General's Goose: Fiji's Tale of Contemporary Misadventure.* Canberra: ANU Press.

Rutz, Henry J. 1978. "Ceremonial Exchange and Economic Development in Village Fiji. Economic." *Development and Cultural Change* 26:777–805.

Sahlins, Marshal. 1962. *Moala: Culture and Nature on a Fijian Island.* Ann Arbor: University of Michigan Press.

———. 2004. *Apologies to Thucydides: Understanding History as Culture, and Vice Versa.* Chicago: University of Chicago Press.

———. 2005. *Culture in Practice: Selected Essays.* New York: Zone Books.

Singer, P.W. 2008. *Corporate Warriors: The Rise of the Privatized Military Industry.* Ithaca, NY: Cornell University Press.

Storey, Donovan. 2006. "End of the Line? Globalization and Fiji's Garment Industry." In *Globalization and Governance in the Pacific Islands,* edited by S. Firth, 217–236. Canberra: ANU Press.

Teaiwa, Teresia K. 2005. "Articulate Cultures: Militarism and Masculinities in Fiji during the Mid 1990s." *Fiji Studies* 3 (2): 201–22.

Tengan, Ty Kawika P. 2002. "(En)gendering Colonialism: Masculinities in Hawai'i and Aotearoa." *Cultural Values* 6 (3): 239–56.

Tippett, A. n.d. *The Vocabulary of Fijian Cannibal Warfare.* Canberra: Tippett Collection of St. Mark's National Theological Centre Library.

Trouillot, Michel-Rolph. 2003. "Anthropology and the Savage Slot: The Poetics and Politics of Otherness." In *Global Transformations: Anthropology and the Modern World.* New York: Palgrave Macmillan.

Turner, James W. 1987. "Blessed to Give and Receive: Ceremonial Exchange in Fiji." *Ethnology* 26 (3): 209–19.

———. 1992. "Ritual, Habitus, and Hierarchy in Fiji." *Ethnology* 31 (4): 291–302.

United Nations Human Rights Council. 2008. "Report of the Working Group on the Use of Mercenaries as a Means of Violating Human Rights and Impeding the Exercise of the Right of Peoples to Self-Determination." A/HRC/7/7/Add.3. Geneva: United Nations General Assembly.

World Bank. 2016. *World Development Indicators 2016.* Washington, DC: World Bank Publications.

SIMON MAY is Adjunct Assistant Professor of Anthropology at Saint Louis University.

FIVE

STORY, BRAND, OR SHARE?

Bafokeng, Inc., and the 2010 FIFA World Cup

SUSAN E. COOK

AS JOHN AND JEAN COMAROFF'S *Ethnicity, Inc.* was going to print in 2009, the top executives at Bafokeng, Inc. were gathering to plan their most ambitious strategy to date to advance the "ethnopreneurial" goals of the Royal Bafokeng Nation in South Africa. As described in detail by Comaroff and Comaroff (2009), the Bafokeng ethnic group had, by the early 2000s, consolidated its political status as a traditionally governed community, its legal status as a private landowner, and its financial status as a major player in the South African mining sector. As such, it became a powerful example of an *ethnic corporation*: a community defined by its ethnic identity while also operating as a commercial enterprise (an "ethnoprise" in the Comaroffs' terms; see also Cook 2005). The process of Bafokeng corporatization, which I began documenting in the late 1990s, was essentially complete by 2006–7, when Royal Bafokeng Holdings (RBH) was registered as a "Pty Ltd" company in South Africa, headquartered in Johannesburg, with assets under management totaling R33.5 billion (approximately USD 4.15 billion). Its sole shareholder was the Royal Bafokeng Nation Development Trust, the community-based entity "responsible for the commercial imperatives of the nation." As the Comaroffs make clear, the boundaries between the Bafokeng "nation" (comprising most, though not all, of the roughly 128,000 people who inhabit twenty-nine villages in South Africa's North West Province as well as the ethnic Bafokeng living elsewhere in South Africa and around the world), the Royal Bafokeng Nation Development Trust, and Royal Bafokeng Holdings became (perhaps intentionally) blurry. Furthermore, the precise contours of Bafokeng ethnicity, its unique identity markers—its culture—were opaque at best to observers of (and participants in) Bafokeng, Inc. When, the Comaroffs (2009, 111) ask, would the dialectic between the incorporation of Bafokeng ethnicity and the commodification of Bafokeng culture consummate itself? In other words, when, how, and—crucially—why would the legal and financial consolidation of the group, its land, and its resources necessarily entail attempts to package and market the group's history, rituals, language and material culture? This chapter seeks to answer that question by exploring the aforementioned Bafokeng executives' planning and subsequent implementation of a massive PR/marketing/branding campaign ahead of the 2010 FIFA World Cup. I argue that the scale, scope, and financial and reputational stakes of the global soccer tournament represented a singular opportunity for the ethnic corporation to package its identity for a global public, and to mold its ethnic brand around specific business objectives. The intended payoff for the Bafokeng: the crafting of a corporate DNA that exudes timeworn values of moral rectitude, collective wisdom, stability, and resilience (to evince "a business with soul" or "social capitalism," as RBH's founding CEO put it). Who better to do business with in the neoliberal marketplace?

BACKGROUND TO THE BAFOKENG, OR, BACK TO THE ETHNOFUTURES

Before describing how the Bafokeng version of ethnicity, inc. played out in the first African FIFA World Cup, let me prepare the playing field by offering some background on the Bafokeng and my own association with the community.

Research on Setswana-speaking communities (*merafe*), including the Bafokeng, by historians and anthropologists has been extensive (Schapera 1943, 1952; Schapera and Comaroff 1991; Breutz 1953, 1989; Coertze 1988; Comaroff and Comaroff 1991, 1997; Legassick 1969). Scholars have long been interested in the Sotho-Tswana cluster for the ways in which their cattle-based economies shaped polities that curtailed the development of internal secondary sources of political power—that is, paramount chiefs (Gulbrandsen 1995) and effectively resisted and shaped colonial forms of administrative authority (Wylie 1990; Landau 1995). Recent research suggests that the people who identify themselves as "Bafokeng" today, as one of approximate fifty Setswana-speaking communities in southern Africa, are most likely descended from Nguni people who migrated to the highveld region of South Africa (formerly known as the western Transvaal) somewhere between the mid-fifteenth and mid-sixteenth centuries.

Archaeologists trace the movement of their characteristic stone-walled build-ing patterns from the Indian Ocean coast (now Kwa-Zulu Natal) to the Free State and then northward to their present location in the Magaliesburg moun-tain range (Hall et al. 2008; Huffman 2007). Bafokeng mythology tells that the current community's forebears chose the Rustenburg valley to settle in because of its fertile pastures and plentiful rain (Phokeng, the seat of Bafokeng governance and administration, is often glossed as "the place of dew"—*phoka*).

The Bafokeng are similar in political structure and cultural practice to most other Setswana-speaking merafe but are singular in their history of purchasing, defending, and leveraging the land they inhabit. This history is well reviewed elsewhere (Cook 2005, 2011; Comaroff and Comaroff 2009; Mbenga and Man-son 2010), but the salient points for this chapter are as follows: the community has enjoyed a relatively peaceful history of leadership succession, with the role of *kgosi* (chief or king) passing from father to son for about fifteen generations. In addition, the foresight of one particular kgosi—Mokgatle, who ruled from 1836 to 1891 (Mbenga and Manson 2010, 14)—resulted in the Bafokeng own-ing their land in such a way that successive waves of attack from the apartheid state, the Bantustan government, the postapartheid state, and various mining companies could not dislodge or displace the Bafokeng as the legal owners of their twelve hundred square kilometers of the North West Province. The discovery in the 1920s, and eventual extraction in the 1970s, of platinum group metals on Bafokeng land further challenged and ultimately strengthened the Bafokeng's claims of land ownership and consequently made the community comparatively wealthy by the end of the twentieth century.

The community's 2016 census counted 128,000 people living on Bafokeng land, roughly two-thirds of whom self-identify as ethnic Bafokeng. Although the Royal Bafokeng Nation comprises part of the Rustenburg Local Munici-pality (the local-most unit of state authority), the Royal Bafokeng Administra-tion, using the community's own coffers, pays for water and electricity, waste removal, and emergency services (fire and ambulance) in its twenty-nine vil-lages, as well as employs its own law enforcement. The administration subsi-dizes the government schools, undertakes its own census and environmental assessments, and provides scholarships for local students who get accepted to university. Unemployment and HIV rates are high in the Bafokeng community (39 percent and 25 percent respectively), but the literacy rate is 97.5 percent and the rate of households with piped water is 97.5 percent (Royal Bafokeng Hold-ings Annual Review 2016). Subject to South Africa's constitution and local magistrate's court, the Bafokeng also observe a complex traditional governance system that extends from the neighborhood-level *kutle* to the biannual mass meeting of the community *kgotha kgothe*. The Bafokeng Tribal Court hears cases that can be resolved under the statutes of Bafokeng customary law.

I first visited Phokeng as a graduate student in 1995 while doing fieldwork for my PhD project on nonstandard varieties of Setswana. As a visiting researcher in 1996–97, I was vetted, as per custom, by the office of the kgosi, and it was the Queen Mother, Mmemogolo Semane Molotlegi, who hosted me and facilitated my research. I met many community leaders in the course of my fieldwork, including Leruo Molotlegi, the Queen Mother's third child (of six). Leruo unexpectedly became kgosi in 2000 at the age of thirty-two, after his two older brothers died tragically in 1999 and 2000. As I was already an informal advisor and friend to the new kgosi, I undertook several research projects at his request to help shape his socioeconomic policy agenda and later accepted his offer to set up a research unit within his administration that would provide a steady stream of empirical data and analysis to inform policymaking in the community. I thus spent six years working full time as the research and planning executive in the Royal Bafokeng Administration (2007–13), and it was from this vantage point that I became part of the story that follows.

THE FIFA WORLD CUP AS GLOBAL STAGE

The FIFA Soccer World Cup is the most widely watched sporting event in the world. Although the sport has a near universal following in Africa, until 2010, the tournament had never been hosted on the African continent. Immediately after South Africa won the bid to host the 2010 tournament, soccer-loving societies in the West began asking, Would an African country have the resources to build the top-quality stadiums, transportation infrastructure, and hotels necessary to host the thirty-two teams and 500,000 fans who attend the tournament? Would fans be deterred by South Africa's high crime rate? Would the country's government, widely criticized for corruption and inefficiency, be able to deliver an event comparable to the well-organized and smoothly executed 2006 World Cup in Germany? Afropessimism was the dominant theme in global sports media coverage leading up to 2010, and South Africans worried among themselves if they could deliver on their promise to FIFA.

In 2004, after winning the bid to host the tournament, South Africa's Local Organising Committee (LOC) proceeded to select the venues that would host the matches. Johannesburg, Cape Town, and Durban were obvious host cities, despite the need to build several brand-new stadiums. In all, ten stadiums in nine cities were selected, including the first rural community ever to host World Cup soccer: the Royal Bafokeng Nation. The Bafokeng had built a stadium under the previous kgosi, Lebone II (1995–2000), and although it required expensive upgrades to meet FIFA requirements, the Royal Bafokeng Nation convinced the LOC that it had sufficient resources to convert its quiet villages and the adjacent (formerly white) town of Rustenburg into a world-class soccer destination.

As a small community grappling with poverty, unemployment, AIDS, failing schools, and more, why take on the huge responsibility of hosting one of the world's premier sports events? To answer that, we need to look more closely at the corporate strategies of Royal Bafokeng Holdings. Early in his reign as kgosi, Leruo established Royal Bafokeng Resources (2002) to manage the community's mining interests (platinum and chrome) and Royal Bafokeng Finance (2004) to develop a nonmining investment portfolio. In 2006, the two companies were combined to form RBH, with the aim of diversifying the community's investment assets away from mining while simultaneously maximizing the Bafokeng's share of the mineral assets within its control. RBH's model is often compared to other intergenerational wealth funds managed by the governments of the Netherlands and New Zealand. In 2009, RBH's investment portfolio was heavily weighted toward mining, with about 85 percent of its value represented by shares in Impala Platinum. The other 15 percent of the portfolio represented a range of shareholdings in about twenty companies. With the "life of mine" for most shafts located on Rustenburg's platinum belt estimated to be about fifty years, the Bafokeng leadership was determined to pursue financial strategies that would protect them from becoming a ghost town in the inevitable postplatinum bust.

RBH's short-term strategy was therefore to move its assets into other classes of investment, using South Africa's black economic empowerment legislation to its advantage (for a more thorough explanation of this, see Cook 2011). But RBH had broader ambitions than just those that could be pursued with cash investments in South African companies looking for black empowerment partners. It sought bigger, debt-financed deals with financial services giants, oil and gas companies, and major real estate holdings, among others. In the absence of a long track record of investment, RBH had to rapidly establish itself as a credible investor with a clear vision, solid principles, and world-class expertise (in addition to substantial resources)—in other words, as a peer to the major South African and international investment firms. How better to demonstrate these attributes than to host six World Cup soccer matches with impeccable planning and flawless execution?

A bit of perspective on the stakes at hand: The viewing audience for the 2010 World Cup included the 2.2 billion people who watched at least twenty minutes of the soccer. (The number is 3.2 billion, or 46.4 percent, of the world's population, if you count everyone who watched at least one minute of the tournament).[1] And beyond the general public, the audience of corporate, political, and cultural elites in attendance is unparalleled (on June 26, when the United States lost to Ghana at Royal Bafokeng Stadium, Bill Clinton, Kobe Bryant, Wolf Blitzer, Katie Couric, and Mick Jagger sat together in one of the VIP suites). The event is a massive staging ground for networking, deal making, and influence peddling—the ultimate soft power occasion. The value of this exposure for a new investment holdings company with cash to spend but no stature in the industry cannot be overestimated, and RBH was determined to make the most of the opportunity.

With the CEO of RBH chairing the "World Cup Steering Committee," the Bafokeng executives (including me, the CEO of the Royal Bafokeng Institute, the head of the RBA's Project Management Office, the CEO of the Health and Human Services Department, the CEO of Royal Bafokeng Sports, the CEO of the Royal Bafokeng Economic Board, the head of the infrastructure planning department, and the head of the Treasury Department) thus sat down to map out our approach for this once-in-a-lifetime opportunity. Through a series of weekly meetings held in Phokeng throughout the second half of 2009 and the beginning of 2010, we established our strategic objectives:

- to rank in the top five venues of the tournament (out of ten)
- to create sixty-five thousand discrete experiences of the World Cup for members of the Bafokeng community[2]
- to generate income for local businesses worth R30 million (USD $4 million) during the tournament
- to generate R250 million (USD 33.3 million) worth of investment, skill, and opportunity for the community within a year of the event

Toward these ends, the Bafokeng Supreme Council (seventy-two hereditary leaders as well as ten elected and appointed councilors, who, together, comprise the community's traditional legislature) authorized funds from the treasury to ensure that the community's short moment in the global spotlight—June 12–28, 2010, to be exact—would yield years, if not decades, of benefits in the form of new investments, both inbound and outbound. The Bafokeng infrastructure department received R700 million (about USD 92 million) to upgrade the Bafokeng Stadium to FIFA standards, build new roads, and design and build a deluxe sports campus featuring a five-star hotel and state-of-the-art training facilities. The Royal Bafokeng Institute received R3.66 million (about USD 480,000) to organize a program for the community's twenty thousand school-age children. Other units within the Bafokeng administration established the first ever trash collection service for the twenty-nine villages, planted trees, trained local entrepreneurs, and established "fan parks" where locals and visitors could watch televised matches live.

Beyond ensuring that the six matches played at Royal Bafokeng Stadium went off without a hitch, with the best possible experiences enjoyed by both local and foreign fans and dignitaries, the bigger objective was to ensure that the world noticed the Royal Bafokeng Nation, and that it would like what it saw. This was an opportunity like no other to influence global business elites: to present the story of a brave and ancient tribe that boasts centuries of strategic, visionary leaders and a forward-looking community that has demonstrated level-headedness in the face of crisis and challenge over and over again. The PR component of the World Cup megaproject was therefore crucial. My role as head of research for the Bafokeng Administration was converted to head of communications and media relations for the duration of the event.[3] My job was, in sum, to research, write, and disseminate "the Bafokeng story" to strategically selected audiences around the world. My department received funds to undertake this work, which included the development and implementation of a PR strategy in partnership with an international PR firm in London, the building of a communications infrastructure, the recruitment and training of a staff of about twenty-five, the establishment of a range of communications platforms and the production of materials ranging from films to books to press releases. It was, in many ways, a conventional corporate communications exercise that aimed to ask and answer two central questions: in this case: "Who are the Bafokeng?" and "What is the Bafokeng story?"

My first task was thus to erect the scaffolding of "the Bafokeng story." Absent any detailed, coherent, or comprehensive sources to work from, my department, together with a team of consultants, commissioned, collated, and synthesized research from historians, archaeologists, anthropologists, and other experts. We held a conference at the University of the Witwatersrand in 2008 where about fifteen South African experts on the history of the Sotho-Tswana peoples, stone-walled construction, the *mfecane*, and its effects on the Transvaal debated the key questions and controversies in Bafokeng history. We soon realized that the most credible academic research on the Bafokeng suggested an origins story that flew in the face of official and received Bafokeng history.

The prevalent migration myth spoke about southward migration from some-where in Central Africa in the eleventh or twelfth century for this branch of the Sotho-Tswana ethnic group, as reflected in this background section on a Facebook page designed by Bafokeng community members:

> Bafokeng (People of the Dew) numbers roughly 300,000 people. About 160,000 live in an area some 150 km North West of Johannesburg, South Africa, with the balance scattered primarily throughout South Africa. They have retained their unique cultural identity and traditional leadership structures and are led by a hereditary Kgosi (king), currently Kgosi Leruo Molotlegi. Bafokeng are descendants of the Sotho-Tswana people that just over a thousand years ago travelled southwards from Central Africa over a period of 200 years. A substantial portion of the people settled in the areas now incorporated into the countries of Botswana and Zimbabwe. Bafokeng, however, continued traveling South before finally settling in the 12th century in an area known as the Rustenburg Valley where the community remained relatively stable.[4]

But contemporary archaeologists argue that Bafokeng arrived from the south, not the north and that their "cluster," which included the forebears of today's Bafokeng, Batlhokwa, and Bapoo (but not other Tswana merafe), introduced stone-walled construction to the highveld, as well as specific aesthetic devices and building patterns (Hall et al. 2008; Huffman 2007). The Bafokeng origin myth was, from where I sat amid previously produced logos, letterheads, and glossy trifolds, more a reflection of colonial and apartheid-era ideologies of eth-nic identity than a story based on rigorous research. Mandated to design the World Cup PR campaign around the most credible research available, I requested that the date cited on official Bafokeng materials be changed from 1140 to 1450. Without further ado, three hundred years were erased from official branding. My team and I then undertook to introduce the new historical findings into the story being produced for local and, crucially, international audiences. We com-missioned two books and a feature-length documentary from Totem Media, a "group of collaborators with a passion for innovative educational media find-ing practical solutions in the form of exhibitions, films, books, archives and museums."[5]

Mining the Future: The Bafokeng Story (Royal Bafokeng Administration 2010) is a highly illustrated, easy-to-read history of the community that tells the story of the community with the not-so-subtle punchline: "Your ances-tors worked hard; you should too." The book offers evidence for the group's Nguni roots and proudly depicts the idea that today's Bafokeng, who are presently led by a practicing architect who oversaw the creation of a strategic blueprint for the community's masterplan and who are increasingly known for their state-of-the-art stadium and other impressive infrastructure, are in fact descended from architectural pioneers of the precolonial era who brought stone-walled construction to the area. My department purchased twenty thousand copies of this book, printed both in English and in Setswana, with the intention of distributing it to every school-age child in the community. The second book was *People of the Dew: A History of the Bafokeng of Phokeng-Rustenburg Region, South Africa, from early times to 2000* (Mbenga and Manson 2010). Two South Africa–based historians, Bernard Mbenga and Andrew Manson, were commissioned by the previous kgosi, Lebone II, to write a history of the Bafokeng. The project foundered when Kgosi Lebone II died unexpectedly in 2000. I recommissioned an updated version from the authors, and shored up by some of the newer research discussed earlier, the updated manuscript went to press in 2010 and was released the same year. To date, this book remains the most widely cited academic source on Bafokeng history.

The third project was a full-length documentary film, *Playing the Game the Bafokeng Way* (Totem Media 2010).[6] The Totem Media team made this film for broadcast on South African television, as well as internationally, in the immediate lead up to the World Cup. In the end, broadcast rights for airing on the South African Broadcasting Corporation were only secured in September 2010, but the film aired several times in South Africa, as well as in Lesotho on June 16, 2010, and Fox Sport in the United States on June 11, 2010. The film seeks to answer the question "How did a state-of-the-art soccer stadium end up in a village no one has ever heard of?" Using the "long line of visionary Bafokeng leaders" as its main trope, the film takes viewers on a journey through 150 years of Bafokeng history, ending up on the pitch of the Royal Bafokeng Stadium, the Bafokeng field of dreams.

The title *Playing the Game the Bafokeng Way* cleverly intimated that Bafokeng culture—a unique set of practices, beliefs, and historical achievements (*the Bafokeng way*)—is entirely compatible with, even a metonym for, the game of soccer and perhaps other competitive pursuits such as business and politics. Niall Carroll, the CEO of Royal Bafokeng Holdings, and mastermind of the World Cup strategy, says it very succinctly in the film: "I do sometimes have to pinch myself and say well, you know, how could that be? How could a small community, in a place that nobody has ever heard of, host both the World Cup and the most celebrated football team in the world? And as a result of that, the world will know about Royal Bafokeng. They'll know about the programs that we're trying to achieve. And they will come, we think, and offer skills and money, to help us achieve that."

This trio of texts was designed to coherently and compellingly answer the question that the soccer World Cup would lead the world to ask: Who are the Bafokeng? Emanating from basically the same set of sources and author(iz)ed in concert with one another, the stories are both complementary and aligned to the Nation's goals for itself. Like more conventional research outputs, these works privileged rigor and accuracy, but because all three narratives were produced in the context of a global PR campaign, they intentionally construct a highly sutured representation of Bafokeng history, ethnicity, and identity: that of a group of related families who migrated to the area in search of good grazing land for their cattle sometime around 1450 and who have survived wave after wave of challenge, conquest, and division through strong leadership, strategic partnerships, and a deep and strong asset base in their people, land, and mineral resources.

For the global PR campaign, we took this basic narrative scaffolding and from it developed fully fledged "messaging." I saw this as extending the answer to the question "Who are the Bafokeng?" into an answer to the question: "Why should I care?"

We started by developing an "elevator pitch" designed to align Bafokeng officials around a common narrative:

The Royal Bafokeng Nation: A Forward-Thinking Traditional Community

The Royal Bafokeng Nation is a vibrant African community where tradition meets modernity in Big Five country. Located in the Rustenburg Valley in South Africa's North West Province, the 150,000 people who reside on the Royal Bafokeng Nation's land are beneficiaries of some of the most innovative approaches to development. These include holistic education reform, the use of sport to generate social and economic momentum, and converting dividends from a single mineral resource into the world's leading community-based investment company.

The king of the Royal Bafokeng Nation is Kgosi Leruo T. Molotlegi, 36th in a long line of visionary traditional leaders. Thanks to the pioneering spirit of the king's ancestors, the Bafokeng community owns 1000 km^2 of land situated on part of one of the largest reserves of platinum group metals in the world. PLAN '35, the strategic blueprint for the community's future, aims to uplift an impoverished community, using long-term strategic interventions to create a socially, economically, and environmentally sustainable region true to its African heritage and traditions.

> The Royal Bafokeng Nation enjoys traditional governance, innovative
> social service mechanisms, and world-leading investment strategies; it
> is a model of progressive leadership on the African continent. Bafokeng
> governance combines elected, appointed, and hereditary leaders committed
> to long-term, future-oriented planning.

Quite a mouthful, I know. Like any piece of strategic PR, this one highlights the attributes for which the community's leaders wish to be known, elides controversy and contestation, is demonstrably correct, and contains a compelling "payoff line," or catchy phrase that audiences are meant to remember and repeat: "a forward-thinking traditional community."

The next step was deciding who our key audiences were. And again, although the Bafokeng people were themselves always considered a crucial stakeholder in the quest for reputational advantage, it was the international audiences that we targeted most aggressively. Recall the objectives: to build a strong reputation for Royal Bafokeng as a serious, professional organization that has stood the test of time, to cultivate new business partners, to bring skills and capital to the region in order to support our work on poverty, education, and health. For these reasons, we targeted the audience in the United States, more of whom watched the June 26 match between the United States and Ghana (19.4 million) than watched any of the first five games of the NBA finals that year. We also targeted the British soccer audience, who we knew would take a special interest in the Bafokeng venue. Shrewd planning on the part of the RBH CEO, Niall Carroll, resulted in the English Football Association (FA), the wealthiest and most famous national soccer team on the globe, choosing Phokeng, a virtually unknown village of twenty thousand people, as its base-camp for the duration of the tournament. Reeling from the scandals that emerged from the behavior of the players' "WAGS" (wives and girlfriends) in Baden Baden during the 2006 tournament, coach Fabio Capello was reportedly interested in sequestering the team in an isolated location in South Africa with no distractions to affect the players' performance. Accommodated at the brand-new five-star Royal Marang Hotel, surrounded by the equally brand-new Bafokeng Sports Campus, David Beckham, John Terry, Wayne Rooney, and the other English mega-celebrities of the soccer world were residents of Phokeng from June 3 to June 28, 2010.

Going from being a tiny community known by few outside South Africa to being the epicenter of the English football fan universe, with both mainstream journalists and ethically challenged paparazzi pouring into Phokeng to get exclusive coverage of the team's African experience, the Bafokeng moment in the spotlight was not without its risks. The British sports journalists who cover the World Cup—renowned for their relentless pursuit of soccer-related celebrity gossip, scandal, and wild fabrications—were a worrying prospect for me and my staff. Could we convince them to depict Bafokeng people as something other than tribal savages living under an outdated form of patriarchal rule, a panorama of ancient human origins as backdrop for their modern sporting gods?

Anticipating that the default Western narrative of Africa as backward would be implicit in much of the media coverage, our PR campaign took a proactive stance in its messaging: "Bafokeng" became the paradoxical signifier of the African World Cup. Chaotic? Bafokeng are organized. Primitive? The Royal Bafokeng Nation is sophisticated and cutting edge. Corrupt? The Bafokeng Nation and its business entities are accountable and transparent. Isolated/marginal? The Royal Bafokeng stadium is at the heart of the action (embodied by the British FA).

These values (organized, sophisticated, accountable, influential)—were woven through the entire campaign and were linked to specific messages around education, business, and leadership. We saturated every media release, fact sheet, news conference, interview, tweet, and post during the tournament with these ideas. In a tactic designed to preemptively take the campaign to the British audience, we organized a media tour of England for the Bafokeng kgosi just weeks before the World Cup to introduce the English soccer public to their "African home-away-from-home." The bruising three-day schedule involved one-on-one interviews between the king and senior English sports journalists, radio and TV personalities, and photo ops such as the one organized by Getty Images at Wembley Stadium.

Speaking engagements and formal meetings took the kgosi and his entourage to iconic institutions of power, prestige, and tradition: Oxford University, Eton College, and the House of Commons, where the king delivered a lecture entitled "The Royal Bafokeng Nation: A New Formula for Africa" sponsored by the Foreign Policy Centre. In addition to answering questions like "which England player is your favorite?" the king had an opportunity to speak about the Bafokeng Nation's history, goals, and achievements. Once back in Phokeng, my team and I proactively managed the media's access to the Bafokeng Sports Campus, the Royal Bafokeng Stadium, and to the king himself. As an example, the following is a memo I sent to the Office of Kgosi in April 2010 regarding interview requests I hoped Kgosi Leruo would consider (see table 5.1). We issued media releases, hosted press conferences and media tours of the village (including a few by helicopter). We screened *Playing the Game the Bafokeng*

Table 5.1. Interview requests for the kgosi (king) of Royal Bafokeng.

Person	Institution	Media Type	Requested on	Possible Dates for Interview
Alex Perry	*TIME* magazine	Print	April 16	Week of April 26
Jane Flanagan	*Sunday Telegraph* (UK)	Print	April 21	Week of April 26
Robyn Curnow	CNN	TV	April 13	May 1–June 1
Jan Ager	TV2 (Norway)	TV	April 19	May 5, 6
Cheryl Vilakazi	Fuji TV (Japan)	TV	April 9	May 5, 6
Archie Babeile	SABC	TV	April 10	May 5
Kai Feldhaus	*BILD*	Print	March 17	June 8–12
Asmaa Botmi	Arte (French TV Channel)	TV	April 15	June 1–4
Jerome Cazadieu	*L'Equipe* (France)	Print	April 2	June 2–5
John Curtis	Sky Sports News (UK)	TV	April 22	June 3–10

Way on the luxury coaches shuttling VIP guests to and from the matches in Phokeng. We designed and installed an "avenue of *Segosing* [Royalty]" featuring large banners displaying the faces of Bafokeng kings. This project was designed to counter (complement? co-opt?) the ubiquitous and legally protected branding for Coke, Visa, Budweiser, and other official FIFA sponsors.

To ensure that our official messaging was both ubiquitous and accessible, we set up our own call center, and made sure that the FIFA media center at the Bafokeng stadium, and the English FA's media tent at the Bafokeng Sports Campus (always swarming with sports journalists awaiting team-related announcements by Coach Cappello), had endless supplies of our press packs.

On June 26, the last World Cup match played in the Royal Bafokeng Stadium took place. My field notes from that day indicate the sharp shift in activity and focus from the frenzy of preparations and implementation of our strategy to the abrupt and deafening quiet of the final hours of the campaign:

> England play Germany today and it's important for the Bafokeng agenda that England win, because there's a negative story brewing at the Sports Campus regarding some employees who apparently stole items from some of the players' rooms . . . there have been two arrests and it's wrapped up, but from a media and reputational point of view, it is not good. So, an England defeat today would get the pack smelling blood and starting to blame us. . . . But if

they win, everybody will be caught up in the victory story, and I don't think the story about the petty theft will be that interesting.

FIFA TV followed me around yesterday to make me a character in their documentary about the 10 World Cup venues and that was sort of funny 'cause they were like paparazzi.

We also had our last media event of the season. We staged a mock USA vs. Ghana pre-game battle, with Bafokeng U11s playing Bafokeng U13s, which Ghana won, 2–1, foreshadowing the outcome of the big match. We got several news crews there who covered it and broadcast it, and it was a lot of fun. Kgosi showed up and the American embassy came with prizes and I think it was a very successful capstone to the media relations project, which has gone well, and I haven't done the formal assessment—that comes next—but I think it's going to turn out to be one of the major successes of the World Cup for us.[7]

England did, in fact, lose to Ghana later that day, and the press did make a meal out of the thefts that occurred at the Sports Campus. But once the English team left on June 28, the Bafokeng Nation was no longer in the public eye, and I myself flew home to the United States to take a vacation. In terms of "the Bafokeng agenda," referenced in my notes, it was indeed a major success. Toward the aim of gaining general exposure, networking with potential new partners, and diversifying the community's business portfolio away from overdependence on Platinum Group Metals, the World Cup PR campaign was an unqualified success. The Bafokeng story became a favorite for sports and feature writers looking for local interest pieces. *TIME* magazine published three stories about the Royal Bafokeng Nation during the tournament, and the *New York Times* published two. We counted twenty-four thousand print stories mentioning the Bafokeng community, including about thirty "set pieces"(in-depth articles that go to great lengths to "tell the story"). The London-based PR company that assisted me and my team, College Hill, won a global media award—the Holmes Report EMEA Sabre PR Award—for their work on the campaign, which they called "Beyond Platinum: Presenting a Nation's Plans for Development."

Negative coverage included hysterical and racist articles in British tabloids intended to stir controversy regarding the English Football Association's choice of base camp, as well as several investigative stories critical of the Bafokeng administration, royal family, and development plans.[8] These were far-outnumbered by coverage that adopted the framework of "a forward-thinking traditional community."

The World Cup drew the Bafokeng into closer cooperation with foreign diplomatic missions, in particular those from the United States, England, Australia, New Zealand, and Japan, and facilitated friendships with countless high-profile visitors, including Queen Rania of Jordan, Princess Takamado of Japan, and US vice president Joe Biden. The National Basketball Association decided to partner with the Bafokeng Nation in late 2010 as part of its strategy to grow the game of basketball and the NBA brand in South Africa. Dr. Timothy Shriver, Global Chairperson of Special Olympics, invited the Royal Bafokeng Nation to host a Special Olympics event in 2012, based on his visit to the community in 2010. The Marriott Corporation sent a delegation to Phokeng in 2011 to look at the Royal Marang Hotel at the Bafokeng Sports Campus, with the idea of acquiring it for its southern Africa collection of properties. The Florida Seminole Tribe, owners of Hard Rock International, invited investment analysts from Royal Bafokeng Holdings to Hollywood Florida in October 2010 to pitch a large tribe-to-tribe investment in Hard Rock.

In short, the word got out and Royal Bafokeng Holdings soon had a wide range of new potential investment partners. Compared to 2006, when RBH's investment portfolio was 85 percent mining and 15 percent other sectors, the proportions are now reversed, with 85 percent invested in nonplatinum assets and only 15 percent tied to mining.[9] On a graphic in its 2016 Annual Report, RBH refers to the period 2010–13 as the time when "diversification grows as excess capital [is] invested in non-platinum assets," a process enabled, or at least facilitated, by the reputational boost that the Royal Bafokeng Nation enjoyed as a result of the World Cup.

Could the Nation's excess financial capital have been invested so successfully without the cultural capital represented by the Bafokeng story? The 2016 Annual Report suggests not. It states, as part of "our value statement," that "the RBN has a long history of wanting a better future for its people and taking innovative action to achieve it. Its leaders' efforts to protect and gain access to the national's hard-won wealth made it possible to foresee a future for the Bafokeng people as a progressive, dynamic and thriving community" (Royal Bafokeng Holdings Annual Review 2016, 3). To reflect for a moment on this remarkable sentence, an arguably historically accurate, if highly condensed, summary of centuries of battles over Bafokeng land becomes the seed of the tribe's future prosperity. Bafokeng history, in other words, makes Royal Bafokeng Holdings possible. Put another way, this ethnic corporation could *only* find outlets for its excess capital by commodifying its culture. What is remarkable in this instance is the unique combination of serendipity, scale, and a sophisticated strategy. With assets under management of around

4 billion South African rands, RBH's challenge was to rapidly establish itself as a known quantity in South Africa and beyond. To position itself as a leading community-based investment company. To engender trust and elicit admiration. The Bafokeng deliberately harnessed the stage provided by the world's largest sporting event to both force the question: "Who are these people?" and to then saturate global audiences with the answer. Both exotic and yet somehow familiar, the Bafokeng story was beamed out to billions of viewers, embedded in classically heroic tropes subtly burnished with the patina of old money values. The Royal Bafokeng Nation (and particularly its stewards of "excess capital") thus garnered the exposure, credibility, and familiarity required to scale new heights of ethnicity, inc.

It is not as though they hadn't tried—or succeeded, albeit on a smaller scale—before. When Kgosi Lebone II was dubbed "the CEO of Bafokeng, Inc.," in 1999 and his brother Leruo generated the same headline shortly after becoming kgosi in 2000 (Comaroff and Comaroff 2009), the nation was already making a concerted effort to commodify its story. Recall that Kgosi Lebone commissioned the first version of the history book that I brought to completion in 2010. The shields, crests, and logos that were redesigned and redeployed for the World Cup campaign had been put together previously by a communications staff who worked without any coherent strategy. Before 2010, the Bafokeng website was understood mostly as tool to communicate to the local Bafokeng diaspora.

Perhaps the most concerted attempt to brand the nation and disseminate its story took place in the context of Kgosi Leruo's enthronement in 2003. A documentary film about Bafokeng history, complete with dramatic reconstructions of Kgosi Mokgatle's land purchasing program, was commissioned and screened at a black tie gala dinner the night before the enthronement ritual. The new king's inauguration speech took as its starting point not his plans to corporatize and modernize the community but rather the values and lessons embedded in Bafokeng history (see Cook and Hardin 2013 for a full analysis of this event).

As important as these attempts to package Bafokeng identity in iconographic and narrative form were to local audiences, none of them came close to the systematic, integrated, full-scale PR campaign that was rolled out for global media consumption in 2010. Billions of viewers, tens of thousands of print stories, countless TV, radio, and social media mentions: the scale of the exposure for the Bafokeng Nation was simply unprecedented.

If I've underanalyzed the local audience's response to the PR campaign, it's because the local audience simply wasn't core to the strategy. The books and film designed to present Bafokeng history were met with broad approval by local Bafokeng. Anecdotally, when "Playing the Game the Bafokeng Way" aired on South African TV, some in the community didn't like the narrator's clothing (contemporary African) or accent (American-inflected). Some complained that there was too much focus on the capital village, Phokeng, and not enough on the other, smaller villages. Some people interviewed for *Mining the Future* wondered why they were not receiving royalties from the project.

Antiroyalist elements in the community were offended by the idea of a corporate communications approach to telling the "Bafokeng story." Skepticism about the motives of those in power who seek to package, polish, and promote the identity of the entire ethnic group is appropriately rooted in questions like: Whose interests are being served by such a campaign? Whose are being marginalized? What's being hidden, smoothed out, or covered up in the process? Many assumed that only elites, foreigners, or the royal family stood to gain from such an investment. While attempts were made to engage these critics and respond to their questions and concerns, persistent poverty in much of the community led many to feel disheartened by the amount of money spent on the World Cup, with little apparent benefit to the people whose "story" was briefly celebrated across the globe. While it is not within the scope of this chapter to examine the wealth distribution model of the Bafokeng, this is a topic of extensive scholarly debate (see Cook 2011, 2013; Kriel 2010; Mnwana 2014, 2015; Capps 2010).

The local critiques of the World Cup PR campaign were also related to a broader set of concerns around chieftaincy/traditional governance/communal land administration. Some argued that ethnicity, culture, and identity are forms of patrimony that belong to the people in the villages, not to the officials sitting in offices. Especially not foreign, white ones. To wit, this Facebook post:

> Bakgatlha Ba Kgafela ba ilo re feta mo tseleng ga re ka seka ra ikela tlhoko. [Gloss: Bakgatlha (a neighboring Tswana community) are going to surpass us if we don't watch out.] Our history and culture is under attack from some elements disguising as historians and anthropologists. Its [*sic*] rewritten to serve certain agendas. We must celebrate our history like other people. . . . Some elements . . . are distorting our history. Our history will only be better told by us. We can't have outsiders telling us where we come from.[10]

Where does this leave those without the power to author-ize a commodified version of their culture and history and where does it leave those *with* that power, including me? The Comaroffs make the important point that "the commercialization of identity . . . does *not* necessarily cheapen it or reduce it to a brute commodity. Quite the opposite: marketing what is 'authentically

Tswana' is also a mode of reflection, of self-construction, of *producing* and *feeling* Tswana-ness" (2009, 9). Replace "Tswana" and "Tswana-ness" with "Bafokeng" and "Bafokeng-ness" and most inhabitants of the Royal Bafokeng Nation would heartily agree. A Bafokeng Digital Archive and Bafokeng Heritage Route both came out of the historical research conducted in the context of the World Cup and plans were hatched to open a Bafokeng Museum at some point. All three of these projects contain ample space for crowdsourced histories that may well contest or contradict the more sutured version used as the basis for the World Cup campaign.

As an anthropologist, I accepted the job of producing and promoting a unitary, noble, and widely accessible "Bafokeng story" for the widest possible audience. This project was not undertaken in the mode of an academic advisor to a local leader (like Malinowski's work for King Sobhuza II of Swaziland) or even Kelly Askew's work as a cultural consultant on the set of the film *The Ghost and the Darkness*, where she tried to ensure that representations of Samburu or Maasai culture in the film weren't inaccurate (or, when they were, not harmful or insulting) (Askew 2004). I was, rather, empowered by the community's leaders to become an author, not just a reteller or packager, of that story, and as Askew rightly points out, "The invention of tradition does not come easy to an anthropologist" (2004, 42).

Although this task forced me to abandon the kind of polyvocality I would privilege in a purely ethnographic project in favor of a more omniscient and heroic narrative, I also welcomed the opportunity to shine a spotlight on the deep inequality bequeathed to South Africa by centuries of colonial rule. To suggest to an audience numbering in the billions that Africans are not "backward" and that traditional forms of governance aren't inherently corrupt or despotic; to raise awareness about the ways in which rural villages in the global South are impacted by global mining operations; this was truly a unique and important opportunity for which I was willing to knowingly elide certain local controversies.

In the process, I found out that having the (economic, political, and positional) power to authorize a "Bafokeng story"—as a researcher, writer of speeches and press releases, executive editor of books and films, and chief steward of the Bafokeng brand—enabled me to influence the way Bafokeng people see themselves, and the way they are seen by others, at least for a time. Influence should not be mistaken for control, however. How those reports, speeches, books and films are received, interpreted, and recirculated over time, is critically important. Voices of contestation abound in the Royal Bafokeng Nation, and both ad hoc and institutionalized platforms for dissent are part of the overall picture that emerges of this small rural community. In the particular context of the FIFA World Cup, however, the goal of seizing a global audience that knew nothing of the Bafokeng, and tailoring a simplified narrative for the purposes of capturing their interest, far outweighed any imperative to win local hearts and minds. And perhaps this portends the next chapter in the phenomenon of ethnicity, inc. Once ethnicity is codified as legal entity (corporatized), and culture is inevitably reduced/elevated to commodity, all in the interest of capital (expanding it, disposing of its excess), what happens when ordinary people newly defined as "shareholders" take seriously their "ownership" of the means of identity production: ethnicity and culture? Will this "forward-looking traditional community" look (forward) to the levers of shareholder activism rather than traditional subjecthood or democratic citizenship, to draw attention to failing schools, soaring unemployment, and uneven resource distribution? Will share capital become less patient, demanding changes in corporate strategy and dividend distribution or perhaps the option of cashing out—converting their ethnic shares into cash? Less metaphor than future likelihood, the path of ethnicity, inc., has not yet reached it legal limits, at least not on the Bafokeng field of play.

NOTES

1. See "Almost Half the World Tuned In at Home to Watch 2010 FIFA World Cup South Africa™," 2010 FIFA World Cup South Africa™, July 11, 2011, http://www.fifa.com/worldcup/news/y=2011/m=7/news=almost-half-the-world-tuned-home-watch-2010-fifa-world-cup-south-africat-1473143.html.

2. "Discrete experiences" refers to individual tickets to matches or fan parks (outdoor viewing venues) distributed throughout the Bafokeng villages, as opposed to saying that sixty-five thousand Bafokeng (half the community) would have access to the matches.

3. As an executive in the Royal Bafokeng Administration, I had dual reporting lines: I reported to the acting CEO of the administration on administrative matters and to the kgosi and his Supreme Council on policy matters. In the context of the World Cup mega-project, I also reported in to the administration's Project Management Office and the World Cup Steering Committee. My team, at its most elaborated, consisted of around twenty-five full-time staff members, interns, and volunteers, most ethnic Bafokeng and many with advanced degrees.

4. See Royal Bafokeng Public Facebook Group, "About This Group" section, accessed March 9, 2012, https://www.facebook.com/groups/8340094333/.

5. See Totem Media's website, http://www.totem-media.net.

6. See Totem Media, 2010, *Playing the Game the Bafokeng Way*, documentary film, accessed December 29, 2016, http://www.youtube.com/watch?v= AeupN4bVD1U.

7. Author's field notes June 27, 2010.

8. For the former, see, in particular, "World Cup 2010: Is There a Snake in the Grass? England's World Cup Base Surrounded by Killer Pythons and Deadly Black Mambas," *Sports Mail*, May 24, 2010, http://www.dailymail.co .uk/sport/worldcup2010/article-1280883/WORLD-CUP-2010-Is-snake-grass -Englands-World-Cup-base-surrounded-killer-pythons.html. For the latter, see, for example, British ITV4 aired a segment entitled "The World Cup's Other Battle—for Platinum," featuring interviews with community members involved in a land claim case against the Bafokeng administration, accessed December 29, 2016, http://www.channel4.com/news/the-world-cups-other-battle-for -platinum.

9. Royal Bafokeng Holdings Annual Review, accessed October 28, 2017, http://www.bafokengholdings.com/images/pdf/annualreview2016.pdf.

10. Posted at Royal Bafokeng Public Facebook Group on September 23, 2011, accessed September 2, 2012, https://www.facebook.com/groups/8340094333/. My translation.

REFERENCES

Askew Kelly. 2004. "Striking Samburu and a Mad Cow." In *Off Stage / On Display: Intimacy and Ethnography in the Age of Public Culture*. Stanford: Stanford University Press.

Breutz, P. L. 1953. *The Tribes of Rustenburg and Pilanesberg Districts*. Pretoria: Government Printer.

———. 1989. *A History of the Batswana and Origin of Bophuthatswana: A Handbook of a Survey of the Tribes of the Batswana, S. Ndebele, Qwaqwa and Botswana*. Pretoria: Breutz.

Capps, Gavin. 2010. "Tribal-Landed Property: The Political Economy of the Bafokeng Chieftaincy, South Africa, 1837–1994." PhD diss., London School of Economics and Political Science.

Coertze, R. D. 1988. *Bafokeng Family Law and Law of Succession*. Pretoria: SABRA.

Comaroff, Jean, and John L. Comaroff. 1991. *Of Revelation and Revolution*. Vol. 1, *Christianity, Colonialism, and Consciousness in South Africa*. Chicago: University of Chicago Press.

Comaroff, John L., and Jean Comaroff. 1997. *Of Revelation and Revolution*. Vol. 2, *The Dialectics of Modernity on a South African Frontier*. Chicago: University of Chicago Press.

———. 2009. *Ethnicity, Inc*. Chicago: Chicago University Press.

Cook, Susan E. 2005. "Chiefs, Kings, Corporatization, and Democracy: A South African Case Study." *Brown Journal of World Affairs* 12 (1):125–37.

———. 2011. "The Business of Being Bafokeng: The Corporatization of a Tribal Authority in South Africa." With CA comments by Steven J Bohlin and Robert L Gips. Supplement, *Current Anthropology* 52 (S3): S151–59.

———. 2013. "Community Management of Mineral Resources: The Case of the Royal Bafokeng Nation." *Journal of the Southern African Institute of Mining and Mettalurgy* 113 (1): 61–66.

Cook, Susan E., and Rebecca Hardin. 2013. "Performing Royalty in Contemporary Africa." *Cultural Anthropology* 28 (2): 227–51.

Gulbrandsen, Ornulf. 1995. "The King Is King by the Grace of the People: The Exercise and Control of Power in Subject-Ruler Relations." *Comparative Studies in Society and History* 37 (3): 415–44.

Hall, Simon, Mark Anderson, Jan Boeyens, and Francois Coetzee. 2008. "Towards an Outline of the Oral Geography, Historical Identity and Political Economy of the Late Precolonial Tswana in the Rustenburg Region." In *Five Hundred Years Rediscovered*, edited by Natalie Swanepoel, Amanda Esterhuysen, and Philip Bonner, 55–85. Johannesburg: Wits University Press.

Huffman, Thomas. 2007. *Handbook of the Iron Age: The Archaeology of the Pre-Colonial Farming Societies of Southern Africa*. Pietermaritzburg: University of KwaZulu-Natal Press.

Kriel, Inge. 2010. "Bafokeng, Inc. Power of the National/Corporation Amalgam." *Anthropology Southern Africa* 33 (1–2): 44–54.

Landau, Paul S. 1995. *The Realm of the Word: Language, Gender, and Christianity in a Southern African Kingdom*. Portsmouth, NH: Heinemann.

Legassick, Martin. 1969. "The Sotho-Tswana Peoples before 1800." In *African Societies in Southern Africa*, edited by Leonard Thompson, 86–125. New York: Praeger.

Mnwana, Sonwabile. 2014. "Mineral Wealth—'In the Name of *Morafe*'? Community Control in South Africa's Platinum Valley." *Development Southern Africa* 31 (6): 826–42.

———. 2015. "Democracy, Development and Chieftaincy along South Africa's 'Platinum Highway': Some Emerging Issues." *Journal of Contemporary African Issues* 33 (4): 510–29.

Mbenga, Bernard, and Andrew Manson. 2010. *People of the Dew: A History of the Bafokeng of Phokeng-Rustenburg Region, South Africa, from Early Times to 2000*. Johannesburg: Jacana Media.

Royal Bafokeng Administration. 2010. *Mining the Future: The Bafokeng Story*. Johannesburg: Jacana Media.

Royal Bafokeng Holdings. 2016. Annual Review. http://www.bafokengholdings .com/images/pdf/annualreview2016.pdf.

Schapera, Isaac. 1943. *Tribal Legislation among the Tswana of the Bechuanaland Protectorate: A Study in the Mechanism of Cultural Change*. London: Lund Humphries.

———. 1952. *The Ethnic Composition of Tswana Tribes*. London: London School of Economics and Political Science.

Schapera, Isaac, and John L. Comaroff. 1991. *The Tswana*. Rev. ed. London: Kegan Paul International.

Totem Media. 2010. *Playing the Game the Bafokeng Way*. Documentary film. https://www.youtube.com/watch?v=AeupN4bVD1U.

Wylie, Diana. 1990. *A Little God: The Twilight of Patriarchy in a Southern African Chiefdom*. Hanover, CT: Wesleyan University Press.

SUSAN E. COOK is Project Manager for Cultural Initiatives in the Division of Social Science at Harvard University.

SIX

THE HUNTER HYPE

Producing "Local Culture" as Particularity in Mali

DOROTHEA E. SCHULZ

IN 2008, WHILE DOING RESEARCH on productions of culture on Malian state television, I attended a performance event in the town Manantali in southwestern Mali, organized by the National Hunters Association (Fédération des Chasseurs du Mali), a cultural organization dedicated to the promotion of cultural activities by hunters. In the different societies of southern Mali, hunters (*donsow*, sing. *donson*[1]) form a distinct social identity. The performance event featured the singer Bala Guimba Diakité, who, from his discovery by national television in the early 2000s until his demise in 2012, was one of the nation's most renowned hunters' musicians (sing., *donson jeli*).[2] Dressed in the typical hunters' garb, a combination of handspun and handwoven cotton trousers and a knee-length shirt to which various animal body parts and other power objects were attached, Bala Guimba moved back and forth in front of us, the audience, singing and playing the *donson ngoni*, a six-string harp, accompanied by two assistant instrumentalists, two men of about thirty years. Moving alongside with him were the cameraman and sound technician who covered the song performance for a documentary to be featured on state television. At one moment, as Bala Guimba passed by, once again stamping the dusty soil and muttering unintelligible phrases as part of his song performance, I overheard an exchange between two older men, who were sitting behind me. Clad in the handwoven apparel that indicated their identity as hunters, they complained to each other that one of Bala Guimba's assistant musicians lacked the necessary qualifications and "clearly had paid for the little knowledge he had" and that this revealed the "sorry state of affairs of hunters' knowledge being passed on for pay."

A few weeks later, I followed the first screening of the documentary on national television in the capital, Bamako, together with my host family, who hail from another rural area of southern Mali. Father and mother, both of them in their late fifties, were visibly thrilled by Bala Guimba's performance. Prompted by my questions, the father observed: "It does not count whose ethnic traditions these are. Fula, Maninka, Bamana, we are all the same. This program teaches us about other people's local traditions. I love to hear Bala Guimba sing, although I grasp little of its meanings. Bala Guimba has a real professional ethos, he does not sing for money. These are the genuine [yèrèyèrè, literally, "truly own"] songs of his locality [kabila³]."

The first episode brings into focus debates among hunters over authority credentials, their acquisition and transmission. It highlights concerns of senior hunters about the transmission of "genuine" knowledge and the corrosive effects of its monetization. The second anecdote shows that to urban television audiences, hunters' musicians articulate genuine local culture. Both episodes present hunters' musicians and their musical performance as the epitome of remote rural culture. They reveal a full disregard of the thoroughly mass-mediated nature of the performance event and a striking lack of concern about the altering influence of state television, media technologies, and mass entertainment. In contrast to a scholarly commonplace, consumers of hunters' music in Mali do not seem to consider mass mediation to introduce a significant break between a genuine cultural performance and its mass-mediated offshoot. Yet they highlight money, and hence commodification, as factors of change and distortion of genuine local culture.

This peculiar conception of the relation between commodification, mass mediation, and the performance—and indeed production—of local culture prompts me to take up two arguments advanced by John and Jean Comaroff in *Ethnicity, Inc.* (2009): first, about the renewed significance of ethnicity as a mode of framing identity, difference, and belonging, a mode whose particular phenomenal forms are characteristic of the contemporary moment, and, second, that ethnicity's ever-growing significance is intricately related to, and effected through, intertwining processes of commodification, incorporation, and juridification, all of which enable collectivities to take on a corporate identity. Theirs is an emphasis on the intricate relation between the making and marketing of identities, as the basis for self-identification and self-construction and for being recognized by others as a group with distinct (cultural) features.

By conceiving of ethnicity as both a modality and a result of differentiation processes in which claims to one's culture play a central role, John and Jean Comaroff sideline earlier efforts to reconcile opposed, primoridalist, and constructionist understandings of ethnicity. Their interest in ethnicity as an emically relevant category of identification opens up highly productive perspectives for the study of ethnicity's lived manifestations under historically and socially determinate circumstances, of the connotations it carries and the practices in which it congeals, and of the peculiar modalities by which ethnic identity claims unfold their affective effects. Their perspective helps make sense of my host's remark, which posited that "local culture" prevails over ethnic identity as the primary marker of identity and belonging and, hence, that in Mali, identity claims are made not in the name of ethnic difference but by reference to the local, as the site of self-making, self-appreciation, and affectively charged belonging. Notably, my host appears to contradict the scholarly argument that as a consequence of recent restructuring of forms of state power, in sub-Saharan Africa and beyond, ethnicity plays a principal role in contemporary politics of citizenship and belonging.

Jean and John Comaroff's conception of ethnicity as a signifier of difference that, although certainly not empty, encapsulates varying phenomenal qualities and affective connotations allows me to move beyond the apparent opposition between ethnic identity as a primarily socially and culturally encoded frame of reference and the category of the local, with its marked spatial overtones. I will show how in Mali's postcolonial history, the two categories have emerged as partly overlapping, rather than mutually exclusive, parameters of framing particularity and difference. Conceived in this way, the meanings of *the local* are not necessarily or primarily defined in territorial terms; they are constantly produced and reproduced in their relation to other social settings and constructions of locality (Appadurai 1996, 178–79).[4]

To explain why locality, rather than ethnicity, has become the dominant metaphor to frame identities in Mali, I will start by tracing the objectification process that, since colonial times, has made culture a key terrain of essentialized difference and invites current identifications of hunters' musicians with local culture.

CONTROL, CIVILIZE, CULTURALIZE: CULTURE AS A MARKER OF HARMLESS DIFFERENCE

Similar to the rationale of colonial administration elsewhere, French colonial policy in the Soudan Français importantly contributed to the construction and reification of ethnic identities and boundaries (Amselle and M'Bokolo 1985; see Vail 1989). Still, in contrast to territories central to the French colonial economy, where the Politique des Races rested on an ethnicized discourse on politicoeconomic inequality, in the Soudan Français, ethnicity (or tribalism) was less important in justifying unequal treatment.[5] Only slowly were these terms integrated into local repertoires of marking and claiming social difference, repertoires that understood identity as flexible and mobile in time and space (Amselle 1990). Except for areas of northern Mali, where the racial distinction between "white" masters and their "black slaves" played a significant role, regional origin, clan affiliation, social status, language, and occupation remained the most important criteria of social identification.

In line with their view of the French colonial mission as an educational and civilizing endeavor, colonial administrators referred to *culture* and its terminological affiliates *custom* (*coûtume*) and *mores* (*moeurs*) to point to what they saw as the essence of colonized subjects and of essential differences between them and the civilized world.

The French conception of *La Culture* as the essence of a people was taken up by Mali's first president, Modibo Keita, himself a product of the French *mission civilisatrice*. Yet whereas French colonial policy had posited a contrast between French civilization and brutish Africans' lack of culture and civility, President Keita and his US-RDA Party were at great pains to demonstrate the historicity of African political and cultural achievements. Sharing founding assumptions of Senghor's negritude discourse in neighboring Senegal, US-RDA Party ideologues conceived of African culture as both a material form and a spiritual essence that needed to be salvaged from the contamination by occidental values and would enable Africans to overcome the "inferiority complex" instilled by colonial rule (Kouyaté 1963; see Snyder 1967).[6] The promotion of culture thus formed a cornerstone of the US-RDA's modernization project.[7]

However, ironically, as much as the US-RDA Party viewed culture as an antidote to the intellectual estrangement prompted by French colonization, it perpetuated the colonial ideological role of culture in justifying unequal treatment of different colonized peoples. Specifically, Keita's government explained the resistance of freeborn, racially "white" clans in the country's north to their forceful integration into the Malian state as a sign of their "stubborn" character and pride, in terms reminiscent of the French colonial lending of mentality, culture, and race as criteria of difference. This rhetoric concealed the violent repression and forceful sedentarization of freeborn Tuareg clans and a policy of ruthless persecution and extinction of those resisting state security forces. It also marked the beginnings of a decades-long political and economic marginalization of Mali's northern regions that continued under subsequent governments, only to be interrupted by separatist "revolts" in which the three confederations of freeborn and noble Tuareg—the Kel Adagh (Kidal), the Illewemedian (Gao) and the Kel Antsar (Timbuktu)—played a role.[8]

THE OBJECTIFICATION OF TRADITION AND CULTURE

To draw on culture as a source of nationalist pride, state officials first had to create it, along with tradition (see Handler 1988). This creation involved a double process of objectification. One was essentially a process of abstraction, of positing the existence of a sociopolitical entity, the Malian nation, whose distinctiveness resided in its culture. The second process of objectification involved the selective identification of practices, objects, and expressive forms as characteristic features of the culture of the Malian nation.[9]

Whereas during the independence struggle, US-RDA Party activists had privileged Franco-African theater as the primary means of political mobilization, after independence, music, dance, and oral tradition became the main expressive forms to target Mali's rural populations, on state radio and public holidays and during biannual youth festivals (Semaine de la Jeunesse).[10] Out of the state-orchestrated making of national culture, a particular notion of tradition emerged. As a term that lacks an equivalent in Malian national languages, the French term *tradition* became a correlate to *culture*, denoting expressive genres, "ways of doing," and practices situated in a mythical past populated by heroic ancestors and empires.[11] Although the staging of culture and tradition was intended to gloss over the nation's internal divisions, it involved a highly contested process of culture making (Nédélec 1992). The logics of competition inherent in the youth festivals prompted the standardization of certain formats of presentation that made these activities legible as instances of regional culture, while simultaneously transforming their form and content (Djebbari 2013, 297).[12]

From the outset, there was a tension in the US-RDA Party's project of forging a national culture. On one side, Malian national culture was implicitly aligned with the expressive forms and political histories of the Bamanakan- and Maninkakan-speaking populations from southern Mali (Schulz 2001, 2007a). On the other side, US-RDA rhetoric celebrated regional cultural diversity, as an effort to encompass internal heterogeneity by alluding to the nation's "diversity in unity" (see Apter 2005). Diversity was constructed in a particular way. Similar to the mapping of ethnic diversity by Zambian state radio (Spitulnik n.d., 231–33), Mali's regional populations were constructed as "equally different" (231)—that is, as different in the same way. To collapse ethnic identity into harmless cultural difference meant to belittle exclusionary mechanisms (justified as mere technicalities) and "euphemize" (Bourdieu 1977) region-based political and economic inequalities. Communication policy mirrored the systematic cultural, economic, and political marginalization of Mali's northern regions, a policy that was by and large maintained under Modibo Keita's successor, President Moussa Traoré (1968–1991).[13]

Even for Maninkakan- and Bamankan-speaking audiences, whose oral and political traditions were privileged in official celebrations, the ruling party's efforts to foster attachment to a shared, national culture did not resonate with their own inclination for particularistic identities.[14] Still, to these select audiences, the broadcasting of national culture initiated a process in the course of which they started to view themselves as members of a broader collectivity, the nation (Schulz n.d., chap. 3).

Starting in the mid-1980s, along with the neoliberal restructuring of the national economy under Traoré's presidency, the commodification of expressive forms fueled an emergent national and international market of art, artisanal products, and, most significantly, Malian music. A notable illustration of this development is the commodification of *jeli* praise. Conventionally performed by a particular socioprofessional group (the *jeliw*, singular, *jeli*) as a client service on behalf of freeborn patrons, it was initially (under Modibo Keita) promoted as emblematic of Malian tradition. Starting in the 1970s, jeli praise increasingly became a commodity purchased by any rich and influential person able to generously remunerate the singer (Diawara 1994; Keita 1995; Schulz 2001, chap. 6).[15] Listeners from the Bamana and Maninka cultural realm made sense of this process by contrasting paid praise to its delivery as a disinterested gift to a patron and by arguing that this client service preserved its "deep meanings" as long as it remained untainted by the corrupting effects of money (Schulz 1998).

The commodification of jeli performances fostered generic formats and styles of praise, deemphasized references to specific family identities and histories, and strengthened the association of jeli praise with national culture rather than with specific ethnic identities. Other instances of commodified culture, such as the fabric *bogolan* and the related fashion style "Chris Seydou" were similarly marketed, not as expressions of specific ethnic identities, but as emblems of Malian culture and of African authenticity (Schulz 2007b; Rovine 2008).

Official celebrations of a nation united by a common cultural heritage clashed with the experiences by northern populations of their persistent economic and political marginality.[16] Their recollection of the state's bloody, ruthless suppression of secessionist attempts by freeborn and noble Tuareg clans (see Lecocq 2010) contrast sharply with the official narrative of peaceful interaction and free-willed integration that has become, in the national arena, a truly hegemonic version of Malian nationhood.

The failed attempts by noble and freeborn Tuareg clans to resist state encroachment led to two different trajectories of opposition that, starting in the 1990s, gained new momentum. Some groupings organized in the National Movement for the Liberation of Azawad to continue with the long-standing aspiration to create an independent Tuareg nation called Azawad. This political program collapses heterogeneous social status groups and clan identities into the ethnic category Tuareg. Other freeborn Tuareg leaders cast their opposition to the central state in a religious idiom (Lecocq and Schrijver 2007) and occupied vast areas of the north after the toppling of President Amadou Toumani Touré (2001–2012) in March 2012. Although pushed back by French and international forces in January 2013, their effort to reform society, domestic life, and the political order in accordance with Islamic prescripts (*shari'a*) is currently the most successful paradigm of ethnopolitical grievances and struggle in the region of Kidal. By presenting the theocratic project as one that unites all "northern people" in their resistance to the Malian state, they downplay the ethnic, racial, and social status specificity of their political agenda (Diallo 2016; Schulz 2016; Schulz and Diallo 2016).[17]

COMMODIFYING LOCAL PARTICULARITY

The onset of multiparty democracy, and the government of President Alpha Konaré (1992–2001) and his party Alliance for Democracy in Mali, prompted the emergence of a diversified market of cultural production.[18] Under a national program of "valorizing culture" (*mise en valeur de la culture*), launched by the Ministry of Culture with the strong support of UNESCO, Mali's different regions and populations were pulled into the same maelstrom of cultural commodification. Key to this process were two political measures, the creation of an infrastructure for ethnotourism and the "festivalisation" (Niang 2014) of local culture—that is, the commercialization of various forms of music and dance and of materials and artifacts during cultural festivals initiated by intellectuals and entrepreneurs from town. The resulting tourist economy targeted various national and international audiences. It furthered the standardization of performance styles and formats of presentation, their objectification as manifestations of Malian cultural creativity, and, finally, the conversion of these practices into a source of income.

Distinctive about the new state-supported valorization of culture is a marked emphasis on *local* culture as the epitome of distinctive *rural* societies, histories, and communities. The new market value of the local is the outcome of a long-standing cultural policy that privileged the promotion of a unifying culture while downplaying—and obscuring—ethnic specificity. As the label "local" rather than "ethnicity" has become the predominant marketing strategy, we can speak of a process of branding local authenticity. Expressive practices and artifacts are now marketed in their capacity to deliver the authentic flair of the local.

Local branding is coterminous with an effort to promote a genuinely Malian or African aesthetics. The common denominator between these two seemingly opposed trends is the centrality of notions of authenticity or genuineness. Regardless of whether cultural practices or artifacts are advertised under the label of the "local" or of a generic African aesthetics, a state-promoted conception of the authentic is still of paramount importance, as an index of market value and as proof of genuine rootedness in local origins.

The new appeal of the local, and its conception as coextensive with the rural, mirrors the restructuring of state-society relations since the late 1980s, prompted, among other processes, through economic reform and administrative decentralization. Starting in the mid-1990s, the creation of new administrative units, the municipalities (*communes*) exacerbated political competition among factions at the communal and intercommunal levels and complicated patronage networks that link local factions to the regional capital and to Bamako (Schulz n.d., chap. 4; see Bierschenk and Olivier de Sardan 2003). Although connections to the central state are still important to gain the upper hand in local political conflicts, vectors of accountability and influence-taking have been partly inverted, as politicians need to cater to the interests of their constituencies back home (see Geschiere 2009, chaps. 6 and 7).

The new valorization of the local-as-rural by government institutions and various cultural initiatives and producers also results from the new entrepreneurial opportunities created by administrative decentralization. To intellectuals from town, the new structures of local government offer a wealth of opportunities for employment and to enter a thriving local industry of aid agency–generated development interventions. Brawls over budgetary autonomy among members of the local and regional administration, and between them and the central state, go hand in hand with calls for greater local autonomy. It is a situation in which struggles over local sovereignty claims hinge on, and simultaneously challenge, the supremacy of the central state. In this situation, governmental efforts to turn culture into a "resource of development" have momentous consequences for conceptions of local tradition, versions of local history, and controversies between local political factions and different generations of men.

WHO'S LOCAL, WHOSE LOCALE?
THE FESTIVAL DE MEDINE

Appadurai (1996, 178–79) has proposed to replace purely spatial and scalar understandings of locality with a relational conception, understanding locality as a "complex phenomenological reality" whose meanings, demarcations and social embedding are constantly produced in the interaction with other settings and practices of producing a sense of locality. This processual conception of locality draws attention to the role of "technologies of interactivity" in specific imaginations of "the local." It also raises the question of how more thoroughly commodified, urban settings and imaginations of locality feed back into productions of local culture in rural settings. The following discussion of a cultural festival's botched marketing of local culture shows the dialectic between rural and urban constructions of locality. A controversial production of locality occurs, in a complex sociopolitical topography structured by multiple scales and vectors of commodification that irreversibly transform the forms and meanings of the local.

The Festival de Medine—organized since 2017 at the castle, or *tata*, of the nineteenth-century kingdom of Dembaya in southwestern Mali—has so far met with limited success. When its organizer, a businesswoman from San (in southeastern Mali) and an outsider to local politics, chose Medine as a platform to "valorize local culture," she chose to ignore the divisive political past associated with the tata and its disruptive potential for the staging of local culture. To descendants of the royal clan of the Dembaya kingdom, the tata symbolizes the center of royal power and past glory. To their local opponents from the kingdom of Logo Sabusère, which resisted colonial occupation and whose tata was razed to the ground by French colonial troops, the Tata de Medine symbolizes the opposite.[19] To them, it is a reminder of Dembaya's treacherous alliance with the French against the kingdom of Sabusèrè.[20]

In organizing the festival, the businesswoman called on tradesmen from Bamako to set up shop and sell their "cultural artifacts" during the festivities. She only invited the elders from the Dembaya clan to join the organization committee and, thus, disregarded the vehemently contested memories attached to the castle and the long-standing resentment between the two clans.[21] After trying in vain to block the festival, the Logo Sabusère royal clan, represented by a youth association,[22] refused to participate, maintaining that the performances they were expected to present during the festival were not part of local culture (which the Dembaya clan had claimed for themselves) but only of their own family history and the kingdom of Logo Sabusèrè.

This reasoning, and the blanket rejection of the local cultural festival by the Dembaya party, illustrates some implications of the commodification of the local through cultural events and through other forms digestible by tourists and other urban middle-class consumers. The commodification of local culture prompts new struggles over local belonging (Geschiere and Nyamnjoh 2001) and over the meanings of *local*—struggles that mirror confrontations or strategic alliances between male seniors and school-educated juniors and competition among entrepreneurs from the area and from town.

The argument of the dissenting Sabusère faction shows that the *local*, not ethnicity, holds special emotive appeal and prevails as the primary trope of particularity claims. Simultaneously, however, the feud renders questionable the very existence of the local as an entity with fixed meanings, and dims down or douses the emotional reverberations that the festival was meant to stage and animate (see Doquet 1996; Schulz n.d., chap. 4).

A similar tension, between the imagination and reification of the local and its concomitant interrogation or erasure, is evident with regard to the cultural forms in which the local is presented and marketed. This marketing requires that certain activities, artifacts and expressive forms are made legible and consumable as instances of local culture or of the local tout court, a translation that requires a process of standardization. For this reason, presenting the local in commodified form, during cultural festivals or on national media, rests on a tension between the assertion of local particularity on one side and, on the other, the simultaneous neutralizing of markers of local particularity through standardized formats of presentation.

This standardization of formats of presentation involves a selection process. Dance steps, songs, and rhythms, which conventionally formed part of initiation rituals, are split off from a larger ensemble of ritual action and are presented to consumers as typically local folklore, music, or cultural performance; other practices and material forms are purposefully withheld from public circulation.[23] This selection process replays, albeit in a different key and to different effects, the process of folklorization prompted by the promotion of national culture under the first president, Modibo Keita, when the standardization of culture similarly involved privileging some expressive forms over others. Both instances demonstrate that selection and standardization are integral to objectification processes. Yet whereas before, the objectification of culture rested primarily on a—largely state-controlled—singling out of certain practices, actors, and material forms, nowadays, objectifying culture needs to adapt to the requirements of mass-mediated circulation and market dynamics. To a greater extent than before, the objectification of culture rests on the standardization of formats of presentation, formats that are crafted on the mode and styles of presenting local tradition on national television.[24] Also, the objectification of culture, now partly decoupled from state directives, is increasingly embedded in a commodity logic that infuses the specific activities, performances, and materials by actors who, located in a continuum of rural-urban connections, produce and consume local culture.

As intimated in the introductory anecdote, the centrality of the commodity logic is reflected in the comments of those who consume local culture, comments that posit essential difference between the "emptiness" of "performances for pay" and the social usefulness and genuinely local nature of non-monetized performances. All of this suggests that whereas ethnicity does not form the prevalent category of mobilization in contemporary Mali, the cultural and economic logics of ethnicity, inc. are indeed operative. They are essential to the emotive appeal and workings of the local. The local is produced by various actors who straddle, and render problematic, the divide between "the rural," as the site where genuine local identity is produced, and its urban consumers. Commodification is essential to the making of local culture yet simultaneously calls into question the existence of the local as a bounded and homogenous social entity by reinforcing divisions within the local population and also reproducing inequalities between different categories of citizen-subjects within the body politic.

PRODUCING LOCAL CULTURE "FROM ABOVE"

What has the mobilizing appeal of the local, and the cultural and economic logics that inform it, to do with changing forms of state power and state-society relations? As elsewhere in sub-Saharan Africa, in Mali a politics of local particularity fostered by administrative decentralization and democratization since the 1990s has reset the conditions for state constructions of citizenship and belonging. Jean and John Comaroff (2004) pointedly refer to these challenges to nation-state politics as a matter of its "hyphen-nation": claims to cultural and religious difference challenge the hyphen that holds together *nation* and *state*. While the link between these terms has always been problematic, nowadays, under conditions of multiparty democracy that invite expressions of dissent and difference, governments are under greater pressure to prove and display the state's efficacy in keeping together a heterogeneous political community.

The new uncertainties of hyphen-nation set new challenges for state cultural politics. Legitimacy for the political order of the nation-state can no longer be achieved through the celebration of shared cultural traditions, and hence through vertical integration, as envisaged by earlier nationalist projects. Instead, governments need to publicly *perform* the state's capacity for horizontal integration and for mending differences through an equitable treatment of its different peoples. In Mali, televised productions of culture vividly illustrate how the governments of Alpha Konaré and his successor, President Touré, have taken up this challenge.

For almost twenty-five years, the television program *Terroir* (from the earth), which stages the "cultural performances," "mores," and "traditions" of (rural) "localities," has enjoyed a remarkable popularity across ages and educational background, and among urban and rural audiences (Schulz 2007a).[25] *Terroir* is produced at the invitation of "villagers from the locale," who, eager to have their own culture broadcast to a national public, cover the production costs. They are assisted by *ressortissants*, urban intellectuals and businessmen who, as natives from the respective localities, often nurture political ambitions and thus have a keen interest in facilitating *Terroir* productions financially and logistically. The ressortissants thus play a central role in connecting villages and local administration to state and nonstate resources in the capital Bamako and in turning *Terroir* into a platform for expressions of local particularity. However, even if *Terroir* is meant to stage the state's equal treatment of its diverse cultural traditions, it features almost exclusively productions from southern and central Mali. The old-standing logic of unequal regional representation prevails, still justified on purely technical and logistical grounds.

The program *Terroir* captures the force of the local, rather than of ethnicity, as the primary frame for representing particularity in Mali.[26] Yet far from instantiating a "politics from below" (Bayart, Mbembe, and Toulabor 1992) prompted by weakened state sovereignty, *Terroir* allows the state to reinvent itself by reasserting its centrality to constructions of local particularity. State media function as a platform and a mediating agent for assertions of local distinctiveness. Thus, paradoxically, local-rural expressions of particularity depend on state institutions and formats of representation from which they seek to set themselves apart.

HUNTERS' MUSICIANS AND GENUINE LOCAL CULTURE

Parallel to the surge in claims to local particularity, since the 1990s a veritable cultural industry has emerged around hunters, leading to the successful marketing of their music, performances, and bodily adornment as tokens of urban consumers' attachment to their rural origins.[27] Hunters' associations are presently mushrooming throughout southern Mali. Inspired by the organizational features of conventional "hunters' groups" (sing., *donson ton*), they integrate new functions related to the urban, ethnically mixed settings in which they operate. In contrast to their counterparts elsewhere in West Africa (Ferme and Hoffman 2004; Leach 2004), Malian hunters' associations intervene primarily in the cultural market (Traoré 2004; Jansen 2008). They claim to valorize culture by hosting musical performances of hunters' musicians. Their self-organization is representative of a broader tendency to 'associationalize' cultural or social activities, in a logic of "incorporation" identified by John and Jean Comaroff (2009) as a correlate to "ethno-commodification." As part of this process of incorporation, hunters and hunter musicians from various southern regions have established themselves as guardians of traditional culture, a culture implicitly associated with Mali's southern oral and musical traditions. The spread of mass-media technologies reinforces this development, allowing musicians to enter a market of commodified hunters' music, where their audio and audiovisual recordings enjoy special popularity among male urbanites.[28]

Conventionally, hunters acquired their notoriously dangerous and beneficial "guarded knowledge" (*dònniya, dònni*)[29] in a years-long apprenticeship with experienced hunters, who, at least ideally, passed on their knowledge not for monetary gain but out of a desire to educate younger men and ensure the continued protection and reproduction of the social and moral order.[30] The same ideal of material disinterest applied to hunters' actual use of their guarded knowledge. Today, the potential for monetary transaction, before entailed in the apprentice-teacher relationship, is more often realized, as many older hunters scramble to make a living from their agricultural activities. They, as well as apprentice hunters, are also interested in the new opportunities of the cultural market to earn some additional cash.

Hunters inspire urban imaginations of the local-as-rural for several reasons.[31] Their physical prowess and esoteric knowledge play a role in many village foundation myths and are a source of personal prestige and family pride. Hunters also personify an ideal of senior masculinity tied to agricultural livelihoods insofar as their occult knowledge allows them to protect humans against the forces of the wilderness. This ideal of masculinity is articulated by hunters' musicians or "hunters' griots" (*donson jeliw*), who, through praise lyrics, singing style, outfit, and bodily display of physical prowess create a multisensory mise-en-scène of what makes a true man. Their songs extol a male ethos built on bravery, endurance, modesty, trustworthiness, and a thirst (*nyinin*) for restricted knowledge of the occult that earns hunters their greatest cachet. A key characteristic of their songs is "hunters' speech" (*donson kuma*), which combines reflections on proper moral conduct with formulaic expressions incomprehensible to the wider public. The opacity of hunters' speech greatly adds to the awe and prestige garnered by hunters' musicians. Their performances take place mainly during the dry season, when agricultural activities come to a standstill and various kinds of musicians and entertainers roam the countryside in search of additional income, generous hosts, and audiences. Whenever hunters' musicians laud individual hunters, they expect a reward in the form of game or some guarded knowledge.

Because hunters' musicians combine entertainment (*njanaje*) and moral edification, they appeal to listeners across the social spectrum.[32] Older listeners are often particularly appreciative of the educational value of hunters' songs, stressing that they strengthen communal cohesiveness and continuity and remind people of the value of respect and material obligation between seniors and juniors. Hunters and hunters' musicians deemphasize particularistic political and social identities and status differences, and instead stress individual achievement and excellence.[33] They therefore invite identification with a rural locale from across the social spectrum. To rural listeners, hunters' musicians articulate notions of locality centered on shared historical experience and that foster a sense of pride in what they consider collective achievements. To urban audiences, on the other hand, hunters' musicians and their performances have a particular affective and aesthetic potential to represent what listeners consider quintessentially rural cultural traditions. The fact the rural traditions articulated by senior hunters are strongly inflected by conventional ideals of male bravery, self-discipline, and power further adds to their appeal, also in the eyes and ears of female urban listeners. The idealized images of male physical prowess may not resonate with their daily experiences with patriarchal power, yet the images nevertheless conjure up a secure traditional social order. What further adds to the popularity of hunters among urban audiences is the aura of threat and mystical danger that surrounds them because of their association with the wilderness and the occult.

There are thus multiple reasons why hunters' musicians have a special potential to epitomize and mediate rural-urban connections and to embody urbanites' affective attachments to an idealized countryside as the locus of genuine social identity. These attachments and imaginations derive additional strength from a situation in which the newly created administrative and political structures and development initiatives of international donors in rural communes offer income opportunities for unemployed family members from town.

The emotive force of hunters' music also needs to be read as a reflection of the growing commodification of cultural expressions of identity and particularity.

I mentioned earlier that conventionally, hunters' guarded knowledge was conceived as an expertise that unfolded its social and moral value in disregard of the monetary profit it could generate. The same idealizing contrast, between the genuine nature of materially disinterested hunters' activities on one side and hunters' performances as their stylistically corrupted and meaningless offshoot on the other, informs the discourse by which hunters position themselves in an increasingly competitive field of cultural production. Senior hunters and hunters' musicians often contrast a true hunter, whose guarded knowledge serves the community, to men who merely employ it for personal monetary gain. They frequently express their concern with the growing tendency to sell guarded knowledge during teaching sessions, in personal reflections on the nature of a good teacher-apprentice relationship, and also in public performances, when they decry the selling of guarded knowledge as a breach of the trustworthiness expected from a man (see Strawn 2011, 96, 296).

With this sinister portrayal, senior hunters attribute the practice of selling or buying guarded knowledge to younger men and assert their own seniority in knowledge and moral authority. Younger hunters, in turn, not only stress the genuineness of their own mystical expertise during performances but intimate (usually in indirect and very generalizing terms) that some senior hunters refuse to pass on their knowledge unless they receive monetary compensation. In short, senior and junior hunters denounce the commodification of culture as a matter of both moral and stylistic corruption. All these allegations reveal considerable competition between seniors and a younger generation of men who have less time and opportunities to learn guarded knowledge and thus fear being excluded from the reproduction of ideals of male sociality, honor, and responsibility. The complaints can also be read as a critical commentary on the increasingly competitive nature of performing hunters' music for urban consumers (see Strawn 2011, 114–15).

The ambivalent assessment of hunters' music forms part of a broader commentary on the growing commodification of social services and cultural practices that hunters' musicians and their audiences associate with urban life. Simultaneously, however, hunters' musicians benefit from this denouncement of the "corrupted" nature of commodified cultural performances. To many urban listeners, the touch of a genuine, uncorrupted culture still inheres to hunters' music, regardless of the thoroughly mass-mediated and commodified conditions under which much of it is nowadays produced.

These ambivalences capture the paradoxical process by which hunters' music unfolds its ever-growing appeal. The market-generated production of local culture generates a new context for urban consumers to imagine the rural-as-local (and rural-as-authentic), imaginations that emerge in a dialectical relationship with rural audiences' identification with hunters' music as a source of local pride. Hunters' musicians and urban consumers celebrate hunters' guarded knowledge as emblematic of a traditional, rural-based culture untainted by the corrosive effects of money, and contrast it favorably to other, corrupted cultural forms, such as jeli praise that, in their eyes, has degenerated into mere entertainment (Schulz 1998; 2001, chap. 6). At the same time, hunters' music owes its success in the urban entertainment market to the very mechanisms of monetization and commodification these critics decry. The appeal and marketability of hunters' music thus emerges in a dialectical process. As once-revered cultural traditions become increasingly commodified, cultural practices, such as those surrounding hunters' knowledge, are imagined and produced as instances of uncorrupted culture that, in consequence, are pulled into the maelstrom of consumption and commodification.

Commodification and a state-orchestrated politics of culture create a new context for the construction of hunters' music as emblematic of local culture; they also affect the meanings, forms and evaluation of hunters' musicians' performances by rural audiences.[34] The transformation of hunters' praise into cultural performance goes hand in hand with a resignification of socially relevant tasks into elements of a marketable cultural performance. Although the entertainment dimension was never absent from hunters' praise performed in rural locales, it has become more prominent in the cultural ceremonies staged for urban audiences. Unintelligible phrases and allusions that remain opaque to urban music consumers serve as further proof of the performer's guarded knowledge and are thus part of his marketable skills.

Taking up Appadurai's (1996) interest in the "social settings" in which "locality" is constructed, we can identify commodification and the state-orchestrated administration of Culture as key processes that affect the production of "locality" in the form of hunters' music. Yet whereas Appadurai (1996, 178–79) stresses the social and socialized nature of locality, we cannot understand constructions of locality in Mali without considering their underlying cultural and economic logic, a logic akin to the Comaroffs' ethnocommodification. The market-generated production of local culture generates a new context for urban consumers to imagine the rural-as-local and as the fons et origo of genuine identity, imaginations that emerge in a dialectical relationship with rural audiences' identification with hunters' music as a source of local pride. As we will see, these constructions of locality in hunters' music are importantly mediated through the sensory-affective (see Luig 1999).

PERFORMING "GENUINE" LOCAL CULTURE
TO TELEVISION AUDIENCES

Screenings of *Terroir* productions demonstrate the program's affective significance as a site for expressions and imaginations of local particularity. For the
first screening, villagers whose culture is captured in the *Terroir* production
flock to the administrative center of the commune or a nearby town, to follow
the event together with relatives who own a television set. Spectators fervently
attend to the smallest detail of the documentary and energetically comment on
performances they consider faithful renditions of their "truly own" (yèrèyèrè)
songs and oratory.[35] Their perception of the accurate character of the televised
productions of local culture raises questions. After all, commodification and
state administration of culture have been integral to the process by which,
in recent decades, the local has emerged as the prevalent frame for claims to
particularity and as the locus of genuine identity. Given the central role of
the state in the production of locality and in mediating claims to particularity, one might wonder how and why these state-mediated cultural forms and
claims resonate with audiences. How, in other words, do forms and activities
so thoroughly subject to the logics of state sovereignty and commodification,
gain the nimbus of genuineness?

To understand how the perception of a faithful rendition of local culture
emerges from spectators' engagements with state television, I draw on Goffman's (1974, 47) argument that "keyings" are essential to the process by which
actions interpreted within primary frameworks of interpretation are trans-
posed to a new setting, recognized as transformations yet nevertheless considered actualizations of essential components of an original act. "Keyings" are
features and formats of *Terroir* productions that prompt spectators' recognition
of a performance as an instance of unchanged local culture. Because keyings
simultaneously attune audiences to (new) perceptive impressions that, over
time, become standards for the presentation of local culture, they allow us to
understand why spectators might assert that a mass-mediated performance
offers a faithful rendition of their "truly own" music and oratory.

Attendees and bystanders of a live performance of hunters' music respond,
viscerally and discursively, to various sensory-aesthetic impressions, such as
sounds; colors; melodic-rhythmic patterning; and the timbre, phrasing, and
other qualities of a voice or instrument. But when it comes to assessing whether
a performance is a faithful rendition of local culture, spectators from the area
highlight two aspects: that a performance reveals a musician's deep knowledge

and a performance's nonmonetized nature, in other words, that its primary objective is not monetary gain but "moral education" (*ladili*).[36]

How does the impression of genuineness emerge for urban spectators, particularly for those not acquainted with the locale in question and whose fascination with the televised staging of local culture stems precisely from their lack of knowledge about it? What keyings prompt their assertions of genuineness if they are unable to judge key criteria, such as a performer's deep knowledge?

Urban television audiences tend to give greater importance to a performance's visual elements, such as dress and bodily posture and demeanor, and to whether and how individual audience members are being covered. Many spectators redirect their attention, away from the hunters' musician's performance and toward the choreographic mise-en-scène of the entire filmed event. To these urban audiences, keyings that mark a performance as untouched rural culture operate primarily at the levels of the sensory-aesthetic and the choreographic, in other words, through elements that lend themselves well to selective rearrangement and manipulation through audiovisual technologies.[37] Also important are presentational formats, such as shaky images and slanted camera angles and shots, that generate the impression of spontaneity and of an immediate—that is, unmediated—rendition of genuine local nature.

Audiovisual recording and broadcast technologies thus create a range of possibilities for the transposition of primary frameworks of interpretation into secondary ones, by condensing keyings into formats that enable the legibility and recognition of visual and acoustic elements as indicative of genuine local culture. When Bala Guimba appears on screen with his blind eyes shut and his head bent to the sky, stirring up dust and sand and pushing his ngoni ahead of him as he moves in small circles in front of his audience, spectators are affected by his performance's multisensory effects. Their visceral experience of immediacy makes the screening event a moment of affective bonding with (imaginary) rural origins.

By inducing, and relying on, the standardization of presentational formats that serve as keyings, state television, as an institution and set of technologies, allows hunters' musicians' performances to be read as the epitome of the local-as-rural. At the heart of this resignification process is a dialectics of inaccessibility and legibility that increases the symbolic value of hunters' music. Television strengthens the sign function of hunters' music performances to an outside world and a world of outsiders (see Comaroff and Comaroff 2009, 142).

CONCLUSION

In contemporary Mali, local culture, rather than ethnic identity, operates as the primary trope of identity processes and claims, as a result of the intertwining of local identity constructions with a powerful legacy of French colonial and early postcolonial cultural policy that promoted culture as the fons et origo of genuine identity. For decades, culture (defined in terms of a people's mores, or expressive genres and artifacts) served as the dominant trope of national belonging and citizenship, leaving little room for expressions of ethnicized difference. The political and economic neoliberal restructuring of state-society relations of the late 1980s has allowed earlier divisions and struggles to emerge more forcefully. Embedded in a thriving cultural economy of expressions of particularity, local culture now forcefully invites imaginations and attachments that bridge and reaffirm the contrast between "the urban" and "the rural."[38] The hype of hunters' music illustrates these cross-scalar, rural-urban dynamics.

However, even if ethnicity has never figured centrally in forms and processes of mobilization in Mali, the means and modalities of ethnicity, inc., are very much at work here. That is, while the local has only recently emerged as a predominant frame for claims to difference and particularity, the processes that have driven its emergence and make its present affective force, most notably objectification, commodification, (incipient) incorporation, and mass-mediatization, are akin to the cultural and economic logics of ethnicity, inc.

Hunters, their musicians, and audiences envision hunters' musicians' performances as an instance of a local culture untainted by the forces of monetization. Yet it is the very process of commodifying these musical performances—of, indeed, turning them into a genre of music—that makes these imaginations possible. The commodification of hunters' music is intrinsic to its spectacular popularity and affective appeal. Commodification, in its intertwining with mass mediatization, has been instrumental in turning hunters into generic, standardized signs of local culture and, hence, into visible proof of its continued existence. Rather than conceiving of commodification as a process that deprives cultural production (or, for that matter, the ethnicization of identity) of its affective weight (Shneiderman 2014), the two processes are predicated on, and feed into, each other. What these "deep affective attachments" reveal, then, is a dialectic between "the incorporation of identity and the commodification of culture" that, according to John and Jean Comaroff (2009, 149, 89), is so central to processes of identification and identity formation in the contemporary era.

As the local operates as a malleable category of framing difference and belonging, similar to ethnicity, autochthony (Geschiere 2009), or other affectively and politically charged tropes, it highlights the necessity of identifying the processes and rationalities operative in *all* these modes of (self-) identification and mobilization. Yet it also calls for attention to potential differences in how these mobilizations of the local in the name of particularity and difference affect and *enable* modalities of reasserting state power and sovereignty. Here, the Malian case seems to offer an interesting contrast to the weakening—indeed crumbling—state sovereignty highlighted in much of the scholarly literature on the state in the era of neoliberal (cultural) economics.

In Mali, the hype of hunters' music and of cultural programs such as *Terroir* attest to the state's ongoing capacity to reinvent itself, as the main architect of representations of local particularity. Mediatization and ethnocommodification are essential to all these processes, to the mode of reclaiming—or affirming—state sovereignty and to the mobilization of local particularity on which this revamped state sovereignty is predicated.

NOTES

1. Unless indicated otherwise, all foreign terms are rendered in Bamanakan, the lingua franca of southern Mali.

2. The literal translation of *donson jeli* is "hunter's griot," but I prefer to refer to them as hunters' musicians because many of them stress their distinctiveness from the socioprofessional category of "griots" (see section "The Objectification of Tradition and Culture").

3. *Kabila* is commonly translated into French as *aire culturelle* (cultural realm).

4. While *locality* connotes relational constructions of place and belonging, *the local* refers to concrete phenomenal instantiations of these constructions of locality.

5. Race and religious identity played a role insofar as they allowed administrators to contrast the "backward," "lazy," or "obtuse" animist "races" of the southern Soudan Français to the allegedly more intelligent and energetic islamized populations of the northern Sahel and the Sahara (e.g., Harrison 1988; Robinson 1999).

6. Because culture was associated with notions of modernity and progress, it played an equivocal role in the US-RDA's state-making project. While party ideologues praised culture as a source of African communal values (Haidara 1992), they labored against cultural mores considered as an impediment to the collectivization of agricultural production.

7. The US-RDA modernization project blended the different meanings of *culture* in European nationalist thought, including the German romanticist notion of culture as the "way of life" of distinct nations, the Enlightenment view of culture as a sign of sophistication and development, and its narrower conception as a collection of expressive forms (see Lloyd and Thomas 1998, chap. 2).

8. The confederations divide into two sub-groups: the formerly nomadic warrior nobility and the free-born vassal groups, the Imghad. Descendants of former slaves are referred to as Bellah or Iklan and form a separate social category.

9. Whereas Handler (1984, 1988), drawing on Cohn's (1987) work on colonial India, refers to both processes as objectification, I suggest that differences between them are critical to our understanding of the distinctive effects they unfold in an expanding cultural market.

10. The festival was revamped as a youth sports and artistic competition event (Biennale artistique et culturelle du Mali) in 1970, suspended after President Traoré's fall from power in 1991, and reintroduced in 2001 (Djebbari 2013, 201, fn2).

11. In Bamanakan, the lingua franca of southern Mali, and in different Dogon dialects, *tradition* is translated as *lada* (a derivative of the Arabic term for non-Islamic conventions), which refers to custom rather than to expressive cultural forms.

12. The top-down perspective suggested by Hobsbawm's and Ranger's now-famous notion of invented tradition (and by studies working in this perspective) does not capture the contested nature of this process.

13. Starting in the 1980s, the reach of national radio was gradually extended to remote rural areas in the south and to some urban pockets in the north, but these changes did not significantly alter stark regional discrepancies in technical infrastructure, accessibility and representation (Schulz 2001, chap. 6).

14. In the late 1990s, older farmers from the Maninkakan-speaking southwest recalled their excitement about hearing their "truly own music" on national radio, which illustrates their eagerness to affirm their cultural and historical particularity rather than being submerged into an all-encompassing, national identity.

15. The transformation of jeli praise from a client service into a commodity went hand in hand with changes in the respective importance of different oral genres and in the gender-specific division of labor among performers (Schulz 1998, 2001).

16. The experiences of the different social status and ethnic groups that inhabit Mali's northern territories cannot be condensed into one single narrative (see Diallo 2016), but their treatment by the postcolonial state nevertheless puts them into a similar structural and political position.

17. The crucial difference to a parallel movement of Islamic renewal building up in the south since the 1980s (Schulz 2012) is that southern Muslim activists seek to influence politics by gaining formal political office. Muslim militants in the north, in contrast, frame their search for a theocratic order as a resistance to a central state run by nonbelievers.

18. The following analysis of state politics of culture since the mid-1990s does not explicitly consider repercussions of the 2012 coup d'etat and the subsequent temporary occupation of Mali's northern territories by Muslim militant groups. The political upheaval prompted by these events did not translate into a significantly modified governmental cultural policy under the current president, Ibrahim Boubacar Keita (in office since 2013).

19. The fact that under President Modibo Keita, the historical date (September 22) of the tata's destruction was chosen as Independence Day and a monument was erected at its site illustrates Sabusèrè's importance as a symbol of heroic anticolonial resistance.

20. Both royal clans belong to the Khassonke ethnic group but stress differences in regional origin and affinity with Fulbe (Dembaya) and Maninka (Sabusère) ethnic groups.

21. The businesswoman thereby dismissed the warnings of an official from the Ministry of Culture, himself a native of the area and a descendant of the Sabusère royal clan.

22. Association des Jeunes pour le Developpement de Médine.

23. In the case of televised productions of local culture, the rationales of selection vary greatly, ranging from the proviso of ritual secrecy to aesthetic considerations.

24. The feedback loop between mass-mediated productions of culture and live performances shows in numerous, subtle shifts in emphasis on various musical and textual elements of a performance event and also, though to a lesser extent, in revised formats of presentation (see also van de Port 2006).

25. Broadcast only sporadically since 1988, *Musique du Terroir* became such a hit television program that in 1993 it was turned into the weekly show *Terroir* (Schulz 2007b).

26. I call it *primary*, not *exclusive*, frame, keeping in mind that members of free-born and noble Tuareg clans frame their opposition to the state in *ethnic* terms.

27. In contrast to authors who understand the practice of everyday life as performative event or "performance" (see Drewal 1991, 1, 10), I use the term to refer to moments that audiences and performers explicitly set apart from routine daily life. Following Bauman (1975), I understand cultural performances as temporarily and spatially bounded and coordinated, collectively shared events that become sites for the ongoing construction of knowledge, bodily skills,

and "ways of doing." They rest on repetition and reiteration yet also involve innovation and the transformation of existing rules and protocols of cultural production (see Schechner 1985; Nunley 1988).

28. Hunters' musicians in rural areas earn only a modest income from their performances, in contrast to hunters' musicians who make music their principal profession. Hunters who live in urban areas also capitalize on a growing demand for their occult services and sometimes draw considerable profit from it.

29. Hunters' guarded knowledge comprises esoteric knowledge and expertise in plant-based medicine (*fura*).

30. Hunters' guarded knowledge is intricately related to their renowned ability to spend extended periods of time in the bush, fending off all kinds of dangers and drawing on the resources around them to make ends meet. Their guarded or, "dark," knowledge allows them to transform organic matter into medicine to treat diverse kinds of afflictions, ranging from physical illness to misfortune (McNaughton 1982; Strawn 2011).

31. Hunters' legendary physical force and prowess also occupy a central place in the foundation epics of different historical polities, or "empires," of Mali.

32. Listeners generally single out three aspects of hunter's music performance as reasons for their success. Firstly, if a song enhances the reputation of the recipient of praise; secondly, when it offers "valuable"— that is, edifying—knowledge about norms and a male code of honor; and thirdly, when it succeeds in "bringing people together" in a shared appreciation of the song.

33. In contrast to the inherited status categories of freeborn or noble people, descendants of serfs, and members of endogamous socio-occupational groups (*nyamakalaw*), becoming a hunter is a matter of personal merit and knowledge. The same applies to hunters' musicians, who are generally, yet misleadingly, referred to as hunters' griots, even though they have become musicians by choice, not birth (see also Strawn 2011, 204, 239ff).

34. Cultural ceremonies organized by hunters' associations prioritize musical performance. Activities by hunters that require secrecy are now minimized and limited to what a broader public is allowed to see.

35. In contrast, *authenticity* (understood as *originality*), so central to state cultural policy, is not a criterion for a successful performance. For interesting parallels to people's assessments of live cultural performances on the Dogon plateau in southwestern Mali, see Doquet (1996).

36. Keyings that prompt spectators to recognize a musician's deep knowledge include references to events and personalities peculiar to the locale of the performance and the use of formulaic phrases indicative of the singer's esoteric knowledge.

37. Sensory-aesthetic keyings include images (e.g., depicting hunters in their peculiar garb and armed with rifles), colors, and sounds (e.g., rhythmic-melodic patterns that stand for a clan identity).

38. The significance of cultural identity, as *one* among several ways of claiming particularity in a multicomposite nation-state, has evolved along separate trajectories in the country's northern and southern triangle. In the north, claims to a Tuareg ethnic identity, sometimes combined with claims to proper religious practice and interpretation, have served high-status segments of the free-born and noble Tuareg population as a mode of political mobilization (Lecocq 2010; Schulz 2016).

REFERENCES

Amselle, Jean Loup. 1990. *Logiques métisses. Anthropologie de l'identité en Afrique et ailleurs.* Paris: Payot.

Amselle, Jean Loup, and E. M'Bokolo, eds. 1985. *Au coeur de l'ethnie: Ethnies, tribalisme et État en Afrique.* Paris: Editions de la découverte.

Appadurai, Arjun. 1996. *Modernity at Large: Cultural Dimensions of Globalization.* Minneapolis: University of Minnesota Press.

Apter, Andrew. 2005. *The Pan-African Nation: Oil and the Spectacle of Culture in Nigeria.* Chicago: University of Chicago Press.

Bauman, Richard. 1975. "Verbal Art as Performance." *American Anthropologist* 77 (2): 290–311.

Bayart, Jean-François, Achille Mbembe, and Comi Toulabor, eds. 1992. *Le Politique par le Bas en Afrique Noire.* Paris: Karthala.

Bierschenk, Thomas, and Jean-Pierre Olivier de Sardan. 2003. "Power in the Village: Rural Benin between Democratisation and Decentralisation." *Africa: Journal of the International African Institute* 73 (2): 145–73.

Bourdieu, Pierre. 1977. "L'économie des échanges linguistiques." *Langue Française* 34 (1): 17–34.

Cohn, Bernhard. 1987. "The Census, Social Structure, and Objectification in South Asia." In *An Anthropologist among the Historians and Other Essays,* edited by B. Cohn, 224–54. Oxford: Oxford University Press.

Comaroff, John L., and Jean Comaroff. 2004. "Criminal Justice, Cultural Justice: The Limits of Liberalism and the Pragmatics of Difference in the New South Africa." *American Ethnologist* 31 (2): 188–204.

———. 2009. *Ethnicity, Inc.* Chicago: University of Chicago Press.

Diallo, Souleymane. 2016. "'The Truth about the Desert': Exile, Memory, and the Making of Communities among Tuareg Refugees in Niger." PhD thesis, Department of Anthropology, University of Cologne.

Diawara, Mamadou. 1994. "Production and Reproduction: The Mande Oral Popular Culture Revisited by the Electronic Media." *Passage* 8:13–22.

Djebbari, Elina. 2013. "La Biennale artistique et culturelle du Mali: La mise en scène d'une culture nationale de l'indépendance à aujourd'hui." In *Une histoire des festivals, XXème-XXIème siècles*, directed by A. Fléchet, P. Goetschel, P. Hidiroglou, S. Jacotot, C. Moine, J. Verlaine, 291–302. Paris: Publications de la Sorbonne.

———. 2014. "Voler, donner, transmettre: Propriété et appropriation chez les artistes de ballet au Mali." *Volume!* 10 (2): 173–93.

Doquet, Anne. 1996. "Décentralisation et reformulation des traditions en pays Dogon: Les manifestations culturelles des communes de Dourou et Sangha." In *Décentralisation et pouvoirs en Afrique: En contrepoint, modèles territoriaux français*, edited by Claude Fay, Koné Y. Felix, Catherine Quiminal, 303–22. Paris: IRD Éd.

Drewal, Margaret Thompson. 1991. "The State of Research on Performance in Africa." *African Studies Review* 34 (3): 1–64.

Ferme, Mariane, with D. Hoffman. 2004. "Hunter Militias and the International Human Rights Discourse in Sierra Leone and Beyond." *Africa Today* 50 (4): 72–95.

Geschiere, Peter. 2009. *Perils of Belonging: Autochthony, Citizenship and Exclusion in Africa and Europe*. Chicago: Chicago University Press.

Geschiere, Peter, and F. Nyamnjoh. 2001. "Capitalism and Autochthony: The Seesaw of Mobility and Belonging." In *Millennial Capitalism and the Culture of Neo-Liberalism*, edited by Jean Comaroff and John Comaroff, 159–90. Durham, NC: Duke University Press.

Goffman, Erving. 1974. *Frame Analysis: An Essay on the Organization of Experience*. New York: Harper & Row.

Haidara, Yero. 1992. *Ländliche Entwicklung und die 'Tòn'-Strategie in Mali. Möglichkeiten und Grenzen des endogenen Entwicklungsansatzes in Afrika*. Hamburg: Institut für Afrika-Kunde.

Handler, Richard. 1984. "On Sociocultural Discontinuity: Nationalism and Cultural Objectification in Quebec." *Current Anthropology* 25 (1): 55–71.

———. 1988. *Nationalism and the Politics of Identity in Quebec*. Madison: University of Wisconsin Press.

Harrison, Christopher. 1988. *France and Islam in West Africa, 1860–1960*. Cambridge: Cambridge University Press.

Jansen, Jan. 2008. "From Guild to Rotary: Hunters' Associations and Mali's Search for a Civil Society." *IRSH* 53:249–70.

Joy, Charlotte. 2011. *The Politics of Heritage Management in Mali: From UNESCO to Djenné*. Walnut Creek: Left Coast Press.

Keita, Mahamadou Chérif. 1995. "Jaliya in the Modern World." In *Status and Identity in West Africa: The Nyamakalaw of Mande*, edited by D. Conrad and B. Frank, 182–96. Bloomington: Indiana University Press.

Kouyaté, Seydou Baidan. 1963. *Sous l'orage (Kany)*. Paris: Présence Africaine.

Leach, Melissa. 2004. "Security, Socioecology, Polity: Mande Hunters, Civil Society, and Nation-States in Contemporary West Africa." *Africa Today* 50 (4): vii–xvi.

Lecocq, Baz. 2010. *Disputed Desert: Decolonisation, Competing Nationalisms and Tuareg Rebellions in Northern Mali*. Leiden: Brill.

Lecocq, Baz, and Paul Schrijver. 2007. "The War on Terror in a Haze of Dust: Potholes and Pitfalls on the Saharan Front." *Journal of Contemporary African Studies* 25 (1): 141–66.

Luig, Ute. 1999. "Constructing Local Worlds: Spirit Possession in the Gwembe Valley, Zambia." In *Spirit Possession, Modernity, and Power in Africa*, edited by Heike Behrend and Ute Luig, 142–64. Madison: University of Wisconsin Press.

Lloyd, David, and Paul Thomas. 1998. *Culture and the State*. New York: Routledge.

McNaughton, Patrick. 1982. "The Shirts that Mande Hunters Wear." *African Arts* 15 (3): 54–93.

Nédélec, Serge. 1992. "1958." In *Les Jeunes en Afrique: La Politique et la ville*, edited by Catherine Coquéry-Vidrovitch and Helène d'Almeida Topor, 204–19. Paris: L'Harmattan.

Niang, Abdoulaye. 2014. "Festivalisation Le Festival de la Jeunesse Africaine de Bamako, activisme et professionnalisation dans les cultures urbaines: L'exemple des festivals Festa 2 H et Festigraff au Sénégal." Paper presented to the workshop "Culture as a Resource: Negotiating the Meaning of Arts and Cultural Practices in African contexts." Point Sud, Ouadagougou.

Nunley, John. 1988. "Purity and Pollution in Freetown Masked Performance." *TDR* 32 (2): 102–22.

Robinson, David. 1999. "France as a Muslim Power in West Africa." *Africa Today* 46 (3/4): 105–27.

Rovine, Victoria. 2008. *Bogolan: Shaping Culture through Cloth in Contemporary Mali*. Bloomington: Indiana University Press.

Schechner, Richard. 1985. *Between Theater and Anthropology*. Philadelphia: University of Pennsylvania Press.

Schulz, Dorothea. 1998. "Morals of Praise: Broadcast Media and the Commoditization of Jeli Praise Performances in Mali." *Research in Economic Anthropology* 19:117–33.

———. 2001. *Perpetuating the Politics of Praise: Jeli Praise Singers, Radios and Political Mediation in Mali*. Köln: Rüdiger Köppe.

———. 2007a. "From a Glorious Past to the Lands of Origin: Media Consumption and Changing Narratives of Cultural Belonging in Mali." In *Reclaiming Heritage. Alternative Imaginaries of Memory in West Africa*, edited by Michael Rowlands and Ferdinand de Jong, 184–213. Walnut Creek, CA: Westcoast Press.

———. 2007b. "Competing Sartorial Assertions of Femininity and Muslim Identity in Mali." *Fashion Theory* 11 (2/3): 253–80.

———. 2012. *Muslims and New Media in West Africa: Pathways to God.*
Bloomington: Indiana University Press.

———. 2016. "'Sharia' as a Moving Target? The Reconfiguration of Regional and
National Fields of Muslim Debate in Mali." In *Sharia Law and Modern
Ethics: Plurality, Contestation, Co-Imbrication,* edited by Robert Hefner, 350–92.
Bloomington: Indiana University Press.

———. n.d. *Probing Legitimacy and Authority in Mali.* (book manuscript under
review)

Schulz, Dorothea, and Souleymane Diallo. 2016. "Political Islam and Competing
Assertions of Muslim Masculinity in Contemporary Mali." *Journal of Religion in
Africa* 46:219–50.

Shneiderman, Sara. 2014. "Reframing Ethnicity: Academic Tropes, Recognition
Beyond: Politics, and Ritualized Action between Nepal and India." *American
Anthropologist* 116 (2): 279–95.

Snyder, Frank Gregory. 1967. "The Political Thought of Modibo Keita." *Journal of
Modern African Studies* 5 (1): 79–106.

Spitulnik, Debra. n.d. "Media Connections and Disconnections: Radio Culture
and the Public Sphere in Zambia." (book manuscript)

Strawn, Cullen Buckminster. 2011. "Kunfe Ko: Experiencing Uncertainty in
Malian Wasulu Hunters' Music Performance and Hunting." PhD diss., Folklore
and Ethnomusicology Department, Indiana University.

Traoré, Karim. 2004. "The Intellectuals and the Hunters: Reflections on the
Conference 'La Rencontre des Chasseurs de l'Afrique de l'Ouest.'" *Africa Today*
50 (4): 97–111.

Vail, Leroy. 1989. *The Creation of Tribalism in Southern Africa.* London: James
Currey.

van de Port, Matthjis. 2006. "Visualizing the Sacred: Video Technology,
'Televisual' Style, and the Religious Imagination in Bahian Candomblé."
American Ethnologist 33 (3): 444–61.

DOROTHEA E. SCHULZ is Professor of Cultural and Social Anthropology at the
University of Münster, Germany. She is author of *Perpetuating the Politics of Praise:
Jeli Singers, Radios, and Political Mediation in Mali, Culture and Customs of Mali,* and
Muslims and New Media in West Africa: Pathways to God.

SEVEN

THE AFFECTIVE POTENTIALITIES AND POLITICS OF ETHNICITY, INC. IN RESTRUCTURING NEPAL

Social Science, Sovereignty, and Signification

SARA SHNEIDERMAN

WHY IS ETHNICITY, INC., PERCEIVED as a tool of hegemonic state power in some contexts and a tool of resistance in others? How do we understand it as both at once? Can we actually see the paradigm itself as a site of contestation between the state and its own margins, which can be manipulated by a range of political actors with divergent ideological and material objectives? Does control over the affective potentialities of ethnicity, inc., understood as the multifaceted nexus between state/market/society/subjectivity, become a deciding factor in larger political outcomes? How are social scientists complicit in such processes? Finally, what compels some groups to frame their struggles in the terms of ethnicity, inc., at certain spatiotemporal junctures, while others do not—even within the same nation-state context?

I consider these questions through a comparative ethnohistorical exploration of two social movements in Nepal over the last half century, and the different ways in which the relationship between ethnicity and territory has figured within both struggles. Although the Dalit movement and other rights-based campaigns are also crucial to understanding Nepal's ongoing political transformation (Darnal 2009), here I focus on the Adivasi Janajati (hereafter Janajati), or indigenous nationalities movement, and the Madhesi movement that has sought full political integration for the Madhesi population who live in the southern plains along the long open border with India. The architects of each of these movements, as well as their cadres, have sustained different relationships to the potentialities of ethnicity, inc., over time.

A careful consideration of these cases helps us understand better how, on the one hand, ethnicity, inc., may be deployed as a state-supported strategy to co-opt more radical agendas for structural transformation while, on the other hand, it may be mobilized from below as a response to the limits of state inclusion. Exploring how actors on all sides of this equation marshal social scientific knowledge in the service of their own agendas additionally reveals the depth of entanglement between scholarship, politics, and the affective production of ethnic consciousness. Recognizing that the paradigm of ethnicity, inc., fuses all of these intentionalities helps mediate overdeterministic arguments about the relative liberatory potential of identity-based versus class-based struggles. Taking a cold, hard look at how political elites may marshal the rhetoric of Marxist modernism to block collective mobilization on the basis of ethnicity is particularly important in political contexts like Nepal's, where communist parties (of various persuasions) set the terms of debate in a context where arguments about the influence of "external actors" on the formation of ethnic consciousness abound.

Consider a September 25, 2015, media interview with Jhalanath Khanal, a prominent leader of the country's "mainstream" Communist Party of Nepal–Unified Marxist-Leninist (CPN-UML, hereafter UML).[1] Providing a window into the polarizing discourse that emerged around ethnicity in Nepal during the process of postconflict federal state restructuring, Khanal described as "meaningless" a wave of violent protests led by Tharu and Madhesi activists from the country's southern plains over the failure of Nepal's new constitution to address long-standing ethnic demands.[2] Khanal's compatriot in the UML, Khadga Prasad Oli, who would soon thereafter become prime minister, similarly dismissed the activists' complaints by stating that the government would only address "genuine demands."[3] In his view, the demands that lay at the heart of the previous month of protest in which nearly fifty people had died (due to both protestor and state violence) did not qualify: demands for constitutional recognition of the deep relationship between a particular category of ethnicized bodies and particular pieces of territory within the nation-state of Nepal's borders.[4]

This chapter makes three interlinked arguments that emerge out of my ongoing research surrounding Nepal's political transformation yet speak to a larger set of questions about the varied potentialities of ethnicity, inc. First, I explore how social scientific debates over the nature of ethnicity, territory, and sovereignty in scholarly contexts may intersect with invocations of meaning and authenticity—and their opposites—in the "realpolitik"[5] of politicians like Khanal and Oli in Nepal or, indeed, anywhere in the world. I suggest that we may want to focus on how the relationship *between* ethnicity and territory is differentially objectified by various actors rather than only on the commodification of ethnicity itself. Second, I consider how specific historical trajectories of territorial integration into the nation-state shape contemporary ideologies of sovereignty among different groups, even within the boundaries of a single contemporary country. These histories in turn shape the specific national and transnational frames in relation to which ethnic claims may be made, a point that leads to an overarching third argument: that the affective and political outcomes of participation in ethnicity, inc. for individual actors are differentially shaped by the range of signifying repertoires available to them. Ethnicity, inc. may mean many things to many people, serving diverse purposes and yielding equally diverse results depending on both *who* controls the terms of ethnicity's objectification and on *behalf of whom* they do that work: the state, their own community, or other organizational forms like political parties or ethnic associations.

In considering these questions, I build on several important interventions made by John Comaroff and Jean Comaroff in their book *Ethnicity, Inc.* (2009): (1) analytically disentangling "the deployment of ethnicity as a tactical claim to entitlement, and as a means of mobilization for instrumental ends, with the substantive content of ethnic consciousness" (2009, 44); (2) revisiting the relationship between "sovereign existence" and antistate assertion; and (3) revisiting how we might consider the role of territory as a key element of ethnic assertion beyond the "ethnic corporation" (2009, 82). In other words, while acknowledging that "the terrain of politics is changing" so that "the notion that culture, politics, and economy might subsist in distinct institutional and ideational domains ... is a thing of the past" (2009, 45), I suggest that constraining our consideration of the political purchase of the ethnicity-territory nexus to market-based concepts of commodification may fall short of the full range of objectifying possibilities, especially in parts of the world that depart from presumed trajectories of postcolonial neoliberalism.

Finally, I suggest that academic critiques of global capitalism grounded in Marxian analysis face particular challenges of interpretation in political contexts that continue to be actively shaped by Marxist ideologies themselves, such as Nepal's post-Maoist, communist-led current moment. In such cases, the confluence of scholarly and political approaches creates a recursive field of fused action and analysis that requires special care if we wish to address this question: do violent, repressive responses from communist governments to the ethnicity-based mobilizations of marginalized communities—as Nepal has seen in recent years—represent a bottoming out of communist ideology's commitment to equality, or a legitimate counternarrative to the global hegemony of neoliberal multiculturalism and its attendant mobilizations of culture (see

Hale 2005)? Ultimately, I argue that we can only answer this question through careful multilayered attention to the question of who controls the terms of ethnicity, inc. in its locationally specific avatars as both instrument and affect.

My own work on these themes to date (Shneiderman 2013a, 2015; Shneiderman and Tillin 2015) has focused on ethnic movements emerging from Janajati communities, not Madhesi movements. While my empirical engagement with the Madhesi movement is limited, some of the analytical approaches emerging from analyses of Janajati contexts, such as the Thangmi community with whom I work, may offer clues toward understanding the affective politics of ethnicity arising in Madhesi contexts and the challenges of signification that they face.

In brief, *Madhes* is a locational term that refers to the long swath of territory inside Nepal that adjoins the open border with India. *Madhesi* refers to the inhabitants of this territory. As such, *Madhesi* literally means "plains-dweller" and is set in binary opposition to *Pahadi*, or "hill-dweller," which is equally a culturally constructed category despite the geographical terminology it deploys. While *Janajati* and *Madhesi* are often seen as distinct supra-ethnicities (see Adhikari and Gellner 2016), in fact their current political mobilizations draw on a shared vocabulary to objectify an embodied relationship between ethnicity and territory. But their divergent locations—in both the geographical and social sense—mean that the implications of their mobilizations for received Nepali nationalist notions of sovereignty are vastly different. It is this difference, coupled with an important set of symbolic variations in self-representational styles, that constitutes the gap between meaningful and meaningless ethnic claims as perceived at the national center, as well as by global political actors. Social scientists are also differentially engaged by each set of actors. Such analysis helps us understand the variegated potentialities of ethnicity, inc. and its relationships with nationality, inc. Even within a single nation-state frame, the conditions of possibility vary between groups, depending on their location, in both geographical and sociopolitical senses. Controlling the affective outcomes of ethnicity, inc. is a constitutive element of larger political arsenals and, therefore, a key site of contestation.

HISTORICAL AND POLITICAL BACKGROUND

On September 20, 2015, Nepal promulgated its seventh constitution. Achieving this took seven years and two constituent assemblies (CAs). The first was elected in 2008 but dissolved in 2012 without achieving its objective while the second, elected in 2013, served as the ratifying body for the eventual document. Devastating earthquakes in the spring of 2015 killed nearly ten thousand

and left over six hundred thousand families homeless, with many more experiencing some damage. The subsequent billions of dollars of reconstruction funding provided the immediate impetus for the so-called fast-tracking of the final constitutional promulgation: the earthquakes offered an opportunity for reconsolidation of a conservative infrastructural state, which conveniently also appeared to meet donor demands for political stability.[6] However, the constitutional process itself was part of a broader "postconflict"[7] state restructuring process. This was initiated in 2006, when a Comprehensive Peace Agreement marked the formal end of a decade-long civil conflict between Maoist and state forces. In this context, the 2015 constitution was supposed to signal the shift to an inclusive polity that would address inequalities through a new federal structure whose territorial boundaries would recognize both historical claims to territory and, perhaps more importantly, the validity of contemporary ethnic blocs as a basis for the demarcation of new political constituencies.

Instead, the seven federal provinces mandated by the 2015 constitution did not build on the recommendations of either the 2010 State Restructuring Committee for fourteen states or the 2012 High Level State Restructuring Commission for ten territorial states (plus a nonterritorial Dalit state to make a total of eleven states).[8] Both of these bodies were composed of lawmakers and experts reporting to the first CA. While both reports proposed provincial names and boundaries that would in different ways recognize historical ethnic claims and establish new political constituencies focused around ethnic and regional blocs, they did not accord "prior rights" to particular groups or offer de jure ethnic autonomy. As such, both the 2010 and 2012 maps seemed to be compromise solutions, which on the one hand symbolically acknowledged ethnic claims but on the other stopped short of offering substantive self-determination. Nonetheless, both of these proposals were ignored in designing the boundaries of the federal map as promulgated in the 2015 constitution, which instead ensured that historically dominant high-caste hill Hindu electoral majorities were maintained in most of the new provinces.[9]

The boundaries as promulgated were of particular concern to members of the Tharu and Madhesi communities living in the Tarai belt along Nepal's southern border with India.[10] The Tarai is home to approximately 50 percent of Nepal's population, but these groups with historical claims to its territory constitute about 30 percent of the country's total population. The rest of the Tarai's population are Pahadi, who migrated south for the most part after 1950.[11] This mass population shift meant that over the last half century, Nepali political elites from hill backgrounds were able to establish dominance over traditional property holders in the Tarai from both Tharu and Madhesi backgrounds. Across both groups, there were both small-scale agriculturalists and wealthy landlords whose success in the agrarian economy was based on exploitative labour practices, but even dominant members of these communities were challenged by growing Pahadi strategies of land appropriation from the 1950s onward. It was this trajectory that Tharu and Madhesi activists—as well as their Janajati counterparts elsewhere in the country—sought to overcome through the vehicle of the new constitution.

The legitimacy of Madhesi claims to historical injustice, and the need for reparation, was acknowledged in a 2007 political agreement made between the interim government and the then-leadership of the Madhesi parties as part of the peace process. It is worth citing several of this agreement's points in full, as they help to demonstrate why activists might feel betrayed by the new constitution and also provide context for discussing the broader relationship between ethnicity and territory in Nepal's state restructuring process. The 2007 agreement included the following points:

4. To ensure balanced proportional representation and partnership of Madhesis, indigenous peoples/janajatis, dalits, women, backward classes, disabled people, minority communities and Muslims who have been excluded for generations, in all organs and levels of government and in power structures, mechanisms and resources.

5. To immediately establish a commission for state restructuring and ensure that it comprises of experts in an inclusive manner.

6. Arrangements will be made for a federal state with regional autonomy while the sovereignty, national unity and integrity of Nepal will be kept intact during the restructuring of the state. The rights, nature and limits of regional autonomy will be as decided by the constituent assembly.

7. To accord national recognition to the identity, language and culture of the Madhesis.[12]

The tenor of this agreement, and a subsequent 2008 one with a broader range of Madhesi parties, reflects public discourse in the years immediately after the conflict came to its formal end in 2006. There was a euphoric sense of possibility about building a "Naya Nepal," or "New Nepal," that would finally overcome long-standing caste, ethnic, and religious inequalities by restructuring the state in a more inclusive manner. Similar agreements were made with Janajati organizations, whose demands also focused on securing proportional representation and a commitment to a state restructuring process that would recognize "ethnicity, language, geographic region, economic indicators and cultural distinctiveness while keeping national unity, integrity and sovereignty of Nepal at the forefront."[13]

In this context, the concept of inclusion was strongly promoted by international development actors from 2006 to 2012 (Shneiderman 2013a). By 2012, a growing backlash challenged the very idea of recognizing ethnicity as a basis for political constituency, affirmative action benefits, or "meaningful" political mobilization. That backlash contributed to the dissolution of the CA by creating political obstacles to the ratification of the 2012 draft constitution (Adhikhari and Gellner 2016) and gained further traction after the 2013 election, which brought in a more conservative body of lawmakers (Gellner 2014).

SOCIAL SCIENTIFIC ARGUMENTS

Social scientists, both Nepali and non-Nepali, have been keenly involved in both sides of this debate in Nepal. One group, comprised largely of scholars who themselves identify as Janajati, builds on in-depth empirical research with specific communities to argue that ethnic as well as "territorial consciousness" (Tamang 2009) is substantively real and must be recognized as such by political boundaries and administrative arrangements. Several of these scholars contributed to the forty-two-volume "Social Inclusion Atlas— Ethnographic Profiles" publication project from 2010 to 2014 funded by the Dutch organization SNV, the government of Norway, and others through the Social Inclusion Research Fund (SIRF), as established in 2005.[14] This was conceptualized as Nepal's answer to the Anthropological Survey of India, necessary to establish a baseline for future affirmative action benefits and projects of territorial recognition. Without a colonial legacy of ethnic classification, that material had never been produced for never-colonized Nepal, as it had been in an earlier era for much of the rest of the subcontinent (Shneiderman 2013a).

The other group of social scientists, largely composed of scholar members of high-caste Pahadi background, has drawn on trajectories of modernist and Marxian social theory to argue against the validity of ethnicity as a political category, emphasizing instead a focus on class-based inequality (e.g., Mishra 2012). Both kinds of arguments have been taken up by members of various communist parties over time.

My point in reviewing these details is to show how seemingly academic debates over ethnicity can have very concrete effects in the real world, especially in a place like Nepal, where the nexus between scholarship, activism, and politics is very tight. As I have described elsewhere (Shneiderman 2015, chap. 1), these two opposed arguments about ethnicity, and the tensions between them (intellectual and interpersonal), were very much on show at a high-profile 2011 Kathmandu conference, "Ethnicity and Federalisation," sponsored by SIRF, at a political moment when the rhetoric of inclusion was still ascendant. Sociologist Chaitanya Mishra, now emeritus faculty at Nepal's national Tribhuvan University, invoked Fredrik Barth to argue, "If ethnicity is not a thing, a set of specific, fixed and distinctive attributes and distinctive blood and semen, the case for separate homelands ceases to hold water. If ethnicity, instead, is a fluid and potentially malleable social relationship, the provision of separate homelands may well be unnecessary at best and counterproductive at worst" (Mishra 2012, 84). Although Mishra's paper is complex and analytically nuanced, these particular claims were simplified and amplified in media coverage of the conference. For instance, a widely circulated *Kathmandu Post* piece a few days later was titled, "Scholars Divided on Federation Model: Some Say Ethnicity Not a Magic Bullet."[15]

The next summer, in July 2012, I coconvened a conference, "Inequality and Affirmative Action: Situating Nepal in Global Debates," which emerged out of a British Academy Partnership grant. In addition to the closed conference sessions, we held a series of public roundtables to which CA members and other political leaders were invited to interact with scholarly participants. One high-ranking UML CA member quickly hijacked the proceedings with what became a filibuster about the nature of caste and ethnic identity in Nepal. He repeated almost verbatim Mishra's arguments from the previous year's conference (which had by then been published in Mishra and Gurung 2012), albeit without any of Mishra's sociological sophistication. At the same time, he invoked several derisive stereotypes of "Janajati" and "Madhesi" communities, highlighting the inconsistency in his position.

On the one hand, the speaker argued that due to the social-scientifically demonstrated fluidity of ethnic boundaries, ethnicity could not be considered as a basis for either territorial boundary demarcation or affirmative action measures. On the other hand, he was not shy about identifying different ethnic "types," to whom he accorded certain characteristics, using their shortcomings to argue that it would not be possible to draw territorial boundaries along ethnic lines: how could certain Janajati groups, for instance, become "self-reliant" when they did not have such inborn "capacity" (to use his terms in English)?

*   *   *

The latter argument drew on the notion of "capacity" from economist Amartya Sen, a concept that moderate Janajati activist-scholars had introduced to the federalism debate to complement the concept of identity. By 2012, their preferred terminology had shifted from "ethnic federalism" to "identity-based federalism,"[16] to a twin emphasis on "identity and capacity." By 2012, this shift in strategy on the part of many Janajati scholars and political leaders was evident: they recognized the need to move away from a focus on individual ethnic claims to "prior rights" in specific territories and toward a shared commitment to recognizing the broader concept of identity as a basis for territorial demarcation, political mobilization, and alliance (Shneiderman and Tillin 2015, 37); however, this had to be complemented by a discussion of "capacity"—meaning human and economic resources that would make territorial units economically sustainable.

Broadening out from the focus on ethnicity to that of "identity and capacity" made it possible for Janajati and Madhesi political actors to begin forming alliances, because it moved away from the rhetoric of indigeneity, which had undergirded previous Janajati claims to "ethnic territory." Indigeneity was not an available trope for Madhesi activists for a range of reasons that I go on to discuss. Indeed, in a 2012 interview, Madhesi leader Upendra Yadav explained, "Firstly states will be made on the basis of identity and capacity, not ethnicity. Secondly, ethnic states are not possible in Nepal . . . everyone living in the Madhes, regardless of whether they are Pahadis or Madhesis will have equal rights. No group will have special rights over the other."[17] Here, the concept of "ethnic state" is equated with that of prior or special rights, while a state "made on the basis of identity and capacity" is seen to have broader appeal. In June 2015, Upendra Yadav's Madhesi Janadhikar Forum (MJF) Party joined forces with a Janajati party, the Federal Socialist Party Nepal (FSPN) to create the Federal Socialist Forum Nepal party.[18] This Janajati-Madhesi political alliance around the shared categories of "identity and capacity" enabled a new round of joint protest that began in May 2016. As political scientist Krishna Hacchethu described the compromise solution that the backers of this party promoted, "identity-based non-ethnic federalism entertains ethnicity at a limited level in naming and the territorial delineation of provinces, but it certainly rejects ethnicity as a constituency for political prime rights, first rights on natural resources, and preferential rights on provincial administrative [sic—read 'administration']."[19]

* * *

Back at that 2012 conference, however, the concept of "capacity" had been twisted to refer to old-fashioned essentialist tropes of high-caste hill prejudice vis-à-vis both Janajatis and Madhesis. The CA member invoked folkloristic stereotypes about Janajatis being "hot-blooded" and Madhesis being resistant to education to suggest that both would be "incapable" of running "their own" states. Yet this was coupled with a discussion of shifting ethnic boundaries to argue that even if they might be capable, "giving" such groups their own states would be "scientifically" incorrect since it would reify boundaries that did not "actually" exist.

Later that same summer, I gave a talk at the UNDP-funded Support to Participatory Constitution Building in Nepal office. Attended by the then UN resident coordinator, as well as several scholars and program officers responsible for carrying out a nationwide consultation process about the state restructuring process, the discussion I presented was an early version of "Restructuring States, Restructuring Ethnicity" (Shneiderman and Tillin 2015). At the conclusion of my talk, a professor of political science from Tribhuvan University raised his hand. Instead of a question, I received a tirade about how foreign anthropologists were responsible for the rise of "ethnicity" in Nepal, because people like me had published work describing individual Janajati communities as distinctive, falsely promoting the idea that cultural difference existed in Nepal while actually all "Nepalis" were the same. The emergence of "ethnicity" as a category of self-identification was the fault of anthropologists and other "external actors," he stated stridently. One of the program officers from a Janajati background responded by stating that this seminar was the first time that he had ever encountered a foreign anthropologist and that nonetheless he had a strong feeling of ethnic affinity with his community. Laughter at this parlay helped relieve the tension in the room, and a serious discussion about how ethnic consciousness might serve as a positive "capacity-building" resource at the local level during the process of state restructuring ensued. The political scientist left the room before long, and I registered the unsettling fact that *both* constructivist arguments about ethnic fluidity *and* ethnographic "community-based studies" that could be read as primordialist were being marshaled to assail the validity of ethnicity as a political category or, even more troubling, as an affective one. Regardless of intentions, social science had clearly become complicit in shaping the potentialities of ethnicity, inc. in multiple political directions.

The broader category of "external actors" that the political scientist had invoked is a common scapegoat used to explain the "real" reasons behind Nepal's instability. In a widely circulated example of such thinking, prominent journalist Kanak Mani Dixit blamed Nepal's ongoing development challenges on "interventionist anthropology-backed social engineering projects during the decade of state restructuring and constitution writing."[20] In addition to anthropologists, commonly demonized external actors included other governments, notably India, and also the full range of international development agencies that, like SIRF, had been involved in promoting the notion of inclusion, in some cases publishing data that provided empirical evidence for historical inequality. The problem with such arguments is that they deny entirely the affectively real basis of ethnic consciousness, as if social scientific attention to such productions calls them into being, rather than the other way around.

One case in point was the long-running World Bank/DFID (the UK's Department for International Development) Gender and Social Exclusion Assessment. After publishing the 2006 *Unequal Citizens*, which summarized earlier data, an even larger 2011 dataset highlighted significant disparities between seventy-eight different ethnic and caste groups on the basis of multidimensional human development indicators such as access to economic, political, educational, and health resources. Hill high-caste males "remained overwhelmingly dominant in all branches of elected and administrative government—either unaware of or failing to take seriously, the resentment of other groups," read the summary of a chapter focusing on access to political participation, which was paralleled by the conclusions of chapters on all other sectors as well (Bennett, Sijapati, and Thapa 2013).

Due for publication in 2011, by summer 2012, when the other events I have described took place, it became clear that the publication of this report had been blocked by an alliance of high-caste activist groups. An August 2012 news article explained:

> The delegation of the Joint Struggle Committee for National Sovereignty and Ethnic Harmony, a front comprising 11 different organizations of Brahmin, Chhetri and Dashnami [high-caste groups] met with head of DFID Nepal Dominic O'Neill in May this year and told the latter not to interfere in Nepal's internal affairs by providing funds to various NGOs, thereby promoting the cause of indigenous Janajatis. The delegation told DFID that it was not right for them to lobby for federalism based on ethnic identity, according to Om Sharma, secretary of Brahman Samaj, one of the members of the struggle committee. "We told them that the international organizations should instead focus on investing for the backward people in general which includes people from different caste, ethnicity and backward regions," Sharma told *Republica*. This even led those in DFID to re-think about using the term 'socially excluded' in their reports.[21]

An independent Nepali trade press finally published a heavily edited version of the report (Bennett, Sijapati and Thapa 2013), composed primarily of tables and figures shorn of political context. The fact that an "external actor" had been intimidated into stopping press on social scientific data that recognized ethnicity as the basis for assessing inequality was notable. Not only had the affective reality of "substantive ethnic consciousness" been subverted through the manipulation of existing scholarship, but new empirical data that demonstrated the materiality of ethnic difference was also actively suppressed.

All this was part of the broader trend that Krishna Adhikari and David Gellner (2016) identify as the pivotal moment "when dominant becomes other," which they assert was the dynamic that led to the dissolution of Nepal's first constituent assembly in mid-2012. In short, as writer Dovan Rai put it, "This is what happens when the dominant group is insecure and uses the dominated group to alleviate their fears."[22] As in discussions about the production of whiteness in the United States, in Nepal dominant high-caste groups began to inhabit the chameleon skin of the ethnic, even in some cases the indigenous. They mobilized social scientific work to argue that since scholars had recognized the constructedness of ethnicity, it could not be a valid basis for demarcating new federal boundaries or political constituency. Yet they also failed to recognize that they themselves were asserting a hegemonic ethnic identity, the reproduction of which was the primary concern behind the territorial boundary lines they promoted (Lawoti 2016). In the classic terms of the unmarked dominant, they argued against the marking of others as distinctive on cultural or linguistic grounds through any legal regime of recognition, while asserting their own entitlement to such recognition. So much so that in the 2015 constitution, a new ethnic group is named, that of the "Khas-Arya," which is an ethnolinguistic term for high-caste Hindus. As anthropologist Mukta Tamang wrote, "The list of the groups is so exhaustive—more than 20 groups—that virtually everyone now qualifies as a marginalised. And to say everyone is marginalised is equivalent to saying that no one is marginalised."[23]

TERRITORIAL CATEGORIES AND ETHNIC CONSCIOUSNESS

Ethnicity as a relational system of social classification then undoubtedly has significant new capital in Nepal, but why? Is this one of the outcomes of constitutional "lawfare" (Comaroff and Comaroff 2009, 56), with everyone seeking entry to "the ethnic" in what I have elsewhere called the "classificatory moment" (Shneiderman 2013a) of constitution crafting, even—perhaps especially—those dominant elites who would have previously distanced themselves from any invocation of "ethnic identity"?

This is part of the story, but there are other key elements as well. These dynamics cannot be fully explained as a one-way process of ethnocommodification driven by a neoliberal shift from the production of labor to the production of culture. Understanding how groups have differentially sought to objectify the relationship *between* ethnicity and territory that Nepal's new constitution was meant to acknowledge will demonstrate how we might view ethnicity, inc. as a multilayered paradigm through which hierarchical relations of power are negotiated. This requires an exploration of both the categories of land tenure through which the state historically recognized the embodied relationship between ethnic and territorial belonging and the political histories that produced Nepal's contemporary borders vis-à-vis India and China. These narratives depart from the emphasis of postcolonial scholarship on the 1947 partition of the subcontinent as the genesis of all contemporary South Asian borders (see Shneiderman 2013b). Instead, they highlight the particular condition of "non-postcoloniality," a term I borrow from Mary Des Chene (2007), surrounding Nepal's sovereignty. Just as the historical administrative categories for land tenure within Nepal's putative boundaries set the stage for contemporary Janajati claims to territorial recognition, the historical condition of nonpostcoloniality, its boundary effects, and its implications for assertions of sovereignty set the stage for contemporary Madhesi ethnic mobilizations. What the two forms of ethnic mobilization have in common, I suggest, is a reliance on demonstrating embodied forms of ethnic distinctiveness, not through the objectification of culture per se, but rather the objectification of a particular set of relationships between ethnic bodies and territory. Where they diverge, however, is in their implications for Nepal's sovereignty, which leads to a difference in their signifying power.

State recognition of ethnic categories has been a strong feature of governmentality in Nepal for a very long time.[24] Consider, for instance, the late eighteenth-century definition of ancestral territory in the form of *kipat* land tenure through royal decrees soon after King Prithvi Narayan Shah's unification of the country (Forbes 1999; Regmi 1976), and the 1854 promulgation of the Muluki Ain. This legal code rationalized the unequal status of individual ethnic communities through the Hindu ideology of caste (cf. Höfer [1979] 2004), recognizing inequality as the legal "basis of the state" (Onta 2006, 305). Such historical moments in the dialectical process of state and ethnicity formation in Nepal have been well documented (Burghart 1984; Gellner, Pfaff-Czarnecka, and Whelpton 1997; Höfer [1979] 2004; Levine 1987), so I will not explore these further here.

The Nepali term *kipat* is most concisely glossed as a "customary system of land tenure" (Forbes 1999, 115); however, its full meaning in Nepal's contemporary political context is more complex. It has become shorthand for "indigenous territory" through a series of ideological and symbolic moves. The quest for historical evidence of territorial rights under the system of customary

land tenure known as kipat occupies a central place in contemporary ethnic activist projects in Nepal (Limbu n.d.; Shneiderman 2015, chap. 6). The
economic historian Mahesh Chandra Regmi explains that "rights under
Kipat tenure emerged not because of a royal grant, but because the owner, as
a member of a particular ethnic community, was in customary occupation
of lands situated in a particular geographical area" (1976, 87). Beginning in
1774, a series of royal decrees issued by Nepal's Shah kings formalized these
rights for several groups who now identify as Janajati. With this move, the fledg-
ling Nepali state reified in legal terms what was until then a circumstantial link
between ethnicity and ancestral territory. Over time, however, as the state
sought to exploit both the natural resources embedded in kipat lands and the
labor of its inhabitants, kipat rights were gradually undermined through a series
of land confiscations. By 1968, all legal distinctions between kipat and *raikar,*
the generic form of state land ownership, had disappeared (Regmi 1976, 16), but
kipat was only legally abolished through the cadastral survey of 1994 (Forbes
1999, 116).

The term *indigenous* was rapidly adopted by ethnic activists in Nepal in the
wake of the UN Declaration of the Year of Indigenous Peoples in 1993 and
the ensuing 1994 Declaration of the Decade of Indigenous Peoples (Gellner
2007; Hangen 2010; Onta 2006). This temporal convergence with the aboli-
tion of kipat highlights how the diminishing recognition of a legal relationship between ethnic individuals and territory, as defined by the Nepali state
through the concept of kipat, was paralleled by an increasing recognition of
an embodied relationship between ethnic individuals and their territory, as
defined through the international discourse of indigeneity. Indeed, the documents of global discourse—most notably the UN Declaration on the Rights
of Indigenous Peoples and the ILO Convention 169 on Indigenous and Tribal
Peoples—conceptualize indigeneity as an essential quality that inheres
in indigenous bodies. Possession of this quality in contemporary Nepal is
expressed in essentialized, embodied terms—"we are indigenous"—rather
than in the territorial terms that might have characterized such assertions of
distinctiveness in the past: "we have kipat." The now widespread use of the
term *indigenous* in political discourse, as well as in legislation like the 2002
Nepal Foundation for the Development of Indigenous Nationalities (NFDIN)
Act that legally recognizes indigeneity, has inscribed the relationship between
ethnicity and territory in the bodies of indigenous people themselves. This puts
the onus on such individuals to develop a new set of techniques to objectify
that relationship and make it recognizable to others, in the absence of state
policies that objectify the relationship between ethnicity and territory in the

legal terms that kipat once did. In the age of indigeneity, the concept of kipat has become refigured as shorthand for evidence of ancestral rights to territory. Although that legal system no longer exists, use of the term kipat now expresses the historical consciousness of having once held such territorial rights, as in the simple Nepali phrase, *yo hamro kipat ho* (this is our kipat). Even groups who do not possess historical evidence of actual kipat grants often use this terminology to describe their relationship to the territories on which they live.

In all these ways, contemporary invocations of kipat must be understood as an assertion of ethnic consciousness on the one hand while, on the other, that assertion is achieved in a manner that implicitly validates the sovereignty of the Nepali state in its role as recognizing agent. Although the historical claim to kipat enables contemporary indigenous territorial claims, it does so within a framework wherein the central Nepali state is recognized as the bestower of an autonomy within its borders that stops short of full self-determination. It also glosses over the interceding decades of state appropriation of kipat through the awarding of land rights to high-caste state officials through the system of *jagir*, which rewarded service with appropriated lands (see Shneiderman 2015, 111–13). Ultimately, Janajati renditions of the ethnicity-territory relationship that emphasize kipat recognize the Nepali state as the key arbiter of recognition, so it recognizes them back: theirs is an ethnic consciousness with signifying power within the existing nation-state frame.

Janajati livelihoods have generally been composed by a combination of subsistence agriculture on small-holdings in rugged hill areas, tenant labor for high-caste landowners, and migrant wage labor. Without adequate land to survive as exclusively agrarian subjects, members of most Janajati communities have had to supplement their resources through mobile trade or labor in various directions including northward to what is now China's Tibetan Autonomous Region, eastward and westward to Indian Himalayan regions, and southward to India's larger cities. Perhaps their best-known and highest-status route of labor migration has been through the British army's Gurkha regiments; however, this is an exclusive opportunity that has led to relatively high incomes (often reinvested in land back in hill areas of Nepal) for a privileged few, which stands in contrast to uncompensated corvée labor for the Nepali state, which characterized the historical experiences of many more (Holmberg, March, and Tamang 1999). Although this is a broad generalization, we might say that Janajatis have existed in a hybrid space where they are not fully alienated from their land yet are also not fully in control of it or able to rely on its material resources for all of their needs. They have long supplemented territorially based livelihoods and identities with other forms of income and identity production that entangle them intextricably with others—particularly high-caste denizens of the Nepali state.

Janajati claims to difference have therefore historically mobilized a symbolic repertoire through which they situate themselves fully within the Pahadi-dominated nationalist vision of what it is to be the ideal type "Nepali." These include items like the *khukuri* knife, made famous as the symbol of the Gurkha regiments, as well as the *madal* (two-sided drum). With their expert objectification of these pan-Himalayan cultural tropes, Janajatis are Pahadis with a difference (from the dominant high-caste norm), but they are still Pahadi—hill-dwellers whose claim to territory at once asserts distinction and validates the central Nepali state's power by recognizing it as the key arbiter of both ethnic classification and property ownership.

Madhesi assertions of territorial belonging do none of these things.[25] The trope of kipat is not available to Madhesi Nepalis because they were never historically recognized as the rightful holders of communal land title by the central Nepali state as many Janajati groups were. Moreover, "the area of today's eastern and central Tarai had been subject to constantly shifting and overlapping claims to political control, tenurial regulation and taxation until the demarcation of Nepal's southern border after the 1814–1816 war with the British East-India Company" (Rinck 2015, following Michael 2012). Parts of the Western Tarai remained under British control until the 1860s, an anomaly in Nepal's nationalist narrative of noncolonization (Gill 2017).[26]

When Nepal's Prime Minister Jang Bahadur finally gained control of these regions in exchange for his complicity in helping the British subdue the 1857 Sepoy Mutiny, he bestowed the label "Naya Muluk"—or "new possessions"—on the area. This term, which is still used today, highlights the historical lack of integration into the central polity that the region has always experienced, and also points to its status as an uncomfortable reminder of what journalist Prashant Jha (2014) has called Nepal's "partial sovereignty." Indeed, the Naya Muluk and its adjacent Tarai regions were always seen as "other," a site suitable for exploitative resource extraction—just as former Janajati kipat areas were—but without the close integration into state mechanisms (such as the army, palace court, etc.) from which Janajatis benefited. At the same time, the lack of integration into central processes of the Nepali state also left the Tarai open to significant Indian political influence.

Following the accession of Naya Muluk, in 1861 Jang Bahadur's administration established the *jimidari* system across much of the Tarai. Revenue officials responsible to the central state "were sent to settle in strategic locations across the Tarai in exchange for collecting a fixed amount of taxes, and providing agricultural inputs. In return, they received a plot of tax-free land for them-selves."[27] This established a multitiered system for land extraction from "trad-itional elites"—Tharus and several middle- and high-caste Madhesi descent groups—as well as from those at the bottom of the pyramid who served as tenant sharecroppers. As Rinck quotes the descendant of an influential local politician from the 1940s–1950s, "Land was the true basis of power at the time" (Rinck 2015).

But this power was not free of identity markers. Those who are now lead-ing mobilizations in the Tarai—Tharus and Yadavs (as well as Jhas)—were traditional landed elites whose power diminished as the central state deployed its own administrators and gradually stripped them of their power. As Arjun Guneratne poignantly sums it up, "The Tharu elite went from being 'little kings' to servants of the state and then to being quite marginal to the state's admin-istration of the Tarai" (Guneratne 2010, 23). We may then begin to see how nested levels of hierarchy situate marginality as relative. The need to objectify the relationship between ethnicity and territory becomes more pressing at cer-tain historical conjunctures. In this case, when a group who was once dominant becomes subjugated to another, the promise of ethnicity, inc. as a means of reas-serting past hegemony at the local level begins to look like a possible bulwark against the vagaries of an unpredictably restructuring nation-state at the center.

FROM TERRITORIAL TO CULTURAL PROPERTY

From this brief summary, we can begin to understand the existence of an embodied relation between ethnicity and territory for those who assert Tharu and Madhesi political identities and the powerful, affectively real dimensions of ethnic consciousness that it encodes. However, a significant problem for these groups has long been that, unlike the hill and mountain Janajati groups, their symbolic repertoire for asserting cultural difference appears (at least to a high-caste Nepali Pahadi observer—such as most officials of the state bureau-cracy) to be "Indian" rather than distinctively "Nepali" in the way that Janajati cultural displays do. Without distinctive expressive or material cultures, items of dress, or food that are recognizable within the Nepali nationalist imaginary, it has been challenging for Madhesis to secure recognition within Nepali state paradigms for acknowledging difference and inequality. Instead, popular dis-course often portrays them as outsiders or noncitizens with an affinity for India who are attempting to co-opt the Nepali polity.

Yet it is participation in the polity that most Madhesi activists want, not secession or overthrow of the system itself.[28] As columnist Apoorva Lal wrote,

"To many of these protesters, their Nepal has never existed; it has merely stood for what they have been deprived of, both legally and emotionally. That they are angry is evidence that they want in."[29] Or, in Guneratne's (2010, 28) account, "the Tharu (and the Madhesi) are Nepali and not Indian, but they seek to be Nepali on their own terms, not those historically imposed on them by the state." In other words, all of these authors concur that rather than seeking a recognition of their own "sovereign existence" in order to "assert it against the state" (Comaroff and Comaroff 2009, 82), Madhesi activists seek to parlay their own stigma as embodied reminders of Nepal's "partial sovereignty" (Jha 2014) into access to the center. Territorial recognition of their historical dominion through the new constitution would not have been a precursor to secession or further ethnocorporatization. Rather, it would have been a stepping-stone to the desired full integration in the state that they have so long been denied and would have likely worked to diminish further development of a cultural-ist ethnocorporate identity. Here we see how territorial recognition of ethnic claims through the paradigm of ethnicity, inc. may not lead toward greater assertion of difference, ethnic sovereignty, or antistate mobilization but rather diminish the desire or felt need for such hardening of boundaries.

Unfortunately, what I have just described remains the path not taken in Nepal. With the 2015 constitution failing to offer adequate territorial recognition, activists began exploring other avenues for mobilization. Madhesi movements have often been understood at the center to be undergirded by political, rather than cultural, motivations. For instance, Chaitanya Mishra (2012, 82) wrote, "The Madhesi protest, thus, was far more political and economic than cultural. The Tarai-Madhesh had acquired a much higher level of economic and financial clout than it was given political and cultural credit for.... There had been building, in a sense, a serious dissonance between the demographic, economic, financial . . . clout of the Tarai-Madhesh on the one hand and its lowly political and cultural status on the other."

In talking with a Madhesi interlocutor in late 2015, I commented that I had indeed not previously noticed much of what we might call "objectification of culture" within Madhesi self-representational strategies. "No," he confirmed, "how could we try that when anything we do is seen to be Indian?" But after a moment's reflection, he described how his father insisted on wearing a *dhoti* to political meetings in the capital. A *dhoti* is the long sarong that constitutes "traditional" men's dress across much of the Tarai on both sides of the border. It's also a derogatory term used by Pahadis to refer to Madhesis. My friend, about my own age, in his early forties said, "My father could just about get away with it, but I never could. In my father's era there was still a sense of legitimate ethnic difference even within the political sphere, while by the time I was coming of age the nationalist idea of 'Nepali' was hardened and I never wanted to emphasize my 'Madhesi' identity."

The next day, a mutual friend of both of ours posted a photo on Facebook showing Madhesi protestors, dressed in dhoti, holding signs demanding a *dhoti pradesh*, or a "dhoti state."[30] I asked the same interlocutor whether he had seen this form of protest before. "Never," he said. "It's only now that we have been rejected as Nepali by this constitution that we are freely claiming our own culture." In other words, after trying for so long to "fit in" as Nepali, but finding that every effort to do so was not reciprocated by the state, there was no longer any logic in trying to downplay the Indian-like elements of Madhesi identity. A self-conscious shift in representational strategy was underway, with a turn toward the culturalist strategies of objectification that Janajati groups had long employed in making claims to indigeneity. Perhaps the dhoti pradesh protestors were bolstered by new political alliances with Janajati groups, as evidenced by the Federal Socialist Forum party described earlier—a confluence of factors that were for the first time encouraging Madhesis to appropriate strategies of ethnicity to make territorial claims, without deploying the trope of indigeneity per se. A widely circulated social media post during the early May 2016 joint Madhesi-Janajati protests showed Madhesis dancing in the streets to Janajati drum beats. Perhaps they were dancing toward meaningful ethnic signification within the nation-state frame, drawing on the existing Janajati repertoire.

CONCLUSION: FROM COMMODIFICATION
TO OBJECTIFICATION

What I have described demonstrates an intense affective politics of self-objectification—both on the part of the Janajati and high-caste scholars described in the first part of the chapter and on the part of the Madhesi activists described in the second part—but how do we understand them as processes of commodification that deepen our understanding of ethnicity, inc?

Some scholars have argued that neoliberalism invited identity to take shape as a major political category in Nepal (Leve 2011), but in such discussions, neoliberalism itself remains underdefined. While Nepal has experienced significant neoliberal influences through the international development apparatus present since the 1950s, which has, indeed, in recent years often pushed toward the understanding of identity as "brand" (Shneiderman 2013a), that apparatus has not encompassed all groups equally. As the Madhesi interlocutor cited earlier put it, "Those NGOs are what has pushed Janajati toward using cultural demonstrations—we have never had those NGOs in the Madhes." Moreover, although development actors may have significantly influenced processes on the ground in specific locations through their programmatic engagement, they seem to have ultimately had relatively little influence on the outcome of the political process at the center. After millions of dollars invested in "postconflict" "good governance" and "inclusive state-building," these key words have left relatively little imprint on the 2015 constitution as actually promulgated. As was already clear by 2012, key political actors were not only disregarding the international community's steer in these domains but also actively thwarting their ability to operate, as in the case of the World Bank/DFID Gender and Social Exclusion Assessment described.

In addition, in Nepal there seems to be little connection in most cases between the production of ethnocommodities for tourist consumption and the kind of political-economic transformation that most ethnic actors, both Janajati and Madhesi, have sought. This is not to say that ethnocommodities do not exist but rather that it is difficult to trace their relationship to political mobilization. Apart from the body of literature on Sherpas that addresses the interplay between tourism and self-representation (Adams 1996, Ortner 2001), there is very little anthropological work in Nepal that explicitly describes the sort of relationships that seem common in African contexts. In the Sherpa context, it is not clear how the economic gains made through engagement with tourism and mountaineering are parlayed into political ones, if at all. Indeed, much recent Sherpa political activity—as in recent highly publicized fights with climbers on the face of Mount Everest—seems to have been directed at undoing the ethnic image of compliant mountain guide that was generated in an earlier era, in favor of forging a newly political identity, critical of both foreign tourists and the central Nepali state.[31] In other words, Nepali ethnic actors may engage with ethnicity, inc., not primarily to produce material objects as ethnocommodities for direct economic benefit through tourist sale, but rather to focus on objectifying the relationship between their own ethnic bodies and the territories they claim in terms recognizable to the state so as to prompt political recognition. Here, we can see ethnicity, inc. as a multifaceted site of contestation between the state and its own margins—one interpellated by external forces but not inherently produced by them.

Guneratne's (2001) description of Tharu encounters with tourists provides a further illustrative example. He emphasized how these experiences of the other are mediated by high-caste guides, resulting not in the increased conversion of labor to culture by members of the Tharu community but rather the conversion of the high-caste guides' labor into exclusive nationalist representations that compel Tharu to retreat ever further from the tourist encounter. As Guneratne put it: "The foreign tourist cannot distinguish between Nepalese unless the differences are pointed out; one native is much like another. The task of differentiation falls to the tourist guide. The Tharus are not only the 'other' in relation to the guides . . . but are also defined by the guides as the 'other' in relation to the tourist" (2001, 535). Ultimately, "While the presence of foreign tourists . . . helps to demarcate ethnic boundaries . . . the discourse this presence engenders also serves to call attention to the relative lack of success in the state's project of creating a sense of common peoplehood among Nepalese. . . . The idea of a Nepali nation thus becomes problematized in this encounter with tourism" (538). I cite this at length to demonstrate how tourism may not always serve as a driver for increased self-commodification, leading to economic income controlled by ethnic communities themselves, but may also reveal incomplete nationalisms and partial sovereignties. It is here that we can begin to see the disjuncture between ethnicity, inc. and nationality, inc. that may exist in many cases. Both may be understood as sets of affective potentialities differentially experienced by variegated actors, depending on the material circumstances that shape their relationship to territory and the signifying repertoires available to them to objectify that relationship.

Although external actors, such as development agencies and tourists, remain part of the story in Nepal, and the country is economically interconnected with global financial flows through the remittance economy—an important additional theme that I have not been able to explore in depth here—I think we will better understand the scenario by focusing on national and regional political histories and the discursive circulation of ideas that they have promoted. It is the Nepali state and its political elites who must provide meaningful recognition of ethnic consciousness in the current political moment, not the global market. It's further possible that the hegemonic communist presence in many Nepali political domains over the last half century has led to the lack of economically desirable mechanisms for producing ethnocommodities in Nepal. With some variation, communist actors of Maoist, UML, and other factional persuasions have understood ethnicity as an epiphenomenon that will disappear in the face of class struggle. Bolstered by the neo-Marxian modernist Nepali social scientific discourse detailed in this chapter that seeks to delegitimize ethnicity as a basis for political claims, it's hardly surprising that the production of saleable ethnocommodities has not been a key strategy for ethnoactivists who rely on political patronage from these communist parties.

At the same time, both the Maoists and UML have been known to promote folkloristic demonstrations of "culture" that demonstrate ethnic diversity in the sense also familiar from China and Russia (cf. Mottin 2010; Stirr 2013). At least from the perspective of communist party leaders, these are "safe" deployments of the "currency of culture" (Cattelino 2008; see also Shneiderman 2015, chap. 5) and historically only ever included Janajati cultural forms, not Madhesi ones, for all of the reasons described.

It is such folkloristic objectifications of intangible culture that are acceptable as legitimate displays of ethnic content from the viewpoint of the central Nepali state, particularly its communist scions. The political objectification of the embodied relation between ethnicity and territory, particularly by Madhesis, is equally unpalatable. This is why the caption for the dhoti pradesh protest photo offered by the Madhesi social worker who posted it online is very apt: "Jhalanath Khanal: here is your worst nightmare come true: a Dhoti Pradesh." Not only is the territorial threat of a Madhesi state a nightmare for this UML leader, whose statement about Madhesi protests being "meaningless" began this chapter, but the notion that Madhesis might find ways to represent themselves in appropriately signifying cultural terms as part of the nation is also a bad dream for communist nationalists.

However, even if such mobilizations of ethnicity, inc. can be read as a powerful response from below to the failures of state inclusivity, the pragmatic pathways that link them to actual state transformation at the administrative level are complex and indeterminate. In early 2017, Nepal's Local Level Restructuring Commission submitted its report to the government. Charged with identifying potential special autonomous areas for marginalized groups within the new federal design, the commission failed to offer any concrete recommendations. A member of the commission told the press, "We needed the actual data and places where such people or communities reside. But we did not get them."[32]

For all of the work to visibly objectify relationships between ethnicity and territory on the part of diverse marginalized communities over the preceding ten years, decisions were ultimately made by bureaucrats who did not even bother to engage with the vast body of discursive and visual evidence in the public domain documenting such labor, let alone to read the wide range of social scientific literature available about these groups. Despite insinuations otherwise in all directions, for the moment it is not marginalized communities themselves, social scientists, or the market that controls the terms of ethnicity, inc. in Nepal but, rather, a resurgent state that at once seeks to ethnicize its own dominance and delegitimize the ethnic claims of its socioeconomically marginalized communities; however, the terms of control remain contested, and the future of ethnicity, inc. may hold affective potentialities that transform both the consciousness of various actors and political structures themselves in ways as yet unknown.

ACKNOWLEDGMENTS

I thank the Wenner-Gren Foundation Grant Number 8988 and UBC Hampton Faculty Fellowship for supporting research that contributed to the arguments here. I am grateful to Jacob Rinck, Deepak Thapa, Mark Turin, and Catherine Warner for their comments, as well as to the participants at the 2015 Ethnicity, Inc., Revisited workshop and to George Paul Meiu and the other editors of this volume for their patience and supportive suggestions.

NOTES

1. The CPN-UML merged with the Communist Party of Nepal-Maoist Centre in May 2018 to re-create a single Nepal Communist Party, after this paper was drafted.

2. "Free Supply Nepal's Right, Says UML Leader Khanal," *Himalayan Times*, September 25, 2015, https://thehimalayantimes.com/kathmandu/free-supply -nepals-right-says-uml-leader-khanal/. The original article was later edited in the online version to use less inflammatory phrases.

3. "India Should End Its Blockade: Oil," *Kathmandu Post*, September 29, 2015, http://kathmandupost.ekantipur.com/news/2015-09-29/india-should-end -its-blockade-to-nepal-oli.html.

4. This chapter was drafted in October 2015 and focuses largely on dynamics up till that point.

5. Following anthropologist Mallika Shakya's comments in the Focaal journal blog, "Ethnicity in Nepal's New Constitution," Focaal, September 28, 2015, http://www.focaalblog.com/2015/09/28/mallika-shakya-ethnicity-in -nepals-new-constitution/.

6. The postearthquake political dynamics in Nepal are in many ways akin to what Edward Simpson (2013) describes for Gujarat, India, after the 2001 earthquake, including Narendra Modi's rise to power. See Paudel and Le Billon (2018) and Harrowell and Özerdem (2018) for further details.

7. See the Cultural Anthropology HotSpots collection that I edited with Amanda Snellinger for a problematization of the term *postconflict*. Shneiderman, Sara, and Amanda Snellinger, eds. 2014. "The Politics of 'Postconflict': On the Ground in South Asia." Hot Spots series, *Fieldsights*, March 24. https://culanth .org/fieldsights/series/the-politics-of-postconflict-on-the-ground-in-south-asia.

8. See Shneiderman and Tillin (2015), as well as Adhikari and Gellner (2016) and Shneiderman et al. (2016) for further context. For maps of the 2010 and 2012 proposals, see Shneiderman and Tillin 2015, p. 32–33. For the actual provincial map implemented by the 2015 constitution and currently in effect, see http://www.election.gov.np/uploads/Pages/1564381682_np.pdf.

9. A constitutional amendment to revise these boundaries in a manner more acceptable to Madhesi constituents was tabled in April 2017 but defeated in parliament in August of the same year.

10. Tharu are an indigenous Tarai community whose leadership has at times joined forces with the Janajati movement, at others with the Madhesi movement, and at others mobilized independently. From a Tharu perspective, Madhesis are also relatively recent immigrants to the area. See Guneratne (2001, 2002, 2010) for details of Tharu ethnolinguistic identities and Fujikura (2013) and Hoffman (2017) on Tharu political mobilization. Madhesi communities often have linguistic, cultural, and kinship ties to populations across the border in India's states of Bihar and Uttar Pradesh. For analyses of Madhesi identity formation, see Jha (2014) and Sijapati (2013).

11. See Guneratne (2010, 24–25). In Chitwan and areas farther west, USAID-funded initiatives cleared the region of malaria, and the Nepali government offered subsidies to Pahadis to settle there. Historian Tom Robertson outlines these dynamics in a lecture available online, "Developing International Development: DDT and US Environmental and Social Engineering in the Chitwan Valley, 1952–1965," Social Science Baha, May 20, 2014, https://soscbaha.org/lecture-series-lxxvi-2/.

12. "Agreement between the Government of Nepal and the Madhesi People's Right Forum, Nepal," August 30, 2017, https://www.scribd.com/document/281944949/2007-08-30-Agreement-spa-Govt-mjf-ENG.

13. "Agreement between the Government and Janajatis," August 7, 2017, http://www.constitutionnet.org/sites/default/files/2007-08-07-agreement_between_government_and_janajatis.pdf.

14. The Social Inclusion Research Fund website no longer exists. For a description of the project see https://cdsatu.edu.np/completion-of-research-project/.

15. "Debate over Federalism in Nepal," *Nepal in a Day's Work*, April 29, 2011, https://nepalinadayswork.wordpress.com/2011/04/29/debate-over-federalism-in-nepal/.

16. The former term was perceived as emphasizing prior rights and therefore potentially polarizing, while the latter was intended to emphasize the positive aspects of "identity" as something that everyone possesses.

17. "Ethnic States not Possible," *Nepali Times*, March 9, 2012, http://nepalitimes.com/news.php?id=19087#.Vhb88RNVhBc.

18. Roshan Sedhai, "Three Parties Merge to Become Sanghiya Samajbadi Forum—Nepal," *Kathmandu Post*, June 16, 2015, http://kathmandupost .ekantipur.com/news/2015-06-16/three-parties-merge-to-become-sanghiya -samajbadi-forum-nepal.html.

19. Krishna Hachhethu, "A Middle Way," *Kathmandu Post*, November 4, 2014, http://kathmandupost.ekantipur.com/news/2014-11-04/a-middle-way.html.

20. Kanak Mani Dixit, "Post-development Era," *Nepali Times*, March 24–30, 2017, http://nepalitimes.com/regular-columns/On-the-way-up/post -development-era,873.

21. Rup Sunar, "Pressure from 'Hill Elites' Halts DfID Exclusion Report," *Blogging My Passion*, August 28, 2012, http://roopsunar.blogspot.ca/2012/08 /pressure-from-hill-elites-halts-dfid.html, accessed September 24, 2017. See also Drucza (2016) for a more detailed discussion of these dynamics.

22. Dovan Rai, "Madhesis among Us," *The Record*, October 5, 2015, http:// www.recordnepal.com/perspective/madhesis-among-us#sthash.62gmjCQV .dpuf.

23. Mukta S. Lama Tamang, "[Constitution Special] Forgotten Promises," *Kathmandu Post*, September 20, 2015, http://kathmandupost.ekantipur.com /news/2015-09-20/forgotten-promises.html.

24. The remainder of this section draws from chapter 6 of my book (Shneiderman 2015) but takes those arguments further by relating them to the Madhesi movement.

25. This section builds on the work of my student Jacob Rinck, a PhD candidate in anthropology at Yale, especially in his 2015 conference paper "Land Reform, Social Change, and Political Cultures in Nepal's Tarai" and his forthcoming dissertation, "The Future of Political Economy: International Labor Migration, Agrarian Change and Shifting Visions of Development in Nepal."

26. See also CK Lal's article, "The Tharu Heartland," accessed September 24, 2017, https://www.facebook.com/archiveCKlal/posts/965774053443018.

27. For further historical detail about livelihoods and economies in the Tarai, see Gaige (1975) and Burghart (2016).

28. A notable exception was Dr. CK Raut, who was imprisoned for his advocacy of Madhesi secession until he signed an agreement with the government in March 2019, giving up his demands in exchange for having all charges dropped.

29. Apoorva Lal, "Cycle of Exclusion," *Kathmandu Post*, September 30, 2015, http://kathmandupost.ekantipur.com/news/2015-09-30/cycle-of-exclusion .html.

30. Indiana University Press declined to publish images of this or other social media posts due to copyright concerns.

31. Peter Hansen insightfully notes that the recent Everest debacles may have to do with Sherpa reassertion of territorial sovereignty within the context of Nepal's state restructuring process ("Have Sherpas Had It?," *Seeker*, May 2, 2013, https://www.seeker.com/have-sherpas-had-it-1767481767.html.

32. Binod Ghimire, "LLRC's Tenure Ends without Completing Task," *Kathmandu Post*, March 14, 2017, http://kathmandupost.ekantipur.com/news /2017-03-14/llrcs-tenure-ends-without-completing-task.html.

REFERENCES

Adams, Vincanne. 1996. *Tigers of the Snow and Other Virtual Sherpas: An Ethnography of Himalayan Encounters.* Princeton, NJ: Princeton University Press.

Adhikari, Krishna, and David Gellner. 2016. "New Identity Politics and the 2012 Collapse of Nepal's Constituent Assembly: When the Dominant Becomes the Other." *Modern Asian Studies* 50 (6): 2009–40.

Bennett, Lynn, Bandita Sijapati, and Deepak Thapa. 2013. *Gender and Social Exclusion in Nepal.* Kathmandu: HimalBooks.

Burghart, Richard. 1984. "The Formation of the Concept of Nation-State in Nepal." *Journal of Asian Studies* 44 (1): 101–25.

———. 2016. *The History of Janakpurdham.* Kathmandu: HimalBooks.

Cattelino, Jessica. 2008. *High Stakes: Florida Seminole Gaming and Sovereignty.* Durham: Duke University Press.

Comaroff, John L., and Jean Comaroff. 2009. *Ethnicity, Inc.* Chicago: University of Chicago.

Darnal, Suvash. 2009. *A Land of Our Own: Conversations with Dalit Members of Constituent Assembly.* Kathmandu: Samata Foundation and Jagaran Media Center.

Des Chene, Mary. 2007. "Is Nepal in South Asia? The Condition of Non-Postcoloniality." *Studies in Nepali History and Society* 12 (2): 207–23.

Drucza, Kristie. 2016. "Social Inclusion in the Post-Conflict State of Nepal: Donor Practice and the Political Settlement." *Global Social Policy* 17 (1): 62–88.

Forbes, Anne Armbrecht. 1999. "Mapping Power: Disputing Claims to Kipat Lands in Northeastern Nepal." *American Ethnologist* 26 (1): 114–38.

Fujikura, Tatsuro. 2013. *Discourses of Awareness: Development, Social Movements, and the Practices of Freedom in Nepal.* Kathmandu: Martin Chautari.

Gaige, Frederick. 1975. *Regionalism and National Unity in Nepal.* Berkeley: University of California Press.

Gellner, David. 2007. "Caste, Ethnicity and Inequality in Nepal." *Economic and Political Weekly* 42 (20): 1823–28.

———. 2014. "The 2013 Elections in Nepal." *Asian Affairs* 45 (2): 243–61.

Gellner, David, Joanna Pfaff-Czarnecka, and John Whelpton, eds. 1997. *Nationalism and Ethnicity in a Hindu Kingdom: The Politics of Culture in Contemporary Nepal*. Amsterdam: Harwood Publishers.

Gill, Peter. 2017. "Days and Nights in Nepalgunj: Life, Politics and Identity in an Underappreciated Border City." *Record*, March 1, 2017. http://www.recordnepal .com/wire/nepalgunj-diary/.

Guneratne, Arjun. 2001. "Shaping the Tourist's Gaze: Representing Ethnic Difference in a Nepali Village." *Journal of the Royal Anthropological Institute* 7 (3): 527–43.

———. 2002. *Many Tongues, One People: The Making of Tharu Identity in Nepal*. Ithaca, NY: Cornell University Press.

———. 2010. "Tharu-State Relations in Nepal and India." *Himalaya: Journal for the Association of Nepal and Himalayan Studies* 29 (1): 19–28.

Hale, Charles. 2005. "Neoliberal Multiculturalism: The Remaking of Cultural Rights and Racial Dominance in Central America." *Political and Legal Anthropology Review* 28 (1): 10–19.

Hangen, Susan. 2010. *The Rise of Ethnic Politics in Nepal*. London: Routledge.

Harrowell, Elly, and Alpaslan Özerdem. 2018. "The Politics of the Post-Conflict and Post-Disaster Nexus in Nepal." *Conflict, Security and Development* 18 (3): 181–205.

Hoffmann, Michael. 2017. *The Partial Revolution: Labor, Social Movements and the Invisible Hand of Mao in Western Nepal*. New York: Berghahn Publications.

Holmberg, David, Kathryn March, and Suryaman Tamang. 1999. "Local Production/Local Knowledge: Forced Labor from Below." *Studies in Nepali History and Society*, no. 4, 5–64.

Höfer, Andras. (1979) 2004. *The Caste Hierarchy and the State in Nepal: A Study of the Muluki Ain of 1854*. Kathmandu: Himal Books.

Jha, Prashant. 2014. *Battles of the New Republic: A Contemporary History of Nepal*. New Delhi: Aleph Book Company.

Lawoti, Mahendra. 2016. "Constitution and Conflict: Mono-Ethnic Federalism in a Poly-Ethnic Nepal." Working Paper. Western Michigan University, Kalamazoo.

Leve, Lauren. 2011. "Identity." *Current Anthropology* 52 (4): 513–35.

Levine, Nancy. 1987. "Caste, State, and Ethnic Boundaries in Nepal." *Journal of Asian Studies* 46 (1): 71–88.

Limbu, Pauline. n.d. "From Kipat to Autonomy: Land and Territory in Today's Limbuwan Movement." Unpublished manuscript.

Michael, Bernardo. 2012. *Statemaking and Territory in South Asia: Lessons from the Anglo-Gorkha War (1814–1816)*. New York: Anthem Press.

Mishra, Chaitanya. 2012. "Ethnic Upsurge in Nepal: Implications for Federalization." In *Ethnicity and Federalisation in Nepal*, edited by Chaitanya Mishra and Om Gurung, 58–90. Kathmandu: Central Department of Sociology/ Anthropology.

Mottin, Monica. 2010. "Catchy Melodies and Clenched Fists: Performance as Politics in Maoist Cultural Programs." In *The Maoist Insurgency in Nepal: Revolution in the Twenty-First Century,* edited by Mahendra Lawoti and Anup K. Pahari, 52–72. New York: Routledge.

Onta, Pratyoush. 2006. "The Growth of the *Adivasi Janajati* Movement in Nepal after 1990: The Non-Political Institutional Agents." *Studies in Nepali History and Society* 11 (2): 303–54.

Ortner, Sherry. 2001. *Life and Death on Mt. Everest: Sherpas and Himalayan Mountaineering.* Princeton, NJ: Princeton University Press.

Paudel, Dinesh, and Philippe Le Billon. 2018. "Geo-Logics of Power: Disaster Capitalism, Himalayan Materialities, and the Geopolitical Economy of Reconstruction in Post-Earthquake Nepal." *Geopolitics,* DOI: 10.1080/14650045 .2018.1533818.

Regmi, Mahesh Chandra. 1976. *Landownership in Nepal.* Berkeley: University of California Press.

Rinck, Jacob. 2015. "Land Reform, Social Change and Political Cultures in Nepal's Tarai", Conference paper presented at the 2015 Annual Kathmandu Conference on Nepal and the Himalaya, Social Science Baha, Kathmandu.

Shneiderman, Sara. 2013a. "Developing a Culture of Marginality: Nepal's Current Classificatory Moment." *Focaal* 65:42–55.

———. 2013b. "Himalayan Border Citizens: Sovereignty and Mobility in the Nepal-Tibetan Autonomous Region (TAR) of China Border Zone." *Political Geography* 35:25–36.

———. 2015. *Rituals of Ethnicity: Thangmi Identities Between Nepal and India.* Philadelphia: University of Pennsylvania Press.

Shneiderman, Sara, and Louise Tillin. 2015. "Restructuring States, Restructuring Ethnicity: Looking across Disciplinary Boundaries at Federal Futures in India and Nepal." *Modern Asian Studies* 49 (1): 1–39.

Shneiderman, Sara, Luke Wagner, Jacob Rinck, Amy Johnson, and Austin Lord. 2016. "Nepal's Ongoing Political Transformation: A Review of Post-2006 Literature on Conflict, the State, Identities, and Environments." *Modern Asian Studies* 50 (6): 2041–114.

Sijapati, Bandita. 2013. "In Pursuit of Recognition: Regionalism, Madhesi Identity and the Madhes Andolan." In *Nationalism and Ethnic Conflict: Identities and Mobilization after 1990,* edited by Mahendra Lawoti and Susan Hangen, 145–72. Abingdon: Routledge.

Simpson, Edward. 2013. *The Political Biography of an Earthquake: Aftermath and Amnesia in Gujarat, India.* London: Oxford University Press.

Stirr, Anna. 2013. "Tears for the Revolution: Nepali Musical Nationalism, Emotion, and the Maoist Movement." In *Revolution in Nepal,* edited by Marie Lecomte-Tilouine, 367–92. Delhi: Oxford University Press.

Tamang, Mukta. 2009. "Tamang Activism, History, and Territorial Consciousness." In *Ethnic Activism and Civil Society in South Asia*, edited by David Gellner, 269–90. Delhi: Sage.

World Bank/DFID. 2006. *Unequal Citizens: Gender, Caste and Ethnic Exclusion in Nepal—Summary*. World Bank and DFID: Kathmandu.

SARA SHNEIDERMAN is Associate Professor in the Department of Anthropology, the School of Public Policy and Global Affairs, and the Institute of Asian Research at the University of British Columbia. She is author of *Rituals of Ethnicity: Thangmi Identities Between Nepal and India*.

EIGHT

—w—

CULTURAL COMMODIFICATION IN GLOBAL CONTEXTS

Australian Indigeneity, Inequality, and Militarization in the Twenty-First Century

EVE DARIAN-SMITH

IN MANY WAYS THE BASIC premise of the book *Ethnicity, Inc.* (Comaroff and Comaroff 2009)—that ethnicity is increasingly being incorporated and culture commodified in our current age of image entrepreneurialism and late capitalist enterprise—is even more globally evident now than it was ten years ago. In this essay, I want to build on *Ethnicity, Inc.*'s provocations and explore the "costs and contradictions" associated with the turning of culture into a marketable product (2009, 139). Specifically, I want to speak to the long histories of colonialism that are still very much in play in the context of neoliberalism. The Comaroffs acknowledge in their conclusion of the book that in the poorest parts of the world "the sale of cultural products, and the simulacra of ethnicized selfhood" may be the "only viable means of survival." That being said, *Ethnicity, Inc.* talks about the wide variety of ways in which "traditional" peoples "constantly find new, often ingenious ways to partake of the identity economy" and in the process become "thoroughly modern" (2009, 149). The account concludes on a rather hopeful tone, arguing that against great odds and long histories of oppression, some indigenous communities have managed to adroitly and astutely find remarkable ways to survive in a global capitalist system and in the process revitalize and perhaps even reinvent a sense of self and community.

Certainly, many of the examples cited in *Ethnicity, Inc.* are uplifting and point to new forms of "self-realization, sentiment, entitlement, enrichment" among some of the most historically oppressed people in the world. Yet these examples are not necessarily reassuring. Indigenous communities constitute some 360 million people, and it should not be forgotten that the number of indigenous peoples who have been able to engage in ethnocapitalism is extremely small. Even in the United States, where some tribes have established casinos and made enormous profits, the vast majority of indigenous peoples in both federally and nonfederally recognized tribes continue to constitute the most impoverished and disadvantaged sector of society. Mass incarceration, unemployment, domestic violence, suicide, disease—all of these societal issues have escalated on and off reservations in recent years. For just as there are growing inequalities in developed Western societies, so is there growing inequality among indigenous peoples worldwide with only a very small number coming up "winners"—the indigenous 1 percent (to use the language of the Occupy movement). The ramifications in the United States is that only the indigenous 1 percent who have parlayed their ethnopreneurialism into moneymaking ventures, which includes establishing Indian-owned casinos, can afford to be involved in what the Comaroffs call "lawfare" against the state. The end result is that the state can blatantly ignore the remaining 99 percent who, not being able to access the legal system, are simply deemed irrelevant.

John and Jean Comaroff (2009, 139) are acutely aware of the costs and contradictions in *Ethnicity, Inc.* They write "it has *both* insurgent possibility *and* a tendency to deepen prevailing lines of inequality, the capacity *both* to enable *and* to disable, the power *both* to animate and to annihilate." Yet throughout the book, they linger on the brighter side—"the promise"—of these contradictions, whereas I want to focus on the mutually constituting relations between enabling/disabling and animating/annihilating that I ultimately see as presenting a darker trajectory that is deeply worrisome. In the first part of this chapter, I present a brief historical overview of the marketing of cultural difference in white Australia. This history is necessary to understand the entwined relations between the country's domestic policies over Indigenous minorities and its international policies with respect to receiving certain immigrants. This history also underscores the significance of the Aboriginal art industry, which emerged in the 1970s and marked to some degree a new era of self-determination for Aboriginal and Torres Strait Islander peoples. Despite the promise of this shift (which in many ways echoes the optimism of *Ethnicity, Inc.*), my interest lies in exploring to what degree ethnopreneurialism in the ensuing decades may have inadvertently aided and abetted insidious forms of neocolonialism that have become one of the hallmarks of today's late capitalist world.

Building on this discussion, in the second part of the chapter, I argue for the need to reframe conversations about ethnicity, inc. to better accommodate contemporary global processes. Since the writing of *Ethnicity, Inc.* it seems that three global concerns have become more pronounced and, I suggest, of particular interest in the context of ethnic-capitalism. These are (1) rising global inequality; (2) mass movements of people around the world fleeing regional wars, conflict, environmental degradation, and natural disasters; and (3) the militarization of nation-states and the justification of particular social policies—both domestic and international—in the name of securitizing national interests. These three intertwined concerns are of particular interest because they cumulatively ensure that increasingly marginalized peoples of the world have less, not more, access and opportunity to take advantage of the manifestations and implications of ethnicity, inc.

With respect to global inequality, the deepening gap between the rich and poor is now listed by the World Economic Forum as its number-one concern because it weakens "social cohesion and security" and hence long-term economic development.[1] Around the world, more and more people are outraged by the decline of the middle classes as expressed by the Occupy movement of 2011. Rising global inequality impacts all countries and regions of the world, be these in the global South or the global North (Collier 2008; Stiglitz 2012). However, given that Indigenous peoples are typically the most impoverished sector of any society and so the most economically and politically vulnerable, global inequality impacts indigenous peoples disproportionally. They are the first to bear the brunt of climate change, environmental devastation, and encroachments on their natural resources (i.e., minerals, water, and biological matter). In times of economic austerity, indigenous peoples are the first to feel the economic pinch and the denial of state-sponsored social services. As a result, livelihoods and cultures are deeply threatened. Moreover, concepts such as indigenous sovereignty and self-determination are profoundly undermined and in a growing number of cases deemed materially irrelevant by financiers, mining companies, development agencies, governments and so on. In short, indigenous peoples are the first to be subject to what Saskia Sassen (2014, 1) calls "a new logics of *expulsion*" from political life.

Rising global inequality underscores that for most indigenous communities, corporatizing and entering the ethnicity, inc. game is the only option available whether they live in the very poorest or the very wealthiest parts of the world. This is because "the current systemic deepening of capitalist relations" reduces all value to economic marketability and increasingly blocks out any other means of social being and economic existence (Sassen 2014, 10). Hence it is increasingly the case that, in most instances, indigenous groups have little choice but to engage in a late capitalism system on terms determined by nonindigenous players (Darian-Smith 2004). The alternative is to face the plight that many indigenous peoples have experienced for centuries under colonial oppression—to be shunned, ignored, silenced, neglected, or ultimately abandoned (Povinelli 2011). In short, indigenous peoples must commodify their ethnic identity or face a very real threat of extinction. Choice—if one can call it such—is limited. Certainly, the Comaroffs are aware in their account of enduring colonial oppression, but I think we need to be more explicit about the engulfing forces of twenty-first-century global inequality in thinking about the forms, processes, risks, and consequences of identity entrepreneurialism.

With respect to refugees and mass movements of people around the world, the figures have risen dramatically since *Ethnicity, Inc.* was published. As reported by the Office of the United Nation's High Commission for Refugees only a few months ago, there are now 68.5 million people on the move (United Nations High Commissioner for Refugees 2018). The numbers of displaced people is the highest recorded in the United Nation agency's fifty-four year history. As a result, we are living in an era of what Steven Vertovec (2011) calls "super-diversity" that is recasting the cultural politics of nation and social organization against a backdrop of mass human migration and the complex melding of religious and ethnic plurality. As we have all witnessed in the European Union's response to Syrian refugees, super-diversity highlights anxieties of state nationalism that are manifesting globally in xenophobia, racism, and brutal state policies of exclusion. The legislation passed by Danish lawmakers in late January 2016 that allows government agencies to seize cash and valuables from asylum seeks (the so-called jewelry bill) is only one instance of the harsh sentiment being expressed by governments across Europe toward refugees. At an international level, populist movements that ushered in Brexit in the United Kingdom and Donald Trump as president in the United States highlight that emerging around the world is the rise of ultra-nationalist ideologies that are in part a response to mass movements of people.

With respect to the militarization of nation-states, this is an artifact of modernity that has taken on specific valence in recent decades (Tilly 1985; Tarrow 2012). Militarization is more than the use of military strategies to shore up state power, the preparedness of a country to go to war, or the sponsorship of military ideals. Rather, it speaks to the deeply embedded cultural values of a given society. "Among those distinctive core beliefs are the notion that the world is a dangerous place, that there are naturally those who must be protected and, conversely, those who must protect, and that every mature and serious government must have a military to secure the protection of its people" (Frühstück 2017, 2). Ramped-up security state apparatuses are usually discussed with respect to the emergence of neoliberal polices that accompanied the global north's policing of the global south through new modes of human security and humanitarian aid. These activities dominated international relations in the 1990s and were supported by the World Bank, World Trade Organization, and the United Nations (Amar 2013). I would add to this narrative by arguing that the same logics whereby the West sought to control the rest can be seen to be operating within Western nations in their dealing with "domestic" foreigners, be these "vulnerable" indigenous peoples, racialized minorities, or criminalized immigrants.

In thinking about some of the risks and contradictions of ethnicity, inc., I wonder how ethnic-entrepreneurialism plays out in the context of a heightened rhetoric of militarization that presents nation-states as seemingly besieged by the impending threat of mass asylum seekers and a dilution of nationalist ideologies, identities, symbolisms, and imagery. In a sense I want to play with the tensions between ethnicity, inc. and nationality, inc.—between indigenous minorities and dominant nationalist majorities competing in a more encompassing global political economy for market share. In Jean and John Comaroff's (2009) book, ethnicity, inc. and nationality, inc. are discussed as discrete phenomena, but I would like to suggest that they are intrinsically and intimately connected. Both forms of commodification speak to what George Yúdice calls "culture-as-resource." In his book, *The Expediency of Culture* (2003), Yúdice refers to the ways culture-as-a-commodity is managed not only through the nation-state but also more and more through a global political economy coordinated "by corporations and the international non-governmental sector (e.g., UNESCO, foundations, nongovernmental organizations). Despite this global circulation, or perhaps because of it, there has emerged a new international division of cultural labor that imbricates local difference with transnational administration and investment" (4). Yúdice's concept of culture-as-resource applies to minority groups as well as nation-states that are both selling essentialized cultural wares and competing for an international economic investment market composed of tourists and corporations. However, it should be noted that what is at stake is more than economic profits since market share equates in many ways with how cultural authority is perceived and power legitimated. So, in a broader sense the successes and failures of ethnocapitalism also reflect the success and failures of marginalized peoples to claim a presence in mainstream society.

Thinking about the essentializing of ethnicity and how different forms of cultural commodification operate through local, national, regional, and global frameworks speaks to my broader research agenda. Indigeneity can be interpreted as a form of ethnicity and for many the choice between an indigenous or ethnic identity is fluid and not mutually exclusive. For other Indigenous peoples, tribal identity may be in tension, or even conflict with a more pan-indigenous ethnic identity. As noted by Duane Champagne (2015), "Often indigenous ethnic groupings are more recognizable to nation-states, since they are willing to conform to the demands and definitions of national political interest groups. In Canada, Métis form detribalized groups with distinct mixed indigenous and European traditions. The Métis seeks rights that are distinguished from tribal Indigenous nations." Notwithstanding the complexities of identity formation and articulation, what interests me are the ways contemporary indigenous politics play out within global contexts that are in turn shifting the terms of conflict between indigenous peoples and state governments.

My underling argument is that too often indigenous politics—and indigenous studies in general—are framed by national borders and classified as domestic issues. But I argue that a country's policies toward its indigenous peoples, and the place of those indigenous peoples within a national imaginary, are constantly being deflected through that country's larger relationship with the rest of the world (Mawani 2009; Darian-Smith 2013; see Ford 2011; Ford and Rowse 2013; Lowe 2015). No nation-state operates as an island, no matter how often and how determinedly the island rhetoric is mobilized (as is the case of Australia and the United Kingdom). In the context of contemporary globalization, the artifice of a nation-state's autonomy and cultural homogeneity is more evident today than ever before. Hence immigration policies seeking to keep certain "aliens" outside the nation-state and maintain the myth of a homogenous national identity are very much connected to a state's indigenous policies seeking to manage domestic "aliens" within (see Parker 2015). And the militarization of state power provides the material and institutional networks to manage these two fronts of security implementation.

These intersecting politics and policies, however, are often overlooked in mainstream political and social thinking. And somewhat curiously, scholars of indigenous studies and scholars of immigration seem determined to keep these arenas of cultural politics analytically separated (cf. Coutin, Richland, and Fortin 2014; Volpp 2015, 291n10). Thinking about the politics of indigeneity—and the mobilization of tribal and ethnic indigenous identities—within a more encompassing global perspective is an approach that explicitly overlays and melds these literatures and scholarly insights.

MARKETING CULTURAL DIFFERENCE
IN WHITE AUSTRALIA

In thinking about global inequality and super-diversity, I turn to the cultural politics surrounding Australian Aboriginal and Torres Strait Islander peoples over the past forty years. Contemporary Australian politics provides an exemplary site through which to think about the incorporation of ethnic groups and commodification of cultural identity for some of the most impoverished peoples in the world. What I argue is that the few indigenous Australians who have participated in ethnocapitalism underscore that it is an enormously ambiguous and risky business, with no ensurance of positive outcomes for either themselves or the wider indigenous population within Australian society. Moreover, as I go on to discuss, when we step back from ethnoenterprise within the nation-state context and take in a broader global picture, cultural capitalism may have unforeseen negative consequences that we are only now beginning to see and appreciate.

The history of British colonialism in Australia, and its impact on the continent's Aboriginal peoples, is very well documented (see Harris 1972; Reynolds 2006, 2013; Gammage 2013; Broome 2010; Hughes 1988). When Captain Cook "discovered" and laid claim to the island continent in 1770, it is estimated that there existed a population of up to 1 million Aboriginal people, making up over 250 different nations speaking nearly as many different languages. Despite the clear evidence of indigenous peoples, Cook declared the continent *terra nullius* (empty land) and established the legal basis for a British settlement to be founded.[2] Under Capitan Arthur Philip, a penal colony was established in Sydney Cove in 1788. Very swiftly European diseases such as smallpox and influenza wiped out many of the surrounding Aboriginal communities. According to Lieutenant Fowell in 1789, only one year after the colony had begun, "Every boat that went down the harbour found them lying dead on the beaches and in the caverns of the rocks. . . . They were generally found with the remains of a small fire on each side of them and some water left within their reach."[3] Those Aboriginal peoples that were not wiped out by disease were driven from their lands as the British settlement grew and land cleared for farming. Many were hunted and killed if they resisted at all, since most settlers at the time considered Aboriginal people akin to dingoes, emus, and kangaroos.[4]

A great deal can be said about Australia's horrifying colonial history. In this chapter, my interest lies in the British and then Australian governments' explicit policies to essentialize and commodify indigenous peoples' cultural difference as a strategy of colonial management. Australia, like other British settler societies, packaged indigenous peoples as backward, uncivilized, violent, lawless, and to a large degree nonhuman. A whole industry of decorative arts for the home featuring exoticized black men and women was established in the colonial era. Quaint silver figurines of fierce spear-throwing indigenous peoples frolicking with kangaroos mounted on blown emu eggs were very popular for the sideboard or tabletop in the latter half of the nineteenth and early twentieth centuries. These and similar decorative pieces deliberately belittled and deni-grated aboriginal peoples, visually categorizing them as part of the country's exotic flora and fauna. This attitude was institutionalized in government policy and enabled the state to keep indigenous communities at an arm's distance, with the prevailing hope that they would eventually die out and become extinct (Har-ris 1972, 13). When Aboriginal people failed in this regard, derogatory imagery helped to substantiate legal policies of land dispossession and justified lack of governmental welfare and support for impoverished Indigenous communities.

Legal, social, and economic forms of discrimination against indigenous peoples continued well into the twentieth century despite pockets of resistance such as the Australian Aborigines' League, which was started by indigenous activists in Melbourne in 1934, and the Aborigines Progressive Association, which was a related Sydney organization that started in 1937 (see Miller 2012; Attwood and Markus 2004). World War II considerably slowed down Aborigi-nal activists' demands for civil and political rights, and it was not until the 1960s that real change occurred with the establishing of the Federal Coun-cil for Aboriginal Advancement (FCAA),[5] which was heavily influenced by the NAACP and black civil rights reforms in the United States (Miller 2012; Darian-Smith 2012). As international media attention gained momentum con-demning Australia's treatment of its indigenous peoples, the 1967 referendum was enthusiastically passed declaring that Aboriginal peoples must be treated as humans and included in the counting of the Australian population. One result was that derogatory images of black Australians went out of fashion, though not out of circulation, as evidenced by the decorative motifs on the country's coins.

It is interesting that at the same time that Australian society expressed a softening of racist attitudes toward its indigenous peoples in the 1960s the country also experienced a softening of racist attitudes toward darker-skinned immigrants. Coinciding with the 1967 referendum was the slow dismantling of Australia's White Australia Policy, which deliberately favored immigrants from English-speaking and European backgrounds. The White Australia policy was officially dropped in 1975. This allowing of more ethnically diverse immigrants into the country coincided with a lesser need to annihilate or assimilate the country's "domestic racial problem." However, while the 1960s and 1970s expe-rienced growth in a more culturally diverse and racially tolerant Australian society, the Australian government was still deeply biased against indigenous peoples and practiced a range of paternalistic and discriminatory laws such as the child removal policy that resulted in the Stolen Generations, which were not entirely abolished until the 1980s (see generally Harris 1972; Broome 2010).

THE RISE OF THE AUSTRALIAN ABORIGINAL
ART MOVEMENT

The modern Australian indigenous art movement can be dated from the 1970s.[6] In 1965, a federal-sponsored tourism report highlighted the possibility of developing Aboriginal arts to sell to foreign visitors. This report helped promote the establishment of a government sponsored company to facilitate the sale of indigenous art called the Aboriginal Arts and Crafts Pty Ltd in 1971. This coincided with a shift in policies toward indigenous communities within the government that sponsored the concept of self-determination and helped promote aboriginal cultures rather than pursuing aggressive former policies of assimilation (Altman 2007, 44).

At the same time that federal legislation was softening toward indigenous peoples, in remote outback communities a new interest was developing among some white Australians in helping indigenous communities who had been devastated by settler colonialism. Against Australia's violent colonial backdrop, a small group of Aboriginal people were encouraged to draw on canvas and wood with acrylic paints provided by a white schoolteacher named Geoffrey Bardon. The year was 1971, and the indigenous community was living in Papunya, a small town in the deep desert outback of the Northern Territory approximately 240 kilometers northwest of Alice Springs. Community members came from a number of different tribes that had been forcibly removed from their ancestral lands and gathered together in the hope of promoting assimilation into white society. Bardon encouraged first schoolchildren and then adult men to paint murals that represented their cultural traditions, body adornment, sacred knowledge, and relationship to the land (see Bardon 1979, 1991). The men expressed themselves in this new European visual medium, painting old cars, hubcaps, and construction debris when they could not afford more conventional canvas and paper. The art was typically executed by a group of artists working together on the ground in a style that came to be colloquially called "dot painting." The original group of artists is widely considered to have started the Papunya Tula Art Movement that included subsequently famous black artists such as Clifford Possum Tjapaltjarri and Kaapa Tjampitjinpa. Dot painting differed enormously from more traditional indigenous art and heralded in what art critic Robert Hughes (2005) later called the "last great art movement of the 20th century."

A large body of literature explores the history and importance of Aboriginal desert art and its influence on subsequent art cooperatives in rural and urban centers around Australia over the past forty years (Bardon and Bardon 2006; Johnson 2007; McCulloch and McCulloch Childs 2008; Kleinert and Neale 2000; Caruana 2003; Myers 2002). What is fascinating here is that, against great odds and with really very few options available, about twenty men at Papunya incorporated and set up their own company (Papunya Tula Artists Ltd.) to help organize the sale of their artwork in 1972.[7] This was necessary given the exploitative nature of white art dealers who slowly, and then more aggressively in the 1980s and 1990s, began marketing dot paintings to national and international art markets. Drawing on the success of the Papunya model, many other art cooperatives were established throughout the 1980s and 1990s. Today Desart, a nonprofit Central Australia Aboriginal organization supporting over forty community-based art centers and ANKAAA (Association of Northern, Kimberley and Arnhem Aboriginal Artists) are the leading networks supporting a vast number of local artists and art centers in rural areas.[8] Within major cities there also exists an extensive network of incorporated art cooperatives, and a good number of these are managed or owned by Aborigines. This successful commodification of culture falls within the optimistic trajectory described in *Ethnicity, Inc.* (Comaroff and Comaroff 2009).

In purely economic terms, contemporary Australian indigenous art is big business, and some pieces are reaching very high prices on the global art market. Within Australia, national galleries now have extensive Aboriginal art holdings and major indigenous art prizes such as the National Aboriginal & Torres Strait Islander Art Award have been established to sponsor and support indigenous artists. Black art is now widely accepted by the nonindigenous society and features in corporate collections, decorates (with unexamined irony) mining company foyers, and greets the visitor to Parliament House in Canberra in the form of a 196-square-meter floor mural. Moreover, Aboriginal art is not confined to so-called high culture, and generic dot images appear on many commodities from T-shirts and clothing, to public transport and airplanes. Dot painting has become a fashionable aesthetic. Despite large problems of art fraud, exploitation, cultural appropriation, and lack of government oversight,[9] as well as various disagreements within some indigenous communities about what sacred symbols and knowledge should be visually presented, there is general consensus by indigenous and nonindigenous peoples that contemporary Aboriginal art has made a significant contribution to the well-being of indigenous Australians. According to Japingka Gallery, located in Perth and representing some of the country's most famous Aboriginal artists for over thirty years, these successful outcomes include:

- Establishing cultural and historic ties to land as part of Native Title transactions
- Maintaining cultural and social cohesion via traditional education methods
- Providing economic stimulus, especially in remote communities
- Engendering cultural pride across generations
- Underpinning return to Country projects in outlying areas.[10]

REVISITING *ETHNICITY, INC.* THROUGH AUSTRALIA'S CULTURAL IDENTITY POLITICS

Given the apparent success of the Australian Aboriginal art movement in both social and economic terms what, may one ask, is the problem? This is the question I asked myself over twenty-years ago when I wrote about competing images of Aboriginal culture in Australian society (Darian-Smith 1993). As a budding intellectual property lawyer, I had taken a graduate seminar on law and the arts and was dismayed by the widespread use of Aboriginal dot painting on a vast range of commodities that did not give due credit to the artists and did not compensate for cultural appropriation.[11] This lack of legal recognition for collaboratively produced art highlighted a clash between a Western art market that promoted and protected the "authentic" work of individual artists, and the implicit depreciation of coauthored artwork that did not sit within a common-law intellectual property regime.

Moreover, I was perplexed by the way white Australian society enthusiastically embraced this new cultural packaging and aesthetic of indigeneity given that at the same time splashed all over the media were horrifying stories of the Stolen Generations and rising numbers of Aboriginal deaths in custody. As I argued back then, precisely because of the horrific tales of discrimination and violence perpetrated by police on indigenous communities, mainstream society in an effort to counter such open hostility latched on to the abstract and brightly colored art as a public expression of its cultural and political inclusiveness of Indigenous peoples into mainstream society.

> Aboriginal art, in the National Gallery or on a cornflakes box, is not politically neutral. It constitutes prejudice by reconfirming the social and legal preconditions by which bias against Aborigines can be considered legitimate. And it does so by steeping the purchase [and display] of black art with moral authority in what James Clifford has called a 'salvaging' operation. In other words, black art is bought because it represents for westerners the illusion of a traditional Aboriginal heritage. It functions to

lock contemporary Aborigines into a historical as well as an ideological past, enhanced by a romanticism of their community artistic experience and production. . . . Championing Aboriginal art is a popular, attractive and effective way of pretending material differences do not exist. Abstract dots and swirls create social distance. Aboriginal art, above all else, symbolizes for white society an identifiable boundary and thus a relationship of cultural difference and, implicitly, continued domination (Darian-Smith 1993, 65–66).

Today, over twenty years later, both in Australia and around the world, decorative Aboriginal dot painting is instantly recognizable as pertaining to the country's indigenous communities. It may well be the most effective packaging and branding of indigeneity in modern history, homogenizing Aboriginal culture under one amorphous aesthetic umbrella, conflating the cultures and concerns of urban and rural Indigenous peoples while blurring the symbols of deserts with rainforests with big cities. Unfortunately, my comment made over twenty years ago, that "Aboriginality in art has come to represent, in a remarkable sense, Aborigines themselves" appears to ring truer today than ever before (Darian-Smith 1993, 61). This is not to say that Aboriginal art should be thought of as a hoax or being inauthentic in some way—far from it. What it does underscore, however, is that in this particular case indigenous peoples are not able to control the interpretation and use of their ethnocommodity once it enters the national or transnational imaginary. This suggests that they are inadvertently participating in a national cultural politics that is quick to lump them together as a homogenous and essentialized group; denies full expression of indigenous peoples' complex and widely diversified cultural, political, economic, and social needs; and downplays claims of colonial racial oppression and contemporary dispossession. At the same time, mainstream Australian society can represent to the world a vision of multicultural inclusiveness and racial toleration.

Ethnicity, inc., as it unfolds in the context of the Australian Indigenous art industry, vividly presents some of its deeply embedded costs and contradictions (Comaroff and Comaroff 2009, 81). On the one hand, the incorporation of Aboriginal companies and the marketing of Aboriginal culture has helped some Indigenous peoples' to make reasonable livelihoods and become "thoroughly modern" (149). It has also undeniably helped to revitalize and regenerate some Aboriginal cultures and tribal knowledge, as well as to introduce into the white national polity positive images of a generalized Australian indigeneity. On the other hand, it can be argued that the costs for Aboriginal peoples as a whole have been significant. The enthusiastic embracing by white Australians of a generic indigenous aesthetics has helped reinforce monolithic images and stereotypes of indigenous peoples living in traditional and premodern circumstances, far from urban centers and the hubs of Australia's political and economic life (Darian-Smith 1993, 2002, 2004). As represented by abstract dots and lines, indigenous peoples have become visually removed as "human" from mainstream society and delegated, once again, out of sight and of mind in a fashion that echoes former colonial strategies of oppression, dispossession and assimilation. At the same time, Aboriginal people as the producers of a circulated commodity within national/international art markets have become very materially relevant but only in so far as they are necessary for the art's authenticity and provenance that in turn correlates to market value.

NORTHERN TERRITORY NATIONAL EMERGENCY RESPONSE—"THE INTERVENTION"

When reading Australia's Indigenous cultural politics against a backdrop of the twenty-first century global inequality and mass movements of people, the costs and contradictions embedded within ethnicity, inc. appear even more pronounced. One event that underscores these costs and contradictions and the heavy-handed militarization of state policies is the Northern Territory National Emergency Response—often referred to as the Intervention. In 2007, the Australian federal government declared the need to enact emergency measures to address claims of sexual abuse and neglect of Aboriginal children. Without consulting with indigenous communities, the government quickly sent the army into the remote Northern Territory.[12] As a result of the emergency action, seventy-three Aboriginal communities and town camps were targeted for a range of changes to welfare services, land tenure, and other civil and political rights. Apart from outlawing the use of alcohol, Aboriginal people's welfare checks were partially quarantined and their income managed, mandatory medical checks were performed on children to ascertain abuse, and indigenous landholdings were initially confiscated under five-year leases, which evolved into forty- to ninety-year lease holds by the federal government in return for essential services (Bray et al. 2012; Bielefeld 2014).[13] Under the Intervention, legal actions against indigenous peoples were exempted from considering customary law and cultural practices, and indigenous peoples lost their right to manage access permits for non-Aborigines to enter their local communities. The net result was that all sense of dignity and self-determination, including control over traditional lands, was taken away from these remote indigenous groups (see Collingwood-Whittick 2012).

In 2007, the Intervention received bipartisan political backing as well as the support of a few indigenous leaders. But over the years, it has been widely and openly criticized by many Aboriginal elders and community leaders, civil society organizations and NGOs, the United Nations, and a broad sector of Australia's public who view it as a failure for failing to meet the real needs of Aboriginal communities. In the ten years since its implementation, there is no evidence or reporting of any person being prosecuted for child sexual abuse, which was the original justification for its implementation. In 2012, new policies were introduced to further extend government powers over indigenous communities under the new "Stronger Futures legislation." This extension incited Malcolm Frazer, the former prime minister of Australia, to declare the legislation one hundred years out of date and fundamentally "racist" and "paternalistic." Despite widespread protests by Aboriginal and non-Aboriginal leaders, Concerned Citizens of Australia and Amnesty International, the Intervention has been extended until 2022. According to Michele Harris, a tireless campaigner against the Northern Territory Intervention and founder of "concerned Australians,"[14] the Australian government took over the management of the Northern Territory as a deliberate strategy of occupation:

> Early inklings of change occurred in 2004 with the management of grants being transferred from communities to government's newly established Indigenous Coordination Centres. More ominous were the Amendments of 2006 to the Aboriginal Land Rights Act and the memoranda of agreements that followed. Government had made it clear that it wished to re-engage itself directly in the control of community land through leasing options, as well as to open up Aboriginal land for development and mining purposes. The plan was to empty the homelands. This has not changed. However, it was recognised that achieving this would be politically fraught—it would need to be accomplished in a manner that would not off-side mainstream Australia. Removing Aboriginal people from their land and taking control over their communities would need to be presented in a way that Australians would believe to be to Aboriginal advantage, whatever the tactics.[15]

A great deal more can be said about the Intervention—its horrors, its failings, its robbing of indigenous communities of their integrity, cultural identity, and land rights as mining companies moved in to dig up minerals and uranium waste is dumped (Altman and Hinkson 2010).[16] Employment is almost nonexistent in the controlled communities and despair is widely evident. Aboriginal artists now find it nearly impossible to produce and sell their work, and many indigenous cultural centers have had to close their doors. Even the art cooperative Papunya Tula Artists Limited that was established back in 1972 to help sell the first dot paintings has had to move its operations out of state to Western Australia.

Experiencing the Intervention firsthand, Ali Cobby Eckerman (2015), an acclaimed Aboriginal poet, helps give a sense of the conditions under which indigenous communities suffered and continue to suffer:

> The whirlpool of public servants continued to crawl across the NT. Without consultation, or the use of local language interpreters, many incidents occurred. A toilet block was built on a sacred site. In some communities the administration offices were totally enclosed in barbed wire. Public servants could drink on communities, within view of residents. A police station was built at Titjkala as promised, but was never staffed. Depression among Aboriginal people escalated, and fatalities suggest the suicide rate has tripled.

She goes on to say that she thinks Australia will never recover:

> With the implementation of The Intervention I personally felt the betrayal of Australia; the moment when 'good' people allowed their neighbors to be treated in a manner they would not tolerate in any form.... This was the moment that any sense of equality and respect, garnered over the previous long years by our grandparents and parents, was abandoned by Australia's majority.

According to Elizabeth Povinelli (2011, 48), the Intervention and its supporters are "symptomatic of a broader conservative agenda in contemporary Australia that sought to, and has been quite effective at, hegemonizing the political and social field by using images of primitive sexuality to figure an absolute difference and hierarchy between the modern and ancient, personal freedom and customary constraint, depersonalized common truths and identity-based prejudices."

Whether or not this interpretation of events would be recognized by mainstream Australian society, it is clear that the Northern Territory Intervention cannot be disentangled from long-standing colonial oppression and attempts by the federal government to install new military strategies to "manage" indigenous peoples precisely at a time when they are beginning to gain modest traction socially, politically, legally, and economically (Ford and Rowse 2013; Fisher 2015). It could also be argued the Intervention, while specifically targeting indigenous peoples, is part of larger regulatory state practices that are "premised upon a neo-liberal combination of market competition, privatized institutions, and decentered, at-a-distance forms of state regulation" (Braithwaite 2000, 222).

How are we to understand the formation and continuing implementation of the Northern Territory Intervention, which is to be kept in place until 2022? For the purposes of this chapter, I am interested in the ways the commodification of indigenous culture and abstraction of indigeneity within the Aboriginal art industry may have helped inoculate mainstream Australian society from responding to the increasing militarization of its indigenous peoples. Did the costs and contradictions of ethnicity, inc. that inadvertently reinforced Aboriginal stereotypes and us/them social distancing in a sense pave the way for the military intervention and forced containment of Aboriginal communities in the Northern Territory? My tentative response is yes. But I think there is more going on than meets the eye and that this only becomes apparent by stepping back from analyzing indigenous issues within a national framework and thinking about Aboriginal cultural politics and the costs and contradictions of ethnic-entrepreneurialism within a more encompassing global political economic context.

Saskia Sassen (2014, 10) argued that land grabbing is the hallmark of our current system of global capitalism and that this has enormously exacerbated global inequality. She wrote that "from the perspective of today's capitalism, the natural resources of much of Africa, Latin America, and central Asia are more important than the people on those lands as workers or consumers." Wendy Brown (2015, 4) added, "The economization of everything and every sphere, including political life, desensitizes us to the bold contradiction between an allegedly free-market economy and a state now wholly in service to and controlled by it." In the context of Australia, and specifically the mineral rich lands of the Northern Territory, indigenous peoples are an obstacle to mining and other forms of extractive industry and in a very real sense need to be cordoned off and blocked from participating in it as either landholders negotiating with companies or as mobilized "mobs" resisting their takeover. So, the federal government's support of private mining industries (many of these Chinese-based companies) is part of the equation in understanding the ongoing implementation of the Northern Territory Intervention. The federal government is inordinately anxious to remove any obstacles to extractive industrial development.

While the Intervention can and should be interpreted as part of a continuing colonial history of land grabbing and land management of Aboriginal peoples (Goodhall 2008; Ford and Rowse 2013), we should not forget my earlier point that all domestic policies relating to indigenous communities must be read against the country's wider global/transnational relationship to the rest of the world. Hence another dimension to understanding the continuing implementation of the Northern Territory Intervention relates to the global challenge presented by mass migrations of people and the "super diversity" of religions and cultures that this mass movement brings. For in a very pragmatic sense, the cordoning off of Aboriginal communities behind barbed wire and under military supervision finds a ready template in the dozens of Australian Immigration Detention Centers that have sprung up across the country in largely remote areas over the past two decades. The government argues that these

Detention Centers are necessary to process so-called "illegal boat people" who have arrived on Australia's shores fleeing war and persecution in conflict zones. Beginning in 1992, all people entering Australia without a visa are mandatorily moved to detention centers for processing. In the 1970s and 1980s refugees came primarily from Vietnam, Laos, and Cambodia. More recently they have been arriving from Afghanistan and Sri Lanka, smuggled across the seas via Indonesia and Malaysia, many of them losing their lives as boats have subsided into the Indian Ocean or crashed along the northern Australian shores.

While the numbers of refugees seeking asylum in Australia is relatively small compared to other receiving countries such as Germany or the United States, refugees have remained a highly controversial issue and have been used by both the right and left political parties to incite racism, xenophobia and serve their respective political objectives. The detention centers, apparently based on Guantanamo and other US offshoring facilities (see Barder 2015),[17] have become a source of extreme political and social contestation within mainstream Australian society. Amnesty International, Human Rights Watch, and the United Nations have condemned practices of indefinite detainment which literally have abandoned asylum seekers to lives of imprisonment. Inside the Detention Centers, there are periodic demonstrations and riots, as well as numerous reports of self-cutting, hunger strikes and suicide. According to Christopher Foulkes:

> Scholars have noted Australians' hardening attitudes toward low-skilled, non-white migrants such as Middle Easterners and Asians for more than a decade, driven by fear the migrants could alter the national identity and culture of Australia for the worse. In a historical sense, Australia's boat people are seem by many as queue jumpers and unauthorized immigrants—not genuine refugees.... Though traditionally seen as a nation of immigrants, Australia has a historical preference for a certain type of immigrant....
> In 1992 the government ... introduced a policy of mandatory detention in the wake of an increase in would-be Chinese, Cambodian, and Vietnamese refugees. The policy—which remains today—requires asylum seekers to be held in mandatory detention while they await a decision on their refugee claims or be deported. The law limits the grounds on which Australian courts can hear matters relating to mandatory detention and places no time limit on detention, making detention indefinite, and, according to the Australian Human Rights Commission, effectively exempt from judicial review. (Foulkes 2012)

The containment of asylum seekers in remote compounds and Aboriginal peoples in remote townships—both sectors ostensibly out of sight and mind from the general Australian public and international monitoring—raises a number of troubling parallels and questions. What are the possible connections between the heavy-handed militarization of the Northern Territory Intervention that clamps down on Aboriginal rights and cordons off remote communities, and the increasingly shrill demands across the political spectrum for patrolling the nation's island borders and incarcerating refugees permanently within the same geographical space of remote outback Australia? These connections were obviously apparent to the Australian federal government when it set up the Department of Immigration and Multicultural and Indigenous Affairs in 2001. This department's specific mandate was to manage both refugee detainment centers and Indigenous affairs. The agency ran between 2001 and 2006, when it was closed down amid controversy for unlawfully detaining a German citizen for ten months and for failing to adequately manage the Woomera immigration detention facility (Whitmont 2003). In hindsight, it may not be coincidental that the year following the closure of the department, the federal government implemented the Northern Territory National Emergency Response Act, which institutionalized a new avenue for managing indigenous peoples.

The point I wish to stress is that both Australia's internal policies toward Aboriginal and Torres Strait Islanders and external policies toward refugees reinforce white paternalism and racial superiority and underscore mainstream society's inability to fully embrace cultural and religious diversity. Moreover, both these policies of political, legal, and economic containment functionally serve to coral certain populations who are often described as unable to work within the standardized norms of white Australian society. Former racialized colonial language—*barbaric, unchristian, lawless*—pepper mainstream and social media about impoverished indigenous communities and detention center inmates. Conveniently, and I would argue not coincidentally, these policies of exclusion speak to what Sassen called a "new logics of expulsion" in that they serve to expel particular sectors of society from participating in the national polity or having access to legal redress and the trappings of democracy.

Returning to ethnicity, inc. and ethnopreneurialism, both internal and external state policies with respect to minority groups shore up the image of an idealized white Australia ringed by empty golden beaches and inhabited by an English-speaking, terrorist-free, tourist-friendly society. Ultimately nationality, inc., trumps ethnicity, inc. in a very real sense—Australia's corporatized national image as expressed through its tourist industry trumps the ethnic entrepreneurialism of indigenous communities. Hence, "world renowned Indigenous artists," as described in the text of a tourist poster, stands in for all Australian Aborigines.[18] This returns us to an earlier discussion about culture-as-resource and George Yúdice's (2003) point that essentialized cultural differences—be these of nation-states or minority peoples—are now being circulated and mediated through a global political economy.

Packaging indigeneity through a robust national tourist industry underscores the myth of a racially "exotic" yet inclusive multicultural Australian society. It papers over with benign imagery the complex and ongoing oppression of indigenous peoples while at the same time serving the global market of the Australian tourist industry. Complementary to this commodification of internal racism is the ongoing need to deter boats carrying asylum seekers (and supposedly Muslim terrorists) from entering Australian waters as well as to keep under lock and key those refugees who have already landed. In this way both permanent Afghani detainees and impoverished Aboriginal communities share a common future in Australia in that both must be kept out of sight and out of mind under policies of neocolonial management.

CONCLUSION

In thinking about the costs and contradictions in ethnicity, inc., I have sought to open up discussion to contexts beyond the nation-state in an effort to more fully understand the ramifications of ethnic-entrepreneurialism among local Australian Aboriginal artists and their communities. While a few indigenous artists have profited—economically, culturally, and socially—from the contemporary Indigenous art industry, the long-term successes are not entirely clear. The vast majority of indigenous peoples continue to live in environments of extreme oppression, marginalization, and racism. Of course, one cannot and should not lump all Australian Aboriginal and Torres Strait Islander peoples into one overarching category, given the very unique kinship identities and the different challenges presented to those living in cities and rural areas in different parts of the country. That being said, the shift toward self-determination and economic, political and cultural revitalization for indigenous peoples that began so promisingly in the 1970s, '80s, and '90s has stalled. The optimism at the time—often associated with the global success of the Aboriginal art industry—has faltered. Australia, like other western nations, is experiencing a cultural backlash against minority peoples both within mainstream society and against those seeking to enter it by way of migration and asylum status.

Around the world, across conventional left and right political lines, the world is experiencing the rise of authoritarian governance and escalating militarization in the name of security. In many cases—in the Middle East, Latin America, Europe, and North America—national governments and state police forces are linking arms with multinational corporations. As a result, there is an increasing convergence if not equivalency between the logics of the security state and the logics of neoliberalism. In these increasingly narrow domains of concentrated power, how does ethno-entrepreneuralism operate? Who has access to marketing cultural difference? Who controls the terms of ethnobusiness? I have argued that ethnicity, inc. has always been an ambiguous and risky business with no assurance of positive outcomes for its minority participants. However, reading *Ethnicity, Inc.* (2009) against today's enormous challenges of global inequality and mass movements of people around the world, the costs of ethnic-capitalism take on a new twist as global economic pressures and political interdependencies sustain the escalation of militarization and security logics. The predominance of militarization, often complemented by the rhetoric of ultra-nationalism, is in turn recasting what is at stake for both nation-states and local communities seeking to capitalize on culture difference. The result in Australia is that asymmetrical power relations between the dominant white settler society and its marginalized indigenous peoples have not been so stark since the times of explicit colonial governance. Against the backdrop of the Northern Territory Intervention, the promise of ethnicity, inc. seems ever more remote.

NOTES

1. Ned Resnikoff, "Global Inequality Is a Rising Concern for Elites," Al Jazeera America, November 11, 2014, http://america.aljazeera.com/articles /2014/11/11/global-inequalityisarisingconcernforelites.html.

2. In 1992, the High Court of Australia recognized in *Mabo v Queensland (No. 2)* that indigenous peoples could hold title over lands and that the common law doctrine of *terra nullius* did not hold. This decision was considered a landmark at the time and gave rise to the Native Title Act (1993). Over the years the courts have interpreted land claims in very limited ways and legally preclude Aboriginal peoples from holding title over their land in ways equal to non-Aboriginal control of landholdings (see Strelein 2010; Smith 2011).

3. "A Brief Aboriginal History," Aboriginal Heritage Office, accessed January 1, 2016, http://www.aboriginalheritage.org/history/history/.

4. There are numerous accounts of settlers shooting Aboriginal peoples, such as that told by Bishop Polding in 1845:

> I have myself heard a man, educated, and a large proprietor of sheep and cattle, maintain that there was no more harm in shooting a native, than in shooting a wild dog. I have heard it maintained by others that it is the course of Providence, that blacks should disappear before the white, and the sooner the process was carried out the better, for all parties. I fear such opinions

prevail to a great extent. Very recently in the presence of two clergymen, a man of education narrated, as a good thing, that he had been one of a party who had pursued the blacks, in consequence of cattle being rushed by them, and that he was sure that they shot upwards of a hundred.

One of the most dramatic instances of indigenous genocide occurred in Tasmania, a small island lying to the south of the mainland. It is estimated that in 1803, prior to European colonization, approximately three thousand to fifteen thousand Parlevar lived there. However, indigenous communities were very quickly decimated by disease, the kidnapping of native children and adults for labor, and the hunting down of those who fought back. By 1833, only two hundred Aboriginal peoples remained alive. By 1876, Truganini, the last full-blood Aboriginal Tasmanian had died, and parts of her hair and skin were dispersed to the Royal College of Surgeons of England. In other parts of Australia, Aboriginal populations continued to decline dramatically throughout the course of the twentieth century, aided by governmental policies of forced removal of native children, who are now referred to as the Stolen Generations. By 1933 the population is estimated to have fallen to only seventy-four thousand native peoples across the whole of the Australian continent.

5. This became the Federal Council for the Advancement of Aborigines and Torres Strait Islanders (1964–1978).

6. Prior to the 1970s, native art was bought, but these items were not produced intentionally for commercial sale. British colonial settlers were interested in indigenous art and sent back to Europe a range of curios and ceremonial artworks throughout the nineteenth and twentieth centuries. The sale of indigenous art was facilitated by many missionaries on the so-called frontier who were keen to show economic development as part of their overall objectives to preserve native traditions and also raise additional funds for their enterprise (Altman 2007).

7. The company is entirely owned and directed by traditional Aboriginal people from the Western Desert, predominantly of the Luritja/Pintupi language groups. It has 49 shareholders and now represents approximately 120 artists.

8. Desart website, http://desart.com.au/; ANKAAA (http://ankaaa.org.au/) is the peak advocacy and support agency for Aboriginal artists and Art Centres located in the regions of Arnhem Land, Darwin/Katherine, Kimberley and the Tiwi Islands.

9. The Australian government initiated a Senate Inquiry into the unethical practices in the Aboriginal art market in 2006. Installing a code of practice, the government sought to bring a stop to widespread forgeries and accusations of exploitative sweat-shop conditions. The degree to which these actions have been successful is not determined (https://www.aph.gov.au/Parliamentary_Business

/Committees/Senate/Environment_and_Communications/Completed
_inquiries/2004-07/indigenousarts/report/index).

10. "Contemporary Aboriginal Art in Australia," Japingka Aboriginal Art,
http://www.japingka.com.au/articles/contemporary-aboriginal-art-in-australia/.

11. I interviewed Judith Ryan, who had been appointed curator of Aboriginal
Art at the National Gallery of Victoria, and she informed me that one of the
criteria for purchasing indigenous art was that it had to come from a regional
community collection since the National Gallery did not buy individual
Aboriginal works. Moreover, she said that the National Gallery did not promote
individual black artists—a reversed approach from all other contemporary art
purchases. This policy no longer stands, but it does reflect prevailing attitudes at
the time and the desire to perpetuate cultural difference through specific forms of
artistic production and legal exclusion (interview with Judith Ryan, July 8, 1991).

12. The Northern Territory population is 220,000, with more than 35 percent
of the population made up of indigenous communities, who technically own half
the land mass of the territory.

13. Similar strategies have been used by the Canadian government against
First Nations, in what Shiri Pasternak has called "colonial forms of fiscal warfare"
implemented through "an army of accountants" (Pasternak 2015).

14. "Vale Michele Harris: A Tireless Campaigner against the NT
Intervention," NewMatilda.com, June 3, 2015, https://newmatilda.com/2015/06
/03/vale-michele-harris-tireless-campaigner-against-nt-intervention.

15. "So began the campaign to discredit the people and to stigmatise
Aboriginal men of the Northern Territory publicly. It would be the Minister
himself who would take centre stage. It seemed that all Aboriginal men
were engaged in paedophilia. The Minister readily gave television and radio
interviews, declaring that he knew there were paedophile rings in every
Aboriginal community. Viewers were asked during their evening news
broadcasts how they felt about Aboriginal children going to bed at night
knowing they were not safe. . . . This was a government Minister engaging in
a sensationalist campaign aimed at demoralising Aboriginal men and was
probably the lowest point in any government behaviour ever seen in Australia's
political history. When challenged by the NT Chief Minister to name the people
involved, the situation deteriorated further" (Michele Harris, "Striking the
Wrong Note," 2015, accessed December 15, 2019, http://concernedaustralians
.com.au/media/Striking_the_Wrong_Note_6_year_NTER.pdf.

16. "Northern Territory Emergency Response (NTER)—'The Intervention,'"
accessed October 3, 2015, http://www.creativespirits.info/aboriginalculture
/politics/northern-territory-emergency-response-intervention#ixzz3nSBmoxl5.

17. Philip Dorling, "Detention Centre Policy Based on Guantanamo," *Sydney
Morning Herald*, March 14, 2012, http://www.smh.com.au/federal-politics

/political-news/detention-centre-policy-based-on-guantanamo-20120313-1uyj7.html.

18. Tourism Australia website, http://www.tourism.australia.com/.

REFERENCES

Altman, Jon. 2007. "Art Business: The Indigenous Visual Arts Infrastructure." In *One Sun One Moon: Aboriginal Art in Australia*. Art Gallery New South Wales, edited by Hetti Perkins, 43–50. New York: Prestel.

Altman, Jon, and Michelle Hinkson. eds. 2010. *Culture Crisis: Anthropology and the Politics in Aboriginal Australia*. Sydney: University of New South Wales Press.

Amar, Paul. 2013. *The Security Archipelago: Human-Security States, Sexuality Politics and the End of Neoliberalism*. Durham, NC: Duke University Press.

Attwood, Bain, and Andrew Markus. 2004. *Thinking Black: William Cooper and the Australian Aborigines' League*. Canberra: Aboriginal Studies Press.

Barder, Alexaner D. 2015. *Empire Within: International Hierarchy and Its Imperial Laboratories of Governance*. New York: Routledge.

Bardon, Geoffrey. 1979. *Aboriginal Art of the Western Desert*. Adelaide: Rigby.

———. 1991. *Papunya Tula: Art of the Western Desert*. Sydney: McPhee Gribble/Penguin.

Bardon, Geoffrey, and James Bardon. 2006. *Papunya: A Place Made After the Story; The Beginning of the Western Desert Painting Movement*. Carlton, Victoria: Miegunyah Press, University of Melbourne.

Bielefeld, Shelley. 2014. "Income Management: Indigenous Peoples and Structural Violence—Implications for Citizenship and Autonomy." *Australian Indigenous Law Review* 18 (1) 99–118.

Braithwaite, John. 2000. "The New Regulatory State and the Transformation of Criminology." *British Journal of Criminology* 40:222–38.

Bray, J. Rob, Matthew Gray, Kelly Hand, and Ilan Katz. 2012. "Evaluating New Income Management in the Norther Territory: The Final Report." Social Policy Research Center UNSW, September 2014.

Broome, Richard. 2010. *Aboriginal Australians: A History Since 1788*. Sydney: Allen & Unwin.

Brown, Wendy. 2015. *Undoing the Demos: Neoliberalism's Stealth Revolution*. New York: Zone Books.

Caruana, Wally. 2003. *Aboriginal Art*. 2nd ed. London: Thames & Hudson.

Champagne, Duane. 2015. "Indigeneity or Ethnicity: A Choice That Could Harm Tribal Identities." *Indian Country Today*, March 22, 2015.

Collier, Paul. 2008. *The Bottom Billion: Why the Poorest Countries Are Failing and What Can Be Done about It*. Oxford: Oxford University Press.

Collingwood-Whittick, Sheila. 2012. "Australia's Northern Territory Intervention and Indigenous Rights on Language, Education and Culture: An Ethnocidal Solution to Aboriginal 'Dysfunction'?" In *Indigenous Rights in the Age of the UN Declaration*, edited by Elvira Pulitano, 11–142. Cambridge: Cambridge University Press.

Comaroff, John L., and Jean Comaroff. 2009. *Ethnicity, Inc.* Chicago: Chicago University Press.

Coutin, Susan B., Justin Richland, and Véronique Fortin. 2014. "Routine Exceptionality: The Plenary Power Doctrine, Immigrants, and the Indigenous Under U.S. Law." *UC Irvine Law Review* 4:97.

Darian-Smith, Eve. 1993. "Aboriginality, Morality and the Law: Reconciling Popular Western Images of Australian Aborigines." In *Moralizing States and the Ethnography of the Present*, edited by Sally Falk Moore, 5:55–77. American Ethnological Society Monograph Series. Washington, DC: American Anthropological Association.

———. 2004. *New Capitalists: Law, Politics and Identity Surrounding Casino Gaming on Native American Land.* Case Studies in Contemporary Social Issues. Boston, MA: Wadsworth Cengage Learning.

———. 2012. "Re-Reading W.E.B. Du Bois: The Global Dimensions of the US Civil Rights Struggle." *Journal of Global History* 7 (3): 485–505.

———. 2013. *Laws and Societies in Global Contexts: Contemporary Approaches.* Cambridge: Cambridge University Press.

Fisher, Daniel T. 2015. "An Urban Frontier: Respatalizing Government in Remote Northern Australia." *Cultural Anthropology* 30 (1): 139–66.

Ford, Lisa. 2011. *Settler Sovereignty: Jurisdiction and Indigenous People in America and Australia, 1788–1836.* Cambridge, MA: Harvard University Press.

Ford, Lisa, and Tim Rowse, eds. 2013. *Between Indigenous and Settler Governance.* New York: Routledge.

Foulkes, Christopher D. 2012. "Australia's Boat People: Asylum Challenges and Two Decades of Policy Experimentation." Accessed July 1, 2019. http://www.migrationpolicy.org/article/australias-boat-people-asylum-challenges-and-two-decades-policy-experimentation.

Frühstück, Sabine. 2017. *Playing War: Children and the Paradoxes of Modern Militarism in Japan.* Oakland: University of California Press.

Gammage, Bill. 2013. *The Biggest Estate on Earth: How Aborigines Made Australia.* Sydney: Allen & Unwin.

Goodhall, H. 2008. *Invasion to Embassy: Land in Aboriginal Politics in New South Wales, 1770–1992.* Sydney: Sydney University Press.

Harris, Stewart. 1972. *This Is Our Land.* Canberra: Australia National University Press.

Hughes, Robert. 1988. *The Fatal Shore: The Epic of Australia's Founding*. New York: Vintage.

Johnson, Vivien, ed. 2007. *Papunya Painting: Out of the Desert*. Canberra: National Museum of Australia.

Kleinert, Sylvia, and Margot Neale, eds. 2000. *The Oxford Companion to Aboriginal Art and Culture*. Oxford: Oxford University Press.

Lowe, Lisa. 2015. *The Intimacies of Four Continents*. Durham, NC: Duke University Press.

Mawani, Renisa. 2009. *Colonial Proximities: Crossracial Encounters and Juridical Truths in British Columbia, 1871–1921*. University of British Columbia Press.

McCulloch, Susan, and Emily McCulloch Childs. 2008. *McCulloch's Contemporary Aboriginal Art: The Complete Guide*. 3rd ed. Balnarring, Victoria: McCulloch and McCulloch.

Miller, Barbara. 2012. *William Cooper Gentle Warrior: Standing Up for Australian Aborigines and Persecuted Jews*. Self-published, Xlibris.

Myers, Fred R. 2002. *Painting Culture: The Making of an Aboriginal High Art*. Durham, NC: Duke University Press.

Parker, Kunal M. 2015. *Making Foreigners: Immigration and Citizenship Law in America, 1600–2000*. Cambridge: Cambridge University Press.

Pasternak, Shiri. 2015. "The Fiscal Body of Sovereignty: To Make Live in Indian Country." *Settler Colonial Studies* 6 (4): 317–88.

Povinelli, Elizabeth A. 2006. *The Cunning of Recognition: Indigenous Alterity and the Making of Australian Multiculturalism*. Durham, NC: Duke University Press.

———. Reynolds, Henry. 2006. *The Other Side of the Frontier: Aboriginal Resistance to the European Invasion of Australia*. Sydney: University of New South Wales Press.

———. 2013. *Forgotten War*. Sydney: University of New South Wales Press.

Sassen, Saskia. 2014. *Expulsions: Brutality and Complexity in the Global Economy*. Cambridge, MA: Harvard University Press.

Smith, Benjamin R. 2011. *The Social Effects of Native Title: Recognition, Translation*. Canberra: Australian National University Press.

Stiglitz, Joseph E. 2012. *The Price of Inequality: How Today's Divided Society Endangers Our Future*. New York: W. W. Norton & Company.

Strelein, Lisa. 2010. *Compromised Jurisprudence: Native Title Cases Since Mabo*. Acton, ACT: Aboriginal Studies Press.

Tarrow, Sidney. 2012. "War, Rights and Contention: *Lasswell v Tilly*." In *Varieties of Sovereignty and Citizenship*, edited by S. Ben-Porath and R. Smith, 35–57. Philadelphia: University of Pennsylvania Press.

Tilly, Charles. 1985. "War Making and State Making as Organized Crime." In *Bringing the State Back In*, edited by Peter Evans, Dietrich Rueschemeyer, and Theda Skocpol, 169–87. Cambridge: Cambridge University Press.

United Nations High Commissioner for Refugees. 2018. "Report of the United Nations High Commissioner for Refugees. Part I Covering the period 1 July 2017–30 June 2018." General Assembly Official Records, Seventy-third Session, Supplement No. 12. New York: United Nations. https://www.unhcr.org/en-us/excom/unhcrannual/5ba3a3854/report-united-nations-high-commissioner-refugees-part-covering-period-1.html.

Vertovec, Steven. 2011. "The Cultural Politics of Nation and Migration." *Annual Review of Anthropology* 40 (1): 241–56.

Volpp, Leti. 2015. "The Indigenous as Alien." 5 *UC Irvine Law Review* 5 (2): 289.

Whitmont, Debbie. 2003. "... About Woomera." Four Corners (Australian Broadcasting Corporation). Accessed January 1, 2016. http://www.abc.net.au/4corners/content/2003/20030519_woomera/.

Yúdice, George. 2003. *The Expediency of Culture: Uses of Culture in the Global Era.* Durham, NC: Duke University Press.

EVE DARIAN-SMITH is Professor and Chair in the Department of Global and International Studies, with affiliated appointments in Anthropology, Law, and Criminology and Law and Society, at the University of California, Irvine. She is author of numerous articles and books including *Bridging Divides: The Channel Tunnel and English Legal Identity in the New Europe, Laws and Societies in Global Contexts: Contemporary Approaches,* and *The Global Turn: Theories, Research Designs, and Methods for Global Studies.*

LIST OF CONTRIBUTORS

TATIANA CHUDAKOVA is Assistant Professor of Anthropology at Tufts University whose scholarly interests lie in the anthropology of medicine and the body; science and technology studies; environmental anthropology; ethnicity, nationalism, and the state; and postsocialist transformations. Having received her PhD at the University of Chicago, Chudakova's research to date has focused on the cultural politics of the formalization and scientization of Tibetan medicine in Russia and on the intersection of moral economies of health care with the politics of indigenous therapeutic and ecological knowledge in postsocialist Siberia; her concerns also extend to the afterlives of Soviet scientific and state-building projects in Russia and Inner Asia. Her current book project, titled *Mixing Medicines: The Politics of Health in Asian Russia*, follows the efforts of Russia's official medical sector to recuperate and regulate therapeutic traditions associated with ethnic and religious minorities. Based in southeastern Siberia, the volume traces the uneven terrains of encounter between indigenous healing, the state, and transnational flows of medical materialities. Her next project will explore the global circulation of cognitive enhancement drugs between Russia and the United States, focusing on emergent concerns with quality control, safety, and notions of efficacy.

JEAN COMAROFF is the Alfred North Whitehead Professor of African and African American Studies and Anthropology at Harvard University, where she is also Oppenheimer Research Fellow in African Studies, and Honorary Professor of Anthropology at the University of Cape Town. She was educated at the University of Cape Town and the London School of Economics. Her research, primarily conducted in southern Africa, has focused on the interplay of capitalism, modernity, and colonialism; the politics of knowledge and the nature of sovereignty; and theorizing the contemporary world from beyond its centers. Her writing has covered a range of topics: religion and ritual, medicine and magic, law and crime, democracy and difference. Her publications include *Body of Power, Spirit of Resistance: The Culture and History of a South African People*, and, with John L. Comaroff, *Of Revelation and Revolution* vols. 1 and 2; *Ethnography and the Historical Imagination; Millennial Capitalism and the Culture of Neoliberalism; Law and Disorder in the Postcolony; Ethnicity, Inc.; Zombięs et frontięres à ère neoliberale; Theory, from the South: or, How Euro-America Is Evolving toward Africa; The Truth about Crime: Sovereignty, Knowledge, Social Order*; and *The Politics of Custom: Chiefship, Capital, and the State in Contemporary Africa*.

JOHN L. COMAROFF is the Hugh K. Foster Professor of African and African American Studies and of Anthropology at Harvard University, where he is also Oppenheimer Research Fellow in African Studies, as well as Honorary Professor of Anthropology at the University of Cape Town and Affiliated Research Professor at the American Bar Foundation. He was educated at the University of Cape Town and the London School of Economics. His research in South Africa, and his writings, focus on politics and law, colonial and postcolonial societies and cultures, crime and policing, personhood and social identity, the workings of the state, and democracy and difference. His authored and edited books, most of them with Jean Comaroff, include *Of Revelation and Revolution* vols. 1 and 2; *Ethnography and the Historical Imagination; Millennial Capitalism and the Culture of Neoliberalism; Law and Disorder in the Postcolony; Ethnicity, Inc.; Zombięs et frontięres à ère neoliberale; Theory from the South; or, How Euro-America Is Evolving toward Africa; The Truth about Crime: Sovereignty, Knowledge, Social Order*; and *The Politics of Custom: Chiefship, Capital, and the State in Contemporary Africa*.

SUSAN E. COOK works in the Division of Social Science at Harvard University, where she was Executive Director of the Center for African Studies from 2013 to 2018. Her scholarship on ethnicity, traditional leadership and the anthropology of the corporation in South Africa is based on twenty years of research in the Royal Bafokeng Nation, where she also served as a senior advisor to the Bafokeng *kgosi* (king). Her journal articles include "The Business of Being Bafokeng: Corporatization in a Tribal Authority in South Africa" in *Current Anthropology*; "Performing Royalty in Contemporary Africa" (with Rebecca Hardin) in *Cultural Anthropology*; and "Chiefs, Kings, Corporatization, and Democracy: A South African Case Study" in the *Brown Journal of World Affairs*. She has also published on urban hybrid languages in Africa and on comparative genocide, including an edited volume, *Genocide in Cambodia and Rwanda: New Perspectives* (2006). Cook has been Associate Professor of Anthropology at the University of Pretoria, Visiting Assistant Professor for Research at the Watson Institute for International

Studies at Brown University, and Director of the Cambodian Genocide Program at Yale University, where she earned her PhD in Anthropology.

EVE DARIAN-SMITH is Professor and Chair in the Department of Global International Studies, with affiliated appointments in Anthropology, Law, and Criminology and Law and Society at the University of California, Irvine. Trained as a lawyer, historian, and anthropologist, her PhD is from the University of Chicago. She is interested in issues of postcolonialism, human rights, legal pluralism, and sociolegal theory. Darian-Smith has published very widely, including eleven books and edited volumes. Her first book, *Bridging Divides: The Channel Tunnel and English Legal Identity in the New Europe*, won the Law & Society Association Herbert Jacob Book Prize, and her *Laws and Societies in Global Contexts* received both the International Book Award in Law and the Kevin Boyle Book Award. Her most recent book is *The Global Turn: Theories, Research Designs, and Methods for Global Studies*. Darian-Smith's other books include *Religion, Race, Rights: Landmarks in the History of Modern Anglo-American Law* and *Ethnography and Law*. She is a former Associate Editor of *American Ethnologist* and the *Law & Society Review*.

ERIC HIRSCH is Assistant Professor of Environmental Studies at Franklin & Marshall College, having previously held a postdoctoral fellowship in Global Governance at the Institute for the Study of International Development, McGill University. He received his PhD in sociocultural anthropology from the University of Chicago. Hirsch's research addresses the relationship between environmental change, economic development, and indigenous livelihoods. His current project, *Investing in Indigeneity*, asks how small-scale development interventions, using ethnicity-based cultural entrepreneurship to secure economic sustainability in Peru's southern Andes, intersect with the country's booming mining sector. Another of his scholarly projects explores the intensifying impact of climate change and the kinds of environmental and economic adaptations being made to it by indigenous communities in the Andean highlands and the Indian Ocean islands. Hirsch has published his work in the *Journal of Latin American and Caribbean Anthropology, Geoforum*, the *Journal of Political Ecology, PoLAR*, and *Global Environmental Change*.

SIMON MAY is a sociocultural anthropologist whose work focuses on political economy, indigeneity, globalization, and the nation-state, founded on ethnographic research in Oceania and the United Kingdom. His current book project, *Are We Not Born Soldiers? Fiji and the Outsourcing of Military Power*, investigates how and why Fijian sociocultural practices and categories precipitated the expansion of a global market in private military force. May is also working on a study examining how climate change in the Pacific stands to transform the concepts of sovereignty and indigeneity across the world. He received his PhD from the University of Chicago, where he was a predoctoral fellow at the Chicago Center for Contemporary Theory. Since 2016, May has been Visiting Assistant Professor at Bowdoin College.

GEORGE PAUL MEIU is the John and Ruth Hazel Associate Professor of the Social Sciences in the Department of Anthropology and the Department of African and African American Studies at Harvard University. His research and teaching focus on sexuality, gender, and kinship; belonging, citizenship, and the state; race and ethnicity; and the political economy of postcolonial Kenya. Meiu's recent book, *Ethno-erotic Economies: Sexuality, Money, and Belonging in Kenya* (University of Chicago Press), received the 2018 Ruth Benedict Prize and the 2019 Nelson Graburn Award from the American Anthropological Association. His work has also appeared in the *American Ethnologist, Ethnos, Anthropology Today*, the *Canadian Journal of African Studies* and in edited volumes on tourism, sexuality, and the history of anthropology. Meiu holds a PhD in anthropology from the University of Chicago.

DOROTHEA E. SCHULZ is Professor of Cultural and Social Anthropology at the University of Münster, Germany. She has previously taught at Cornell University and Indiana University and has published widely on media practices and public culture in the Sahel, gender studies, and Islam in West Africa. She is currently conducting research on Muslim practices of mourning and coming to terms with death in the context of continued ecological disaster, social dislocation, and irruption in Uganda. Her publications include *Perpetuating the Politics of Praise: Jeli Singers, Radios, and Political Mediation in Mali* (Rüdiger Köppe), *Culture and Customs in Mali* (ABC-CLIO), and *Muslims and New Media in West Africa: Pathways to God* (Indiana University Press).

SARA SHNEIDERMAN is Associate Professor in the Department of Anthropology and the School of Public Policy & Global Affairs/Institute of Asian Research at the University of British Columbia (UBC). She is the author of *Rituals of Ethnicity: Thangmi Identities between Nepal and India* (University of Pennsylvania Press), winner of the 2017 James Fisher Prize, and editor of *Darjeeling Reconsidered: Histories, Politics, Environments* (Oxford University Press). Shneiderman, who received her PhD from Cornell University, has also published essays and book chapters on Nepal's Maoist movement; ethnic classification, affirmative action, and the politics of recognition in South Asia; and borders and citizenship in Himalaya. Her current research includes a project titled "Expertise, Labour and Mobility in Nepal's Post-Conflict, Post-Disaster State of Transformation";

an ethnography of postconflict state restructuring in Nepal that focuses on lived experiences of citizenship, territory, and religiosity since 2006; and an exploration of trans-Himalayan citizenship across the historical and contemporary borders of India, China, and Nepal. Shneiderman is Codirector of UBC's Centre for Indian and South Asian Research (CISAR), and Cocoordinator of the UBC Himalaya Program.

INDEX

A page number in italics refers to an illustration.

www.ingramcontent.com/pod-product-compliance
Lightning Source LLC
Chambersburg PA
CBHW031415270326
41929CB00010BA/1463